AFRICAN C

Cameroon Studies

General Editors: *Shirley Ardener, E.M. Chilver* and *Ian Fowler,*
Queen Elizabeth House, International Development Centre,
University of Oxford

Volume 1
*Kingdom on Mount Cameroon. Studies in the History of the
Cameroon Coast, 1500-1970* – Edwin Ardener. Edited and with
an Introduction by Shirley Ardener.

Volume 2
*African Crossroads. Intersections between History and
Anthropology in Cameroon* – Edited by Ian Fowler and
David Zeitlyn

AFRICAN CROSSROADS

Intersections between History and Anthropology in Cameroon

Edited by Ian Fowler and David Zeitlyn

Berghahn Books
Providence • Oxford

First published in 1996 by

Berghahn Books

Editorial offices:
165 Taber Avenue, Providence, RI 02906 USA
Bush House, Merewood Avenue, Oxford, OX3 8EF UK

© 1996 Ian Fowler and David Zeitlyn

Library of Congress Cataloging-in-Publication Data

African crossroads : intersections of ethnography and history in
  Cameroon studies / edited by Ian Fowler and David Zeitlyn.
       p.   cm.
    Includes bibliographical references.
    ISBN (invalid) 1-57181-859-5 (cloth : alk. paper). -- ISBN
  1-57181-926-6 (pbk. : alk. paper)
    1. Cameroon--History. 2. Ethnology--Cameroon.   I. Fowler, Ian.
  II. Zeitlyn, David.
  DT570.A35   1996
  967.11--dc20
                                                      96-2120
                                                      CIP

British Library Cataloguing in Publication Data

A catalogue record for this book
is available from the British Library.

Printed in the United States on acid-free paper.

Dedication

For Sally Chilver
'Mama for Story'

TABLE OF CONTENTS

LIST OF FIGURES

ACKNOWLEDGEMENTS

The Editors gratefully acknowledge the help and support of Lady Margaret Hall, Oxford, Royal Holloway and Bedford New College, London and the Institute of Social and Cultural Anthropology, Oxford in making this publication possible.

FOREWORD

The Catalyst:
Chilver at the Crossroads

Shirley Ardener

Those who are interested in African affairs or have a committed interest in Cameroon history and society are immensely fortunate, for this area provides exceptionally varied and vivid experiences. Moreover, the area generates themes of much wider than local relevance for consideration.

As the title of this volume implies, Cameroon is a meeting ground for a wide diversity of cultures and polities both native to Africa and intrusive from Europe. Its unique history is reflected in the range of ethnic affiliations of the academics – Cameroonists – whose energies have been drawn to it. Foremost amongst these are Cameroonians themselves, so many of whom have demonstrated a deep scholarly interest in their past and in their present societies and cultures (see Fanso, Langhêê and Banadzem below). This has occurred at the local level with individuals (including traditional dignitaries), with teachers and others working in small area-based groups, or with academics or administrators in national and overseas institutions. The co-operation and the generous welcome they have unfailingly shown to Cameroonists from abroad has been remarkable. For Cameroonians too, the chequered history of their country must sometimes seem to drive it close to the danger of falling between a number of international stools. So there is special exhilaration when and wherever Cameroonists get together at workshops and conferences where colleagues from many continents meet up.

Happily, the international network of Cameroonists has grown stronger and stronger in recent years. It goes back a long way. Cameroon studies were fostered to some extent in schools, in teacher-training colleges and at the school of administration at Yaoundé. Many other initiatives were taken in Cameroon, including an informal group of returnees trained abroad who met and gave papers at a small seminar in Buea convened by Edwin Ardener in 1963.[1]

A significant step forward in the international field was taken by Claude Tardits who in 1973, with the backing of the CNRS (Centre National de Recherches Scientifiques), organised a large international conference in Paris on the contribution of history and ethnology to the civilisations of Cameroon. This occasion drew in many scholars from Cameroon, and out of this colloquium the Grassfields Working Group (GWG) emerged and has since met on a number of occasions in France, Cameroon, Britain, Holland and the United States.

Meanwhile, in Cameroon, the pioneering work in the Grassfields of the anthropologist Phyllis Kaberry was honoured in the mid-1980s by the formation of the Kaberry Resource Centre (KRC), the research wing of the Association for Creative Teaching, itself founded only shortly before. Cameroonists have also been able to keep in touch through a Newsletter edited in and distributed from the United States by Eugenia Shanklin, which has book reviews and short notices of conferences and other activities. More recently Cameroonian professionals and students working and studying abroad have established an international electronic bulletin-board system to exchange gossip, and report on affairs back home in Cameroon. The 'Camnetters' carry on a vigorous debate on an extensive range of social, political and sporting issues, which enables the Cameroonian (and Cameroonist) diaspora to keep abreast of current affairs back home (see Fowler, in prep.)

All of the study groups mentioned above have produced publications.[2] It was no surprise therefore that at a meeting of the GWG in Oxford in November 1991 another publication should be planned. In this case, however, there was to be a special feature, the book was to be dedicated to a key student of Cameroonian culture and history and a founder member of the working group: E.M. Chilver, known to friends and colleagues alike as Sally. It is important to note, however, that this book is not a Festschrift containing a motley of papers with only a tenuous link between them. It is written and edited by Sally's friends who, while bringing their distinctive expertise to their contributions, precisely share with her an interest in Cameroon studies; it is therefore well focused. Indeed, so many excellent contributions were offered that the editors perforce found themselves editing, not one volume in honour of Sally, but three collections of papers (see the editors' Preface below.) Thus this volume has been preceded by the publication of a set of papers in the 1995 issue of the journal *Paideuma* entitled 'Perspectives on the State: from Political History to Ethnography in Cameroon. Essays for Sally Chilver', and will be followed by a special edition of the *Journal of the Anthropology Society of Oxford* (*JASO*). Together the three publications reflect the state of Cameroon studies today.

Why, though, should Sally Chilver have been given this accolade? As she now occupies a niche in Cameroon history a biographical word or two are merited here, although a much fuller account by Mitzi Goheen and Eugenia Shanklin provides a fascinating biographical essay which can be found in the special edition of *JASO*. The authors have kindly permitted me to draw briefly upon it here to add to my own knowledge, but for more details of Sally's colourful life the longer text is essential reading. Sally Chilver's full bibliography (liberally drawn upon by the authors herein) is also found in *JASO*.

Sally Chilver's first contact with Cameroon came in the summer of 1958 when she accompanied her friend Phyllis Kaberry on a tour of the Grassfields to work on the divisional records for a case study of the local administration. Sally was well-equipped for the task. She belonged to a well travelled and scholarly family, her father, Philip Graves, being a *Times* correspondent who had lived and worked in Turkey and travelled to other parts of Europe and the Middle East; Sally had a multicultural upbringing. After her mother's tragic and early death in 1935, the recently graduated Sally Graves set off independently 'on a tour to the Middle East and Bulgaria, just as people go to Nepal these days' (Goheen and Shanklin, 1996). Olivia Manning's *Balkan Trilogy* gives a flavour of the exciting times and milieu in which Sally then circulated. It gave her the chance to begin her writing career as a freelance 'stringer', sending back stories to *The Times* in London.

Two years before the war she married Richard Chilver and set up home in London only to be conscripted into war-work as a civil servant in the Ministry of Economic Warfare. It was then that she first heard of the French Cameroons, as the war effort required her to encourage the export of West African products. After the war, and a brief spell at *the News Chronicle* newspaper, she returned to the civil service and eventually became Secretary of the Colonial Social Science Research Council, an advisory body which sponsored overseas research.[3] In this job she came into contact with various social anthropologists, including Phyllis Kaberry who in 1951 was completing the draft of her book *Women of the Grassfields* (1952). Soon afterwards she met Edwin Ardener, who had just completed a field research trip among the Igbo with the aid of a grant from the Council. Sally was responsible for implementing the policy of establishing research institutes in East and West Africa (The East African Institute for Social Research [EAISR] and The West African Institute for Social and Economic Research [WAISER], now The Nigerian Institute for Social and Economic Research [NISER]). It was WAISER that first took Edwin Ardener to Cameroon, and it was Sally to whom he handed the manuscript of *Plantation and Village in Cameroon*, to which Richardson, Warmington, Ruel, Morton-Williams and myself had also variously contributed.

Sally Chilver's interest in social studies and her curiosity about Africa grew to the point that she decided to see it for herself. So in 1958 she accompanied Phyllis Kaberry on a ten-week visit to the Grassfields. It was almost a case of game warden turned poacher! Sally herself has explained that Phyllis Kaberry wished to restudy the political systems of the polities in the western Grassfields which she had first encountered in the 1940s. 'These systems were now faced with the new pressures of recent political, fiscal and economic reforms, the take-off of smallholder coffee production and the emergence of a nationalist leadership' (Chilver and Berndt 1992: 34).

Describing herself with typical modesty as 'an apprentice historian in stout boots' Chilver returned for further stints with Kaberry in 1960 and 1963 to continue their study of 'the interplay between German and British administrations, and the political structures they found and tried to manipulate' (Berndt and Chilver 1992: 35). During this period Chilver and Kaberry engaged the interest of local people in their work, circulating drafts among them for their comments.

She recalls:

whatever resthouse or *manjong* house or whatever we stayed in ... became a
port of call for the literati of the area, and conventional fieldwork was amplified by results and hypotheses being constantly discussed with them...
(Berndt and Chilver 1992: 35)

The circulation list of the first 1966 draft of the volume
Traditional Bamenda (published in 1968) included not only
administrative and education department officers, but also two
local historical societies. This publication was originally intended
as part of a larger project initiated by Claude Tardits for which
Edwin Ardener was to supply a text on the western Grassfields
and on the forest areas of the then West Cameroon down to the
Coast. The project was never completed, but Ardener arranged
publication of *Traditional Bamenda* in a series he issued[4] on his
annual visits to the archives office which he had established at
Buea.[5] Recently Sally Chilver has returned the favour by preparing for publication a section of text written by Edwin Ardener for
the original project, which covers a stretch roughly from Esu
across part of the Mamfe Overside.

Sally Chilver and Phyllis Kaberry produced a string of publications both jointly and individually. A biography by Berndt and
Chilver of Phyllis Kaberry, and a full list of the latter's writings,
can be found in S. Ardener, (1992) which also includes two
essays written in Phyllis Kaberry's honour (one by Sally herself,
another by Caroline Ifeka).

By now Chilver had irretrievably crossed the bridge between
the civil service and academia; first, from 1958 to 1961, she was
Director of the Institute of Commonwealth Studies at Oxford
before it was merged with Queen Elizabeth House. It was during
this time that she lured Edwin Ardener, as a visiting Oppenheimer
Scholar, to Oxford. In 1964 she became Principal of Bedford
College, London University, but in 1971 she was back in Oxford
as Principal of Lady Margaret Hall. On her retirement from the
latter she plunged full-time into her work on Cameroon studies.
The task seemed urgent; sadly, Phyllis had died of a stroke six
years earlier. Sally set about sorting and editing their field notes
in order to make them more accessible to others.

When I first knew Sally, Edwin and I, back from the bush, had
just set up home in two rooms in the Caledonian Road in London,
and we had the cheek to invite her round to sit in our made-in-the-
bush deck chairs (I still have the detachable raffia backs) which
were our only seating for some time. I am still fortunate in living
only a stone's throw from Sally in Oxford. I run round always to

find a ready ear and an encouraging word. She has the latest news from Cameroon, which she garners from her extensive correspondence, and which she tells eagerly as if it were local gossip from just up the road. Someone has got a new job, another has just published a paper, a third has recently got married. Details of a new piece of research have arrived, another gap in the cultural jigsaw is filled. This I learn as Sally looks up from her dining table, long since given over to the spread of manuscripts she is perusing or editing at the request of some Cameroonist, young or old, despatched from some village in Cameroon, or Yaoundé, from across Oxford or perhaps from Holland or the World Bank. Being an historian Sally takes a long view and respects the value of archives. Between these activities she assiduously continues to render the ethnographic notes that she and Phyllis made in the 1940s and 1960s into readable condition for others to use.

The papers below easily demonstrate the continuing relevance of the issues which concerned scholars who worked in the 1950s and 1960s, among them Sally and Phyllis, and also Edwin Ardener and Claude Tardits and others whose initiating roles Sally has acknowledged (1992: 105). Many years ago I noted that I was unhappy at the dismissive approach of some writers (e.g., Onwuka Dike) when referring to the coastal dignitaries who coped with the complex economic and situations of their period (S. Ardener 1968: 21). Whether the political leaders did this well or badly, were knowledgeable or out of their depths in international affairs, they deserved respect for their attempts to negotiate a way through the confusions of their time and situation. They were certainly taken seriously by those with whom they engaged in dialogue. That some may occasionally have been out-manoeuvred is not surprising given the overwhelming forces of change they had to face. How many heads of state do better today? Happily this book carries forward the meticulous unravelling of nineteenth- and early twentieth-century political issues undertaken by Phyllis Kaberry, Sally Chilver and many others, including the heirs of those Cameroonians involved at that time.

Those of us who worked in Africa through those early optimistic years, when bright futures for Africa were forecast – and believed in by all of us – were fortunate. Today the whole world seems more complicated. That Cameroon is still at a crossroads today is all too clear. The political experiments, the economic ups and downs, the social revolution as generational and gendered relationships change, and other pressures within and from outside the nation – all these impel Cameroonians to reflect on their cultural and political history.

How did Cameroonians cope in the past? What can be learnt for the future? Human nature does not vary much, if at all, from time to time nor from place to place: conditions do. However, freedom for action is never unrestrained. We all carry our past with us, and peoples and nations do the same. In a multicultural community such as Cameroon, with its international links, the diversity of many cultural and political histories still have to be taken into account. None of us starts with a blank sheet on which to write our future.

Furthermore, if Cameroonians can learn from the course of the events in which they and their forebears have been involved, so can others. For the human past belongs to us all. It is by the telling of other peoples' tales that we learn about ourselves: what to do and what to avoid. The history of Cameroon therefore is everyone's. It is an exciting one. It is a story of princes and powers, of wars and peace treaties, of disasters and achievements. Fons and commoners, Queen Mothers, Governors and warriors in and out of uniform, wielding spears or guns, diviners and mission converts, all play their parts in the presentations in this book, each now is accorded the attention merited. We must be grateful to Ian Fowler and David Zeitlyn for undertaking their task, which comprises three publications, and to Sally Chilver for inspiring it.

Notes

1. The Buea 'Seminar on Social Problems' covered topics including matrilineal succession, social mobility and the family, migration, demography, settlement and land tenure, statistics, development and women's roles in voluntary organisations. The material presented at this informal seminar is still quoted (notably Francis Nkwain's account of *anlu* [women's war] in Kom). In addition to Nkwain, the members included Benedicta Ngu, Elias Matthew Nwana, Tambi Eyong Mbuagbaw, Benedict Simo, Gwen Burnley and Patrick Sine. Many of the participants have since risen to prominence.

2. For example: Geary (ed.)1979, Tardits (ed.) 1981, Chilver (ed.) 1985, Mbunwe-Samba, et al. (eds) 1993.

3. On support for scholarship on Africa in the 1950s and 1960s see Chilver 1951, 1957 and 1958.

4. 'One of the aims of the series of booklets, started in 1965, [was] to make available historical source material not otherwise easily obtainable in West Cameroon' (E. Ardener, in S. Ardener, 1968). Other titles in the series included Chilver (1966), E. Ardener (1965), and S. Ardener, (1968).

5. Edwin Ardener's search for local documents had led in October 1959 to an invitation to collect together the archival material he had come across, often mouldering away in cupboards in various government offices. He had been particularly concerned about a collection which had been bundled up by Professor Onwuka Dike some years earlier for despatch to Nigeria, which still lay among mounds of collapsing files and stray documents, all deteriorating in the dirty, hot and humid loft of the Secretariat in Buea. Eventually, on the foundation of the Federal Republic, and at the far-sighted initiative of the then West Cameroon Government, he was asked to establish a government Archives Office. First temporarily housed in an old German building (and for a time in his absence in its old, rat-ridden kitchens!), the archives were finally moved into a purpose-built office in Buea. For this Ardener selected the site, drew up plans with the Public Works Department, installed fitments, and equipped and trained staff. Special mention must go to the devoted duty of Mr Kima, the first Cameroonian member of staff, who shared the discomforts of the Secretariat loft, and who worked with his later colleagues to save many documents from the predations of insects and of man. The office was officially opened by the then Prime Minister of West Cameroon, the Honourable S. T. Muna, in 1969. More recently the fine collection of German books and records was moved to Yaoundé, but the administrative history of western Cameroon is still, largely, available to scholars in Buea. Some of the contributors to this volume have made good use of it.

PREFACE

Ian Fowler and David Zeitlyn

The published work and continuing correspondence of Sally Chilver have marked several generations of research in the Cameroonian Grassfields in the overlapping subjects of anthropology and history. This book is part of a broader project that celebrates that work.

The genesis of an idea for such a project, much like the history of the foundation of an African kingdom, is often difficult to elicit unambiguously – it too may become imbued with a foundation myth. We, as western liberal academics, may sometimes appear to claim undue proprietary rights over intellectual projects of diverse provenance. To continue the metaphor – and in this instance it is a very apt one – claims to unitary African dynastic origins frequently mask great diversity in the composition of populations, communities and polities.

Issues concerning cultural and political representations of identity have always been a strong undercurrent in anthropology. However, since the collapse of the Soviet Union and the eruption of conflict in Europe seemingly based on, or at least played out in, terms of ethnicity this has become the object of more focused attention. It is sometimes said that Africa exists in its very own temporal space, but in this instance there is simultaneity in the chronology of events and their interpretation. Here, too, the qualities and meaning of identity in cultural practice and political representation are deeply questioned in the context of the post-colonial African state. There are fascinating convergences and parallels here, in the events of Europe and Africa and the knowledge that is created in the interpretation of them, that remain to be explored.

Sally Chilver's personal life and her academic endeavour touch upon all of these things. Her contribution to the Africanist world-view and the knowledge contained and generated by it is also highly significant. At a time when it was perhaps less than fashionable, Sally collaborated in field research and in print with the anthropologist Phyllis Kaberry. This personal and academic alliance flew in the face of the established academic bias in anthropology that eschewed the knowledge of missionary, administrator and trader in favour of the monopoly of the professional ethnographer. Happily for those of us who have followed them into the field, Chilver's work with Kaberry did more than simply help neutralise the effects of this disciplinary bias against history. (For two instances of the consequences of this see Burnham and Warnier below).

The Grassfields area of Cameroon appears to exemplify Ardener's formulation (1967: 298) that 'self-classification never ceases' or, similarly, Appadurai's notion of the continuous production of locality. However, Kopytoff's work on the Aghem presents a picture of an anomalous marginal society, an example of recent ethnogenesis (1981) and Geary, on the We, also interprets her data in terms of recent ethnogenesis (1981). It is not entirely contradictory to suggest that identity in the Grassfields has been constantly reworked across a range of groups of quite different orders of magnitude. In this sense all Grassfields communities are recent, irrespective of how long they have been around.

Ethnography and history are nowhere more tightly bound up with identity and ethnicity than in the broad field of colonial and post-colonial African studies. This is particularly well illustrated in the historical and ethnographic studies of Cameroon undertaken by Sally Chilver, associated Cameroonian scholars and other colleagues influenced and aided by her. The enormous diversity of Cameroonian culture, language and history is well known. Its geographical position makes it a true African crossroads, a microcosm of the continent. Chilver's precise area of study, the Grassfields of Cameroon, is itself a microcosm of this microcosm. We have already noted that it has a host of linguistically diverse and independent polities, reworking a common core of ideas and practices into distinctive individual formations.

Ardener has stressed the complexity of this picture in the light of the large number of named sets for the wider region of anglophone Cameroon (1967: 295–6). It is clear that anthropologists and historians may play significant roles in the production of the kinds of knowledge that tie in to the emergence of broad social and political groupings in the colonial context. It is perhaps also the case that such knowledge becomes a part of the armoury of action in the contemporary struggle for definition of locality and its articulation with the agents and offices of the post-colonial state.

The partnership of Chilver and Kaberry, the early work of Kaberry, and Chilver's continuation and enhancement of this up to the present day span a crucial period in the history of Europe and Africa. Effective administration of the Grassfields by the mandated British regime was very much in its infancy when Kaberry arrived in the 1940s. An example which illustrates this point is furnished by Chilver's reworking of Kaberry's 1947 field notes from the Funggom area in the north of the Grassfields:

> 16.vi.47: Chief and Court Messenger (interpreting in Pidgin) informants…
> Atshaf is distantly related to Atshaf in Kom, similarly Akee to the Kom Ake village. Meeku is related to the Ekwu of Laikom, the chief's lineage there. In Mme Meeku is 'like a chief' and has 'nggumba' (presumably nkwifoyn). The first Atshaf chief of Funggom took it from Meeku and brought it here. In Mme the QH of Meeku not that of Atshaf is head of 'nggumba': here he does not have it but is recognised as being 'distantly related' to the Chief's family. (Chilver 1995a)

Complex clan relationships and claims to hierarchy and ownership of the symbols of ritual power and political authority are presented in terms of a straightforward narrative of the past. In representing the ongoing interplay and negotiation of relationships of power and dominance in this framework of historical narrative the past is frozen as an eternal validation of the present. Fixed units of administration are created. Simultaneously, one version of history is recorded and becomes a contestable validatory text for political action or representation. Our own activities as historians and ethnographers of Africa lead to the production of knowledge that has dual currency in academic and political realms.

It is rare, however, for any one individual, or that individual's works, to straddle or pass freely between these spheres. Knowledge produced at one time in academic endeavour becomes political usually only after many peregrinations and transformations. It may take considerable time to pass into the box marked 'history' from which contemporary combatants for power may select their costumes and props for the theatre of conflict. Individuals concerned with the actual production of knowledge move on to other things, or at the very least shift into a different kind of relationship with their subjects and the knowledge produced about them, as time goes on. In her work Sally Chilver incorporates processes of reanalysis and reflection not usually carried out by one individual. For a considerable period her work has problematised the relationship between ethnographic knowledge and cultural and political representations of identity. Meticulous attention to detail, to source and archive, are in Chilver's case happily married to a personal longevity and a historical view of the long term; much that is academically crucial to the twentieth century is embodied in her life and work.

If identity is constantly reworked, it is nonetheless 'fixed' in narratives of the past; if classification is continuous it has, at least since the early colonial period, not usually been framed by one side alone. In these two key and related areas Sally Chilver has played, and continues to play, a major and dove-tailing role in the production of knowledge for and of the Grassfields. She adopted an early, if discordant, stance against the short-sightedness of contemporary professional ethnographic practice. She has retained a focus on historical issues in her archivist reworking of her own fieldnotes and those of Kaberry, and in ongoing correspondence with Cameroonian colleagues and dignitaries. Yet she has become far more of an anthropologist than she might perhaps care to admit. A recently published paper on thaumaturgical belief in Nso' (Chilver 1990) is a case in point. Not only has it been widely quoted in literature on the Grassfields but, more importantly, it has significantly advanced our knowledge of African religious belief in a region for which such knowledge has until now been sorely lacking.

Certainly, many of us associated with Sally Chilver have given thought to ways in which her very significant contributions to Cameroon studies might be satisfactorily acknowledged. At the last meeting of the Grassfields Working Group in Oxford (organised by Sally Chilver) a number of us, notably Miriam Goheen, Eugenia Shanklin, Shirley Ardener, Claude Tardits, Charles-Henry Pradelles and Jean-Pierre Warnier, took the opportunity to conspire. The project of which this volume forms a part is the welcome product of that happy conspiracy.

In order to thematise what we initially envisaged as a single volume we requested that papers should focus on the convergence of ethnography and history in the field of Cameroonian studies. The voluminous and overwhelmingly positive response to our call presented us with the 'problem' of a wealth of contributions that could not easily be meshed into a single unit. The very high quality of papers submitted meant that we would have been unable, should we have been so bold, to exclude any on the basis of relative merit. Dividing the contributions into connected themes produced three sets of papers.

The first set of papers focuses on contemporary views of the state, its emergence through partition and reunification, the developing role of the chieftaincy, and key issues of gender and accumulation. This set of papers has now been published as a major section of the 1995 issue of *Paideuma,* the journal of the Frobenius Institute. This is an appropriate place for papers in honour of Sally Chilver, since Leo Frobenius is considered by many to have been largely responsible for bringing West African art and culture to the attention of contemporary western intellectuals. In a similar, if more humble, way Sally Chilver has brought the complexity of the Cameroonian Grassfields in its history, material culture and ethnography to the attention of Africanist scholars. The direct German connection also fits very well with Chilver's historical focus on the German colonial period and with her ethnographic studies of Bali-Nyonga, the earliest and main ally of the nascent German colonial regime.

A second set of papers deals with topics such as witchcraft, divination and religion in a more or less straightforwardly ethnographic way.[1] Sally Chilver's links with Oxford encompass both formal and informal academic sectors. As an Africanist historian and ethnographer she has enriched the Oxford academic scene while nurturing young Cameroonist and Cameroonian students and scholars.

The third set of papers, published in this volume, is more tightly focused and theoretically orientated in analyses that combine historical and anthropological perspectives. Again it is highly appropriate that this volume should be produced by an Oxford-based publisher of German origin. This reflects the incorporation in the person of Sally Chilver of a combination of a productive Oxford academic base with a long-term interest in German colonial history.

The individual chapters adopt a set of interrelated approaches to the study of African societies, drawing deeply on the complex interrelationship of history and anthropology. We touch on some of the problems of 'ethnic' identity in the case of the Tikar and the Chamba below. This is discussed in Fardon's chapter with which this volume begins. His explicit target is 'the incommensurability between anthropological and local models' and 'the numerous historical links between them'. He treats this through an examination of the chiefdom of Bali-Nyonga, which while located within the Grassfields maintains a Chamba identity. Hence this chapter in its theoretical and methodological perspectives, as well as in its use of ethnographic data, keeps to the path laid down by Sally Chilver. In a complex argument Fardon explores the theoretical underpinnings of the conceptual clusters of the interrelationships between persons, ethnicity and identity in both 'traditional' and modern types of West African society. His examination of the Bali-Nyonga case 'largely derived from Sally Chilver's meticulous historical work' analyses the use of history as part of the transition to modernity. In so doing he draws out the complexity of the relationships between local history and anthropology. He poses the question 'who is writing whom?' which sets our discussion firmly in contemporary anthropological theory and debate.

Burnham presents a reanalysis of the historiography of the early relationships between the Gbaya and the proto-colonialists, the explorers and traders, that presaged formal colonisation. He uses the results of anthropological research into the history of slave-raiding in the region to interpret the documentary evidence of the first French expeditions to the area in the late nineteenth century. In this he acknowledges the pioneering role of Chilver and Kaberry in breaking down barriers between history and anthropology. Burnham complements Chilver's archivist work in his use of the Gbaya material to highlight the problems of interpreting early colonial documents and the difficulties in dealing with built-in biases. In this light he stresses the need to eschew disciplinary boundaries and confront contemporary European colonial documentation with, for example, data from oral tradition, archaeological evidence, historical linguistics and title systems.

Austen pursues this theme by considering both sides of the German-Duala relationship early in the period of German rule. His paper complements Chilver's (1967) studies of the Germans

in Cameroon and offers an interesting parallel to (and some convergence with) her focus on the so-called 'Bali-Frage'. In each
case initial German alliances led to subsequent difficulties.
Ambiguities in relationships gave rise to serious problems with
groups such as the Moghamo (see O'Neil below) and others who
sought redress against the injustices that resulted from these
alliances. Austen analyses the mythic representations of the
German-Duala relationship in the light of three themes. These are
first the *Sonderweg*, the exceptional historical path of Germany;
secondly extreme oppression, the dramatic and oppressive climax
of German rule in Douala; and thirdly the 'golden-age' myth that
contrasts in a positive light the German period with that of the
French. In reconciling these different threads Austen demonstrates both the ambiguities and the banalities of colonial history,
and also how these underlying contradictions connect with ongoing confrontations between Africa and Europe. This material is of
even greater interest since accounts of this period now figure in
local debates about rights to land and power in the metropolis of
the city of Douala and figures such as King Akwa bulk large in the
creation of Duala identity. We start with political history and end
with the contemporary processes of identity and its making.

Similar concerns underlie O'Neil's study of the relationships
between Bali-Nyonga and the Moghamo people in the early years
of German penetration of the Grassfields. O'Neil presents a strik-
ingly dramatic account of this key historical moment. Local informants recall great excitement upon hearing first reports of the
arrival of Zintgraff 'an unknown thing… skin red like fire' and the
great drama when the Fon of Bali took the white man by the hand
and declared to the assembled chiefdom that he was indeed a
human being, since his skin was cool and not like fire. Through
the eyes of Franz Hutter we are offered the startlingly vivid picture of the bloody mayhem of a slave raid 'over which shines the
tropical sun from a deep blue sky'. And the words of those so
enslaved, such as Simon Peter Nguti, provide an insight into
experiences of enslavement and subsequent life-histories.
Alongside this rich and descriptive account are deeper concerns
of history and contemporary ethnography. From the point of view
of the Moghamo villages, Bali-Nyonga are now represented as
tools of the Germans, and the uprisings of the early years of the
twentieth century (especially 1908) are the seed from which contemporary nationalisms (note the plural) can grow.

Fanso and Chem-Langhêê present an account of Nso' military organisation and warfare. They demonstrate how a key innovation occurred in Nso' military organisation after about 1825. Nso' was divided into northern and southern sectors, each under a military leader, based in the capital. This facilitated and channelled a flow of information from lineage to village to the wider kingdom in one direction, and of directives from the centre to the periphery in the other. The individual elements of this military organisation are present elsewhere in the Grassfields but in the case of Nso' these have been assembled in an innovative and effective configuration. The authors link the characteristics of this configuration to the reputation of Nso' in the nineteenth century as a strong regional military force. Nso' had resisted the intrusions of mounted northern raiders; it had defeated the larger and more centralised neighbouring kingdom of Bamum, and in victory had killed and taken the head of the Bamum paramount Nsa'ngu. On one level this is a straightforward historical reconstruction of nineteenth- and early twentieth-century systems on the basis of documentary and oral sources. However, this, like the two papers just discussed, has significant contemporary implications. Grassfields polities resemble no one as much as each other. This lends greater urgency to the pressure to claim uniqueness or distinctive differences from their neighbours (who are up to the same thing). Both Nso' and Bali-Nyonga pride themselves on their military prowess. Nso' rejoices in the memory of the wars against the far larger and more powerful state of Bamum, and Sally Chilver has been part of the intellectual wing of such movements.

Warnier's paper analyses a little-known historical phenomenon, the revolt of the 'Kamenda Boys' in the early years of German colonial rule. This was a multiple revolt of African against white colonialist and young African against elder. The latter monopolised Grassfields political systems in which young males were powerless. In a reflexive vein Warnier notes how at the time that he recorded these events he felt embarrassment at the revelation of disorder and violence unleashed by European colonialism, and also that he could not easily use the material in what was essentially a functionalist exercise in reconstructive ethnography. Moreover, Warnier's account is of wider interest and great current relevance – there are significant resonances with descriptions of young guerrillas in Liberia, Somalia and the Highlands of New Guinea, and also in the politics of contemporary Cameroon versions of the revolt by the young against the old guard that are being played out even as we write. The *villes mortes* or boycott campaigns of the early 1990s were largely taken up by the current dependent male youth very much in opposition to customary chiefs and elders who largely support the current regime and the status quo.

The papers by Joseph Banadzem and Claude Tardits tackle the issue of conversion to world religions, in Nso' and Bamum respectively, but from very different perspectives. It is of note that Banadzem has used documentary sources from the early Christian missionaries to help reconstruct the Nso' pre-colonial religious system. While this is an increasingly common method in anthropological practice, it must be remembered how unusual it was when Sally Chilver first encouraged other scholars to use a wide variety of sources including missionary documents. The recent publication of one of her papers (Chilver 1990) is a testament to a lifetime's interest in this topic. Banadzem astutely makes the point that not only is it of little use to examine religious developments simply in terms of the play of foreign influences on an inert mass, but also that fictional sources such as the novels of Kenjo Jumban and Jedida Asheri may be even more revealing than historical and missiological literature. If this rejection of academic authority represents a form of post-modernism, it is nonetheless very welcome. We must note that while mention is made of the Fon of Nso's leanings towards Islam in the 1960s, this account of conversion is not presented in terms of a paramount doing this or that, but rather in terms of the choices made by individuals in the light of personal experiences and knowledge of the opportunities for healing and advancement. Banadzem parallels Horton (1971) in his formulation of the Nso' situation. The critical factor for Banadzem is the opening up of Nso' by the Germans to the outside world. At the same time as individuals are confronted with new experiences in a freshly unbounded world they are presented (through world religions) with a means by which to accommodate themselves to it. He goes beyond Horton in emphasising the significance of what is termed inculturation, in which core symbols of local belief are incorporated into official Christian practice. Banadzem also presents some new data that bring together the hitherto disparate strands of apotropaic hunting rituals and beliefs in animal transforms (i.e., the shape-changing powers of titled elders); this throws important light upon a broader range of Grassfields ritual practices. Indeed, Banadzem's contribution to this volume together with another paper on funerary rituals

(Banadzem forthcoming) and Chilver's (1990) discussion of 'thaumaturgy' enable us to fill a great gap in Grassfields studies, notably in providing an account of Grassfields belief systems.

Claude Tardits presents the first published discussion of the short-lived attempt by the Bamum paramount, Njoya, to syncretise Islam. Tardits discusses the document that the King wrote in 1916 entitled *Pursue to Attain*. This was written in the script '*a ka u ku nfa mfo*' devised earlier by Njoya and his court. In order to explain this document, and Njoya's motives, Tardits presents a short summary of Bamum history and religion in the nineteenth century. He uses a rich body of history, ethnography and oral tradition stemming from extended research in Bamum. Tardits focuses on Njoya as an individual, a paramount aware of the beliefs and ritual practices of his people. We see a ruler striving to manoeuvre between the different belief systems of his erstwhile northern Islamic allies and the newly arrived Christian colonisers from Europe. A third dimension to this struggle is that of customary belief and practice, from which the position of the paramount derives. The physical and symbolic space in which this takes place is the Palace. Tardits presents the striking image of individuals attending Njoya's court but only substituting their customary dress for the required Islamic dress when they reach the Palace precincts. For a very brief period between 1916 and 1918 the Palace at Fumban became a very special space in which the paramount and his immediate entourage attempted to control, through mediation and interpretation, relationships between Bamum and the world. In so boldly seeking to syncretise local and world beliefs, we may perhaps see in the figure of Njoya an overreaching personal ambition of great intellectual proportions that was to culminate in the tragedy of his subsequent death in exile under later French rule.

Finally, the paper by Christraud Geary is firmly set in the crucial proto-colonial period of early contacts between German colonisers and local rulers (already discussed for the Duala [Austen] and the Moghamo [O'Neil] as well as by Warnier [see below]). At this time there was a distinct shift in the focus of colonial activity from Bali-Nyonga to Bamum, as well as increasing concern about maintaining control over allies given advantages (including weaponry) during the initial German penetration. Many Grassfields paramounts had adopted German-style military uniforms, and were not slow to show them off to visiting Europeans. The German cartographer Max Moisel visited Babungo in 1907 and recounted that: 'Whenever a bath, meal or work intervened to interrupt the conversation with the inquisitive and chatty chief, he came back in a new uniform be it white or khaki coat or Green Litewka (German officer's undress jacket); it was always spotlessly clean.' (Chilver 1995b: 7)

Geary picks up the theme of military and political dress in the court of the Bamum paramount Njoya. She treats dress as a cultural artefact that may generate multiple meanings in the construction of identity. She uses early colonial photography as well as Bamum ethnography to explore the shifting relationship between dress and identity at a moment of great and intense change when Islam, Christianity, and the German colonialists came dramatically together with Bamum in the court of Njoya.[2]

Notes

1. These papers are due to appear as the 1996 issue of the *Journal of the Anthropological Society of Oxford*.

2. Readers should note that *Pursue to Attain*, the document considered by Tardits, was written at the end of the period of amicability between Njoya and the Germans which was marked by gifts of uniforms and other goods.

Introduction:

The Grassfields and the Tikar

Ian Fowler and David Zeitlyn

The Grassfields in History

Chilver and Kaberry brought to light the complexities of the societies of the Grassfields of Cameroon. These comprise a multiplicity of political communities predicated on heavily stressed linguistic singularity, varying modes (and extent) of centralisation of powers and the seemingly idiosyncratic parcelling up in individual polities of elements from a common core of cultural forms and practices. While not unique, this multiplicity of fiercely independent and linguistically distinct groupings is clearly distinct from other broader and more homogeneous ethnic blocks such as the Yoruba or even the Tikar (see below) from whom, paradoxically, many Grassfields dynasties claim origins.

The political and linguistic diversity of Grassfields societies is susceptible to differing interpretations. If the word 'fragmentation' were substituted for that of 'diversity' in the sentence above, we might be led to consider the Grassfields as an example of a 'shatter belt' phenomenon. In other words, as some formerly more homogeneous entity that has been fragmented into the great multiplicity of sets observed by the first European travellers to the Grassfields in the late nineteenth century. This is a negative view of Grassfields society and history. It is paralleled by a negative linguistic view of small language populations in the Grassfields as instances of language death or decline.

Explicitly 'negative' views of the diversity of sets and multiplicity of languages in the Grassfields are exemplified in the recent historical works of Eldridge Mohammadou (1990 and 1991) and the earlier work of the anthropologist Jean-Pierre Warnier (1984). In their studies a picture emerges of a hammer-blow from the north, in the shape of mounted raiders sweeping in and shattering a homogeneous and politically relatively uncentralised population. The historically attested incursions of Chamba (Jeffreys, 1962), and later Fulani raiders are taken to have disrupted local organisation leading to compaction of mixed groups in defensible positions and increasing political centralisation. We examine Eldridge Mohammadou's development of these ideas below in a discussion of the Tikar origins claimed at one point in time by certain Grassfields groups.

That mounted raiders penetrated the Grassfields in the nineteenth century is undeniable, but the actual forms of Chamba and Fulani activity were very different indeed, and moreover, the nature of their respective impacts susceptible to conflicting interpretations (Fardon 1988). There is no space to go into this in detail here, but in principle the Chamba incursions did lead to permanent settlements in the heart of the Grassfields while Fulani returned whence they came. However, it is important to stress that the largest of the Chamba successor states in the Grassfields, Bali-Nyonga, is highly composite, includes non-Chamba elements from within and beyond the Grassfields, and presently speaks Mungaka, a Grassfields language (Chilver 1967). The smaller, less powerful Chamba successor states, notably Bali-Kumbat and its small neighbours the Bali-Gashu and Bali-Gangsin, retain their Chamba-Leko dialect. This is an indication that the Grassfields have, in many ways, assimilated the Chamba; and further that the greater the degree of this assimilation the more successful the Chamba successor state, especially the Bali-Nyonga, has proved to be (see Fardon [below] and Pradelles [1995] for further discussion).

Later Fulani raids were not associated with settlement. The pastoral Fulani only arrived in the first decades of the twentieth century (Chilver 1989). Fulani raids seriously disorganised northern groups but their greatest influence was on Bamum in the later part of the nineteenth century. Between 1895 and 1897 forces from Banyo were sent to support the young king Njoya against a palace revolt led by the retainer Gbetnkom (see Tardits below for a discussion of wider Fulani influence on Bamum). This example of Grassfields elements inviting mounted military forces from the north to support local factions competing for power represents an alternative and more positive view of Grassfields history and relationships with the exterior. Indeed, rather than seeing the multiplicity of political sets and languages of the Grassfields as an outcome of processes of fragmentation by external forces, we can offer an alternative and more positive view.

When the Germans arrived in the Grassfields in the late nineteenth century they perceived it to be a distinct region. They made this judgement on the basis of the material culture, architecture and political forms they encountered. The region was not culturally homogeneous but it was perceptibly different both from its southern forest neighbours and from northern groups on the Adamawa Plateau. The kinds of groupings that the Germans found included individual chiefdoms ranging in size from 200 to 60,000, often physically bounded by large-scale earthworks and fixed in dynastic time by lengthy chief-lists.

The Germans encountered chiefs, palaces, elaborate forms of retainerdom and secret male associations with political functions. Nonetheless, these communities varied considerably in the degree of centralisation of political powers, which correlated inversely with population density so that the largest and most centralised polity, Bamum, had lowest densities whereas groups such as the Meta' or Moghamo on the western margins of the Bamenda Grassfields, described in the literature as acephalous (and in some oral traditions as slave-marches) had the highest densities of all (Warnier 1985). Patrilineal succession and virilocal marriage, large compound units with sons, brothers and their wives were predominant. However, a large section of the Bamenda Grassfields practised matrilineal succession. Put in these terms it hardly sounds like a region that was culturally, politically or socially homogeneous. Indeed, when it comes to economic activity the diversity is even more striking, with locally specialised production of a wide range of craft and agricultural products apparently unconstrained by ecological factors.

Whence then a distinctively Grassfields character given all this diversity? It is clear from early German written material and photographic records that the Germans were very much taken with the material culture of the region they called the

Grasland. Christraud Geary presents astonishing accounts of German collecting activity at the beginning of this century when 'booty' was sent home in the form of masks, stools, thrones, et cetera in order to win medals from the Kaiser (1988: 85–6). Indeed, it is precisely in these material realms, of domestic architecture, carved portals, masks, iron-ware, decorated cloth and beadwork that things, people and places become distinctively 'Grasland'. Materials, objects and skills were the substance of an intense system of exchanges that served to negotiate status between individual descent-group heads and between communities and chiefs. Hence, no one is innately Grassfields; rather, one becomes more or less Grassfields relative to one's position in the regional structure of exchanges and the opportunities that this presents.

This pattern of economic specialisation upon which participation in exchange networks was based is distinctive of the region. Jean-Pierre Warnier (1985) represents this pattern in abstract as a series of concentric rings. On the periphery is a surrounding belt of palm-oil production, then an inner ring of cereal and agricultural production associated with entrepreneurial trading houses. Finally there is a central zone characterised by production of high-value low-unit-volume commodities, such as fine ceramic-ware and wood carvings, woven caps and decorated raffia-work, and a great deal of iron-ware. Physical – topographic, edaphic and climatic – factors do not account for this regional specialisation. We may, as Warnier does, adduce Ricardian notions of comparative cost advantage – we may point out the apparent ordering of production according to relative transportation costs – but there is no reason to expect that the conditions that brought this pattern of economic specialisation into being should necessarily survive its continued existence.

Central to all of this is the nature of control by male seniors over access to women, prestige, ancestral favour and other mystical sources of power; for instance, at the centre of the Grassfields in the Ndop Plain. At the end of the nineteenth century, with very few exceptions, all the necessary materials – palm-oil, salt, cowries, camwood, et cetera – which a junior male required to progress through society to social adulthood through participation in recreational and political associations, marriage, et cetera – were not produced locally, and were obtainable only through regional trade networks (Fowler, 1990). These networks were jealously guarded by senior males.

In order for juniors to get anywhere it was necessary for them to contribute raw materials and labour to seniors in the specialised production of local commodities. The advantages to senior males in this scenario are clear, and it is interesting to note that this goes hand-in-hand with an extraordinary degree of economic control exercised by the secret male political associations linked to the palaces of Grassfields chiefs (Warnier 1985).

Harter (1986) has argued that specialisation in the production of high-value objects at the centre of the Grassfields is an outcome of economic necessity: i.e., since they had nothing else they were obliged to make all this fine craftwork to sell in order to make ends meet. There is evidence to support an opposing view (Warnier 1975). Early reports from the western Bamenda Plateau talk of the chiefdoms of the Ndop Plain in terms of great wealth. Administrative reports suggest that there were on average twice as many people per compound unit than in the very much larger chiefdom of Nso' to the east of the Plain (Anon. 1929).

The small chiefdoms of the northern Ndop Plain were no smaller than individual settlements anywhere else apart from Fumban. They were fiercely independent both from each other and from the larger neighbours that surrounded them. Chiefs engaged in more or less continuous bouts of exchanges with other chiefs that had dimensions of competition and alliance. In their production of high-value, low-unit-volume items of material culture, that incorporated powerful immaterial forces of transformation, chiefdoms at the heart of the Grassfields were extremely powerful in terms of local cosmologies (Fowler 1990).

This is the nature of competition for regional power here; it has little to do with population size or military clout. The intense competition between chiefdoms was on the whole not warlike but centred on the competitive exchange of materials and objects. People also entered this arena of competitive exchange, and recent research points up the highly composite nature of their populations. There were winners and losers in this ongoing regional game for power. The multiplicity of political sets in the Grassfields may be viewed less as a result of fragmentation by external forces and more as a result of local processes of competition for people and other resources.

The Problematic Tikar: Questions for History and Ethnography

The issue of the Tikar origin claimed at one time by many of the kingdoms of the Bamenda Grassfields provides the perfect case with which to introduce a collection of essays that celebrate the work of E.M. Chilver. Each of these essays concerns a different aspect of the relationship between history and anthropology, taking Cameroon as the case in point. History is illuminated by, and in much of Africa cannot be practised without appreciation of, the methods of anthropological fieldwork. So too, ethnography is enriched and enabled by the depth and awareness of change that is comes from a historical perspective.

What has become known as the 'Tikar Problem' has been raised (Jeffreys 1964), allegedly solved (Chilver & Kaberry 1971; Price 1979) and yet it will not go away (Mohammadou 1990). The problem has to do with the construction of identity in the colonial period and the regalisation of chieftaincy. This constructed royal or 'Tikarised' identity retains limited currency in local contemporary dynastic contexts and in some western academic discourses, particularly art-history and museological studies. It has also been subject to a curious reversal in the context of recent political debate over the future of the post-colonial state (Fowler forthcoming). Hence, this problem is a useful exemplar of the collaborative nature of the production of knowledge and construction of identity, and also of the incorporation of academic or historical knowledge in contemporary political conflict.

What then is the Tikar problem? At its crudest it may be presented as follows: many Grassfields dynasties claim Tikar descent, yet neither the languages spoken nor the cultural traditions of the groups concerned bear much relationship to the language and culture of the Tikar who presently occupy the Tikar Plain. This situation contrasts starkly with the dynastic origins of the intrusive Bali-Chamba chiefdoms (see Fardon below). In Bali-Kumbat, for example, the royal lineage unquestionably originates from the Chamba of northern Nigeria and Cameroon. Language lists from the royal court clearly reveal that the Samba-Leko language was spoken. Further, some ritual continuity can also be demonstrated for Bali-Nyonga (Pradelles 1995).

The question of Tikar origin, by contrast, rightly deserves the label of 'problem'. First, and perhaps most telling, is the linguistic issue, itself linked to a puzzle (Warnier 1979). The puzzle concerns the co-existence of two major groups of Grassfield languages, Mbam-Nkam and Western Grassfields, which in their common lexical innovations and basic vocabulary counts are closer to each other than to any of their neighbours. However, the evidence from innovations in noun classes gives a different picture; on this basis Mbam-Nkam would be included in Bantu, but Western Grassfields would not be so easily placed. In other words the lexical and grammatical evidence is contradictory. One hypothesis is that the Bantu Mbam-Nkam moved into the region splitting the Western Grassfields language group from their grammatic cousins, and that intense interaction between Mbam-Nkam and Western Grassfields led to a relexification of both language groups; hence the puzzle. According to what we know of the intensity of exchange and contact between Grassfields groups (see above) this is not an implausible solution. The intensity and long-term nature of this situation is highly relevant to the Tikar problem.

Whatever view is taken of the set of Grassfields languages, it is an inescapable conclusion that they are distinct from the language spoken by the Tikar of the Tikar Plain, the 'true' Tikar. Price makes the point that, although 'following the 1953 census, the Tikar were regarded as the largest ethnic group in the former Bamenda Province', (McCulloch, Littlewood and Dugast 1954: 11), 'there is no linguistic, ethnic or truly historical evidence that justifies using the term "Tikar" in relation to any of the Grassfields peoples' (1979: 89).

There are in fact two questions at stake here, and failure to distinguish between them has been the main cause of the persistence of the problem in the literature. Question one: how should we explain the Grassfields polities' claim to a Tikar origin? Question two: what is the origin of the Tikar people themselves? Recall that we term 'Tikar' only those who speak the Tikar language, and the separation between the two questions is *prima facie* absolute, in theory if not in practice.

We have briefly summarised the argument in light of Eldridge Mohammadou's recent work which raises once again the issue of Tikar origins for the political formations of the Grassfields. This is far more than mere origin fetishism. It is a live political issue with great currency today, just as it had a

quarter of a century ago when Chilver and Kaberry found themselves confronted with origin claims that were both relatively
new and unsubstantiated, indeed contradicted, by the available
evidence. At that time the key political question centred on the
political trajectory of that section of the former German colony,
Kamerun, which was administered by Britain. *The* question
then was whether the British Cameroons would remain effectively under Nigeria or enter into a process of 'reunification'
with that part of Kamerun that had been administered by France
(see discussion in *Paideuma* 1995). The Tikar live immediately
across this colonial divide, in the French section of Cameroun.
Before considering in more detail why Grassfields rulers claim
linguistically and culturally unlikely Tikar origins, let us look
briefly at the more recent work of Eldridge Mohammadou
which, albeit from different perspectives, reaches much the
same conclusion.

Eldridge Mohammadou has devoted many years of research to
the oral traditions of local groups in the 'middle belt' of
Cameroon. His work constitutes an unparalleled survey of historical traditions through a wide, and largely undocumented swathe
of central Cameroon. Eldridge Mohammadou has been conscien-
tious and systematic: we know whom he interviewed, when and
where. This allows us to be critical of the results and we must
emphasise how much it is to his credit that we are able to be so.
For what he presents is a set of official histories by those holding
power in the Cameroon of the 1970s and 1980s. While these are
not all warrant chiefs (Afigbo 1979) or their French equivalents,
there is little doubt that some contemporary holders of traditional
posts do so by warrant of the French administration and their successors (the best documented case is probably Geschiere [1980
and 1982] on the Maka chiefs further south in the forest zone).
These chiefs are particularly keen to legitimate their positions by
reference to history and the weight of tradition.

The historical impulse, widespread in this area, that has
received a century of encouragement from colonial and post-colonial administrators and researchers, is to account for identities
(however fragile, shifting and situationally defined) in terms of
historical origins. These origins are usually elsewhere. The
autochthones appear to have received short shrift in the received
accounts. Just what is being explained is rarely questioned. To say
'we come from ...xx' where 'xx' may be nearby, or as far away
as Palestine in some celebrated local accounts, is to make a com-

plex claim that may mean different things to different people. As such Eldridge Mohammadou reproduces political discourse without analysing the varieties and purposes to which it is put. Colonial officers conducted historical research with a view to establishing hierarchies of chiefs and structures of tax collection. The effective power of a village head could be radically altered by convincing an administrative officer that a neighbouring village was descended from a sister of his founding ancestor. What the population outside the royal palaces thought was rarely asked, and it was not important in any case.

The mere concept of subaltern studies changes this. One of the ways in which progress has been made is that we are far more sensitive to the political significance of narratives be they our own or those we report (and, according to some, expropriate). As anthropologists we are committed both to the multiple voices and varying narratives of the people with whom we work, and to the academies within which a large part of our audience is found.

Hence we are led to ask what function does a claim of Tikar origin have in a Grassfields kingdom? First of all it does very little for most of the population that owe allegiance in some form or other to the Fon in question. Yet for the Fon the claim leads to being one of the major players in the political arena, or at least to be as worthy. Grassfields claims to Tikar origins are dynastic claims both in the sense of descent ties with Tikar kings, but also in that these claims are made by Grassfields chiefs in Grassfields palaces to outsiders addressing themselves to chiefdom-wide issues through the chief and council.

Hence, a claim to Tikar dynastic origin may also be a claim to the qualities of kingship attributed to Tikar kings. The Tikar remain poorly documented. Apart from the early publications of Thorbecke we have the field research of David Price in the 1970s but unfortunately relatively little of this has been published to date. Enough is known, however, to be clear that Tikar society as described by Thorbecke (1914–24) and Price (1979, 1985, 1987) is *not* a Grassfields society. For Price the distinguishing feature of Tikar political organisation is the very high degree of concentration of powers in the king who had the power of life and death over his subjects. He sees the Tikar king as a truly sacred form of kingship. The king selected his six senior councillors and they might not overrule him; he could not be dethroned as there was no formal mechanism to do so. Unlike the Grassfields case the regulatory association of the Tikar could not act against the king but was a straightforward executive branch of government under his control. Accordingly, although political and ritual institutions of the Tikar appear to parallel 'similar sounding descriptive titles' in the literature on the Grassfields a very major difference lay in the nature of the king. Hence it is not insignificant that claims to Tikar origin were made by Grassfields chiefs and paramounts certainly not unaware of the quite different dimensions of a sacred and absolutist Tikar kingship. The latter almost certainly represents a pole to which the Fons were strongly attracted.

The regalisation of Grassfields chieftaincy is expressed in terms of an increasing separation of individuals and groups on the basis of presumed powers of agency (largely mystical in our terms) recast in the imported European binaries of royal and commoner. This works alongside a complementary restriction on the expressive use of objects (precisely those collectibles that adorn our museum cabinets) to allow for the creation of a new class of beings ('Fons'), with shared characteristics that are bounded in time and space. Collective dynastic origins are thus projected both backwards in time and outwards in space.

The exercise of contrasting the geographical spread of such dynastic claims with the total picture of claims to origins of individual patrilineages that make up individual chiefdoms reveals a very interesting scenario. It appears that the regional pattern of dynastic claims to origin mirrors the diverse composition of the individual communities. If we introduce language into this equation a very important point emerges. Common claims to dynastic Tikar origins cross-cut internal Grassfields linguistic groupings and have no significant relationship with languages present on the Tikar Plain. Yet claims to diverse origins in the composition of the general population have very real expression in terms of multilingualism, trade, exchange and marriage relationships with chiefdoms of origin.

Real, or, perhaps imagined transformations of some other principle or relationship, such common dynastic claims have been picked up quite uncritically by art-historians such as Northern (1973) and raised up to the level of tribal groupings into which local forms and styles of art-working can be bound up for expositional purposes. In some ways this is an advance over the earlier efforts of collectors and documenters of local material culture who often erroneously conflated point of acquisition with provenance. A good example of this is the chiefdom of Bali-Nyonga. The material upon which Bali's earlier false reputation as a centre of artistic excellence was based came largely from the central zone of the Grassfields, from Kom, Babanki, Oku and the Ndop Plain or recent Bamileke immigrants. By the 1970s these real centres of production had long since[1] been recognised as such. Yet they are still referred to in some of the literature as the so-called Bamenda-Tikar (see e.g., Northern 1984). Part of the complexity confronting visitors to the area is that some local cognoscenti who have had feedback from the literature may well articulate such claims. However, any such claim can really only be based on an uncritical reading of the existing literature.

In fact the Bamenda part of this nomenclature derives from a very small chiefdom, called Mandankwe, quite near Bali where the Germans built a fort and set up an administrative station around 1902. From this point on the region administered from here becomes known as Bamenda. The Tikar element of this curious tribal nomenclature reflects what has been outlined above regarding common dynastic claims to origins. In other words inclusion in this group does not follow linguistic lines, nor do the languages of the Grassfields chiefdoms claiming Tikar origins bear any meaningful relationship to that of the actual Tikar, a relatively small group living either side of the Mbam river. It is worth pointing out that the art of the Tikar is scarce and little known by comparison with the arts of the Grassfields chiefdoms that this version of history would have them to have spawned.

We can read this in two ways. Firstly, these claims only appear in the administrative records of the 1920s in the historical context of a new and British colonial regime seeking to establish some form of effective administration. Hence this may constitute a specific form of representation to that nascent colonial administration by individual communities as associational groups of relatively equal value. However, there is a wider context – that of the partition of the former colony of Kamerun, and just as in Europe post-Yalta, the political debate did not cease. The Tikar lie to the east in the francophone region. Hence, claims to Tikar origins may reflect a desire to reject incorporation into Nigeria.

There may, of course, be a material kernel from which such claims have been elaborated. Bamum, the largest Grassfields chiefdom claims dynastic links with the Tikar, and borders the Tikar area with which it maintains some ritual ties. Geary (1983a) recounts Bamum traditions that up until the reign of an early Bamum chief the material symbols of the chieftaincy – especially the double-gongs and other iron sacra came from the

east, from the Tikar area rather than the centre of the Grassfields as was the case in more recent times. So, in one sense,
powerful objects of material culture may well come to 'transmit' identity independent of movement of peoples although it
may be represented as the latter rather than the former.

Bamum had become a major regional power by the end of the
first quarter of the nineteenth century with an absolutist monarchy
firmly established at the time of German contact in 1902 (Tardits
1980). The Bamum, like their neighbours the Nso' and some others, recognise the 'ritual' ascendancy of the chief of Bankim. New
paramounts must be blessed at Rifum, a sacred lake near Bankim,
and during these rites only the chief of Bankim sits on a stool. To
sit on the ground in his presence is a clear symbol of sub-
servience. Such ritual power does not correspond to political
power, and has not done so this century, and, we can say with
some confidence, for last century also. Such conundrums do not
mean in any simple sense that the Bamum, or the Nso' *are* Tikar
or come from Bankim. There may be parallels with the origin
claims made for North American identity. We do not know how
many Americans claim to be descended from the passengers on
the Mayflower, but one suspects that it is a demographic impossi-
bility (one that parallels the total number of fragments of the True
Cross to be found in churches throughout Europe).

We are ethnographers. Our strength lies in detailed knowledge
of areas that are tiny by comparison with the span encompassed
by Eldridge Mohammadou's survey (1990 and 1991). What our
detailed knowledge reveals are some of the complexities that any
survey must miss by its very nature. To take but one example
from the history of the Mambila on the Tikar Plain – if one talks
to the heads of the hamlets that fall within the authority of the
major villages, one receives a very different history from that
obtained in the central palaces of those villages. Mambila immi-
gration onto the Tikar plain appears to have occurred in several
waves, each one conquering less of the Tikar than those Mambila
that preceded them. A historical text that makes this point from
Duabang hamlet has already been published (Zeitlyn 1992). The
degree of complexity of the problems of local population shifts
and the changing patterns of political allegiance, let alone political structures, is such that it cannot be done justice by a broad picture of invaders from the north who sweep in on horseback and
change all those that they touch.

What Eldridge Mohammadou argues, in essence, is that not the bulk of the population but the ruling Grassfields dynasties come, in some sense, from Bankim. Why else would their coronations have to be confirmed at the sacred lake outside Bankim? Let us push this argument to its logical extreme and consider the following scenario. Were it the case that some hypothetical Grassfields paramount should claim a European dynastic origin, would then the necessity to register the succession with the post-colonial administration (itself ultimately of European colonial origin) similarly confirm the claim? To describe the Bankim rite as 'confirmation of coronation' may be misleading and perhaps 'endorsement' is a more useful way of describing what is going on. Certainly we have no reason to preclude the existence of various ritual ties between some Tikar kingdoms and some Grassfields groups. For instance, following the death in 1913 of the noted Bamum queen-mother, Njapdungke, emissaries were sent from Rifum carrying fire and smeared with the white clay of mourning. Jeffreys suggests that sacred water from Rifum was also sent at the death of the Bamum king (1964). Therefore, such ritual endorsements may take many forms and may also be ongoing between paramounts who continue to exchange gifts and to send masquerades to each others' important ritual and ceremonial occasions.

The mutual dependency of Grassfields Fons may reach far deeper even than this – to the extent of a neighbouring Fon coming to occupy the stool of the deceased paramount until the succession has been assured (Chilver pers. comm.) – but this is not public knowledge and may well be concealed, especially from outsiders. One reason that the problem will not go away is that since the Bamum and Nso' do have a visible link with Bankim this serves as a model for other Grassfields groups with aspirations to wider political influence. The argument is almost syllogistic in form. High-status groups have historical links with Bankim. We are a high-status group, therefore we have historical links with Bankim.

Similar processes can be documented at work among the Mambila (immediately to the north of the Grassfields) where origin accounts which include mention of founders coming from 'The East' may be re-interpreted as meaning 'coming from Bankim'. For instance, in the 1970s Adda (1975) and Hamman (1975) documented some Nigerian Mambila as claiming Tikar origin. They say they come 'from the East' from Bankim (the centre of the Tikar living on the Tikar Plain) or from 'Shomi'. Yet one of us, as an intermittent resident of Somie (Shomi) for the past ten years, can state with some confidence that the population there claims to come from the West, descending from the Mambila Plateau in several waves over the last 150–200 years.

The general picture presented by Eldridge Mohammadou is one of Bare-Chamba raiding groups mounted on horseback sweeping down from the north in the late eighteenth or early nineteenth century, i.e., long before the Fulani raids of the eastern-most wing of the Sokoto *jihad* arrived in the area. The subsequent Fulani raids have often obliterated memory of the earlier Bare-Chamba raids. These raids are considered by Eldridge Mohammadou to have radically changed the political and demographic map of north and central Cameroon, pushing local groups on to mountain fastnesses or into nucleated polities that were centralised as a defensive strategy against the raids. This is the picture presented of the 'crystallisation' of the Tikar from the more or less acephalous indigenes of the Tikar Plain. Though here it proves necessary to introduce the complicating factor of the Mbum. Once the Tikar proper were established raiding continued with Bankim as its base. These raids went further south into the wider Grassfields, giving rise to what we now recognise as the Bamum, Nso' etc. Our argument with this is in the detail of the final sentence, 'giving rise to' is deliberately vague. We believe it cannot be fleshed out satisfactorily. Similarly Bamum, Nso', etc. The *et cetera* is a movable feast.

The problem for Eldridge Mohammadou is that he is either trying to explain too much or too little. The high degree of lexical convergence among Grassfield languages implies that they have been spoken in the same area for a long time, far longer than the few centuries covered by Eldridge Mohammadou's reconstruction. Thus he cannot claim to be accounting for the origins of the languages spoken in the area. Along with language we could include a greater or lesser amount of 'cultural baggage', but we leave that argument for another place. What he could still claim to be describing is the origin of the main institutions of the main polities. Although this is a far lesser claim it is itself weakened by the evidence of Tikar ethnography. Eldridge Mohammadou's raiders seem to have carried little with them, and, especially by contrast to the Chamba that established Grassfields Bali chiefdoms, left little behind them. The best comparison does seem to

be that of the Lumbee of the United States (Blu 1980): the Grassfields 'Tikar' are the Lumbee of Cameroon – they are united by
an assertion of identity that is its own warrant!

In 1971 Chilver and Kaberry themselves considered the issue
of claims to Tikar origin as a Malinoswkian charter, as a political
statement legitimising sacred kingship. In seeking legitimacy
there is implied both a claim for validation as well as a claim to
certain qualities of kingship or chieftaincy and the context in
which it is manifested.

It is the case, as we have noted, that both Tikar kingship and its
social and cultural context differs markedly from its Grassfields
neighbours. Price states that 'there is a high degree of cultural
homogeneity amongst the six Tikar kingdoms. They share similar
institutions... They are quite distinct from their neighbours...
They speak one language...' (1979: 91). None of these characteristics are easily applied to Grassfields chiefdoms which are to a
much greater extent linguistically and culturally heterogeneous. It
is perhaps not insignificant that the Tikar strongly exhibit the
characteristics of 'tribe', i.e., they speak one language, share common culture characteristics that mark them off from their
neighbours. Fardon (1987) has proposed that ethnic identity as a
universal class of difference is not necessarily present until it is
learnt or introduced. May we extend our reading of Grassfields
claims to Tikar origin as a response to the introduction of ideas to
do with tribe, bounded identity and so on? In other words the
Tikar present a model 'tribe' and the Grassfields chiefdoms seek
to emulate this condition by claiming a dynastic link or origin
from them. This, of course, begs the question why the Tikar
should have achieved, or be perceived to have reached, the status
of tribe or discrete ethnic identity. One clue may be the many
mentions in early exploration literature of the Tikar from a northern perspective. These include accounts of brave and successful
resistance by Tikar kingdoms, such as the Ngambe, against Fulani
sieges. It seems plausible that the Tikar may have acted as both
buffer and intermediary between northern and Grassfields groups
during the course of the nineteenth century. In this respect we may
concur with the thread of Eldridge Mohammadou's argument that
stresses the significance of the role played by Tikar groups as
intermediaries between Grassfields and northern polities.

Notes

1. First by Ankermann in 1910.

CHAPTER ONE

The Person, Ethnicity and the Problem of 'Identity' in West Africa

Richard Fardon*

Argument

The similarities between people with common attributes of 'ethnic' and 'personal' identity can be recognised only once such attributes are conceded as essential features of the way 'people are made up'. When these features are anticipated to constitute 'human kinds', novel inductive arguments may arise (arguments unthinkable were such features not conceded). However, following Goodman,[1] similarity is never given; resemblance is institutionalised and enjoys a virtuous relationship with rules of induction that demonstrate how similarity becomes operative. As such rules are mute about the grounds for sameness, the success of induction merely demonstrates the workability of grounds for sameness – not how well found those grounds are – or, indeed, how they are found at all. 'Ethnic' and 'personal' identities are productive, allowing novel kinds of inductive argument to be made, thus confirming by their very productivity the well-found, or argument-rich, status of the categories. This is evidently circular. Instead, 'whenever we reach any general conclusion on the basis of evidence about its instances, we could by the same rules of inference, but with different preferences in classification, reach an opposite conclusion' (Hacking 1992:181). In making new attributes of human kinds, as it were, speak to one another, a redefinition of the past is effected. Rather than pursuing these propositions abstractly, I want to explore two related instances that are, again to borrow Hacking's terms, 'lively and complex' (1992:192).

The first example involves a sketch of a pair of polarised 'conceptual clusters' (Bloch 1990) concerning interrelationships between person, ethnicity and identity in 'traditional' and 'modern' types of West African society. I argue that this contrast is attributable to the way in which social anthropological method has found novel human attributes problematic in West African societies. The second part of the chapter develops an example, largely derived from Sally Chilver's meticulous historical work on the chiefdom of Bali-Nyonga in the North West Province of Cameroon, of the way in which novel human attributes have been handled in the societies. I am not concerned here to argue the rightness or wrongness either of the categories themselves or of the arguments they make thinkable. My target is the discreteness, or incommensurability, of anthropological and 'local' models. I suggest instead that these models are historically connected in numerous ways, and that contrasts between them derive largely from what seems 'not to fit' in the two cases. As the boundedness of personal identity and 'collective belongings' (such as ethnicity and nation) were not novel to European and Euro-American anthropologists, they were struck by the degree to which the bounded entities failed to fit West African materials and interpreted this 'resistance' in terms of earlier (traditional) and complex states of affairs. West African accounts focus instead upon the work involved in attaining a modernity conceived in terms of bounded identities. It might seem that I am suggesting only that anthropologists tended to over-traditionalise the West African societies they studied. I believe that this argument has some truth, but that it involves claims more complex than its current status as conventional wisdom implies. The hinge between my two examples is supplied by a brief discussion of the idea of identity in which I note the slippage of that term's range of connotations from sameness to unique difference. I argue that it is this slippage (though not necessarily around the English-language term) that fundamentally connects my two examples. If this is so, no case can be made for an argument that would oppose, in simple-minded terms, the European imagination to African realities.

The 'Traditional' West African Model: a Synthesis

I follow well-known sources in seeking a 'traditional' model in southerly West African societies, described in an 'ethnographic present' that precludes the influence of major world religions (both Islam and Christianity). My use of 'traditional' is twofold: applying both to the pre-modern African situation which the models describe and to the 'traditional' status the model has achieved in West African ethnography. Relatively low population and high land availability; relatively invariant agricultural technology in terms of tools but not technique; political relationships made problematic by the scarcity of supporters; relationships between people differentiated by status categories; and a capacity for societies to be made anew at the frontier – these form a scenario[2] to which to relate the attributes of the person in West Africa. Each generalised feature is produced by contrast to a European, or modern, counter-instance which causes it to become discernible (as the use of 'relatively' suggests). Although the contrasts are diverse[3] their net effect is to produce an ideal-typical West African scenario at variance with both 'traditional' Europe and 'modern' West Africa.

If control over people, as this background scenario argues, was the foundation of West African political systems, how were these people spoken about? The main generalisations on this subject aver to a composite, unsynthesised nature of the person ('human being' might be a closer translation of most West African concepts). If we ask: in relation to what was the West African person composite as opposed to unitary (or unsynthesised as opposed to synthesised), the obvious answer is in relation to one particularly influential European idea of the person as unitary and internally consistent. The West African person was an internally organised composition, but each element of the composition was unlike any of the others and derived from a source initially external to the person. The elements could not be conflated with one another and, by virtue of the original externality of elements, the person embodied numerous relations of derivation. These derivations were both the antecedent condition of the individual's conception, formation, birth and development, and the intrinsic form taken by continuing relationships with those who shared or transmitted the same qualities. The widely reported instance of the donation of bodily substance by the mother, by virtue of her retention of blood after conception and subsequent suckling of an infant with milk, was both the antecedent condition for individual corporeal existence and the continuing basis for recognising identity, in terms of this component, with the mother, with her matri-siblings and, more distantly, with matrikin. The living individual was a cathexis where numerous connections were made, some transiently and others more permanently, in ways that might outlive the individual. The person was thus a field of tension between elements (Horton 1961). From the viewpoint of European conceptions of a unitary self, the West African person plausibly resembled the jural concept of the corporation (Strathern 1985). Formalised behaviours related the person to others in terms of the rights and obligations anticipated between particular categories of people. Positions might be heritable: for instance, a son could succeed to features of his father's being (most evidently under systems of positional succession). Similar features are described throughout West Africa.

Françoise Héritier (1977) has presented what may be a limiting case of complexity in the Samo distinctions between nine elements of the person. Each element: blood, bone, shadow, et cetera, led diversely away from the individual and, correlatively, each element in the world of agencies (gods, other people, animals, et cetera) led back to the person. The person was not simply an analogical model of the social and cosmological world but an instantiation or actualisation of it. Regionally widespread features of this actualisation include:

a) Parentage: a person has different relationships to each parent. Frequently, bodily relationship (often literal consanguinity or consubstantiality) is stressed in relation to maternity ('one mother', 'one womb', 'one blood', 'one breast suckled us' and such-like idioms are widely reported). Maternal kinship comes closest to what Europeans often mean by kinship, i.e., consanguinity. Paternity is envisaged as contrasting with maternity (sperm, bone, skull, name, incarnation, potential ancestrality, et cetera). Quite *how* paternity and maternity are defined matters less to the present argument than *that* they are defined differently.

b) The living and the dead: this distinction is not defined in quite the same way as in European systems of thought (a conclusion following the debate initiated by Kopytoff 1971). Elders and the dead converge, partly because the dead continue to play a role similar to that of the elders. How this happens is quite variable: in particular, the degree of individual 'ancestrality' accorded the dead, either individually or collectively, varies with the conventions for tracing descent, and the significance attributed to doing so at all (McKnight 1967). However, the continuing influence, in some form, of individual or collective dead upon the living is typical of West Africa, as is some degree of identification between the dead and elders in particular, and between the dead and the living more generally.

c) Forces emanating from 'society' are typically counterposed to forces from the 'wild' (Horton 1983). This is not a singular distinction, but has complex interrelationships with other distinctions to which it can be likened with varying degrees of flexibility (Jackson 1989, chaps 5–7). However, there is typically a distinction between village and surrounding bush. Relative wildness is also a characteristic of forces which play upon the individual (in the form of spirits) and of elements internal to the composition of the person (sometimes associated with maternity, animality or both).

d) Gender polarities are complexly articulated with attributes of parentage, relationships between the living and the dead, and the contrast between village and bush. Components of the individual are gendered by association with their derivation. This means that men and women are both masculine and feminine in certain respects (Amadiume 1987b). Particular attention to the complex gendering of sexual subjects is marked at turning points of a sexual subject's gender career: defeminisation for boys at initiation, correlative demasculinisation for girls, and remasculinisation for women at menopause are common. Particular gendered attributes, otherwise treated as non-dominant in sexual subjects, are foregrounded under particular circumstances: in relation to some rituals, offices, inheritance procedures and so on. This is feasible because the sexuality of subjects is treated apart from the gendering of their personal components; there is near-universal local opinion (whether presumptive or factual) that homosexuality was not thinkable in the types of society I am discussing. By contrast with, for instance, documented Melanesian examples (Strathern 1988), the sexuality of a person seems to follow unproblematically from human sexual dimorphism. However, gender discriminations, distinguishable here from sexuality, are highly complex, far from dimorphous, and relate to the gendering of the component elements of the person. In contrast to Melanesia, the relationship between sexual partners was less important for the definition of the person than the relationships between generations involving parentage. Parentage was predominantly defined in terms of gender (elaborated symbolically) rather than sexuality (relatively unelaborated, but of no less concern for that). Elaborated parental relationships and sibling seniority – rather than conjugal relationships and egalitarian siblingship – make West African kinship systems appear hierarchical relative to Melanesian examples.

e) Some forms of personal anomaly were regularly explained by slippage of the normal relationships between categorisations: shape-changing, witchcraft, twins, breech births, anomalous dentition, fear of particular diseases (notably leprosy, smallpox, epilepsy and madness), returnee children who refused to remain among the living and so on.

Idioms of relationship, and possibilities for changing them, are prefigured by these suppositions about the person. Two frequently noted features of West African societies follow from this. The second, derivative, feature illuminates the first. The composite nature of the person allows the detachment and reallocation of certain personal elements: the best known feature of this is the partibility of rights in women which could be transferred between kin groups (e.g., the Bohannans' [1953] distinction between rights *in uxorem* and *genetricem*). Different marriage regimes transferred different types of rights in women; for instance, rights to filiate children could be withheld and the mother treated as a male link in the continuation of agnatically defined descent (e.g., Amadiume 1987a 1987b). The co-occurrence of different marriage regimes was almost a West African norm (e.g., Fardon on Tiv and middle-belt societies of similar type [1984/5]; Muller on secondary and other marriage systems [1982]). The partibility of rights to be transferred was prefigured according to the definition of the components of the person (their detachability or permanence). Thus, the cumbersome terms patriliny and matriliny, or worse patriarchy and matriarchy, were led into paradox when attempting to track more subtle West African thinking on the subject (Amadiume 1987a). Does relatively high transference of rights in a woman indicate the strength of patriliny (relative to her husband's group) or its weakness (relative to her father's group)? As the nature of the operation of transference had been misconstrued, the question could not be resolved; it required acceptance of presuppositions about the unitary nature of the person. West Africans operated with a more flexible concept allowing greater complexity of personal allegiance.

The routine transference of rights in components of women's personhood was only one of a number of such operations: transference of people to settle blood debts, pawning, adoption and so forth. West African systems were notably inventive in these respects. The prevalence and general form of these institutions concerns us here; local instances can often be interrelated with other features of the bricolaging of sociality by the application of transformational analysis at a regional level.

Kopytoff and Miers (1977) have noted, controversially, that West African slavery can be fitted into this series of rights and obligations vested in corporate, composite persons as an extreme of kinlessness – an extreme detachment from their usual moorings of aspects of full personhood. Significantly, where slaves were not commodities such detachment could be reversed by a process of reattaching components of the person over two to three generations. Kinlessness was a transitory, not a permanent condition; and it was a relative rather than absolute condition: most people were more or less securely moored to most sources of their personhood.

From what were components of personhood detached? This goes back to the relational idioms of personhood. The components of the person were related in different appropriate ways to the domains from which they derived. To each component of the person corresponded a network of socialities: matrikin to maternal derivation, patrikin to paternal derivation, relationships to singular and plural divinities to a 'divine' component, relationships to the wild to a wild, animal side and so forth. Very often, the closest kinship was defined in terms of maternal commonalities, and paternal commonalities were envisaged in terms of place. These qualities might bifurcate not just in terms of matrikin *versus* patrikin, but on a repeated internal basis: for instance in a 'patrilineal' system where special recognition was accorded to mutuality with a mother's patrikin. Patrilineal and matrilineal are potentially misrecognising terms, since they fail to address the constant feature, the recognition accorded to complementary and different features of paternal and maternal parentage. These fields were complexly articulated with one another and with features of the dead, anthropomorphised agencies and so forth. At more abstract levels, human proclivities corresponded to relationships of sociality: humour to the relationships defined by privileged abuse, respect to those defined by degrees of avoidance or highly circumscribed behaviour.

What follows from this model of the person as a corporate personality, made up of juxtaposed elements, derived from outside the individual and instantiated in a particular human existence? First, I would suggest, a situational sensitivity to similarity and difference. In the African languages of which I have knowledge, similarity and difference between people are most commonly spoken about in terms of 'one' and 'different' – discussions of West African kinship in close translation suggest this to be a common feature ('we have one father and one mother', 'one father and different mothers', 'one mother but the father divides us', and so forth). It is as if identities and differences are established starkly, but only for very particular situations. Those who are completely 'one' in a particular context are different in another. It would be difficult to know how to clinch this impressionistic point but, if it is conceded momentarily, it could be argued that this relatively definite way of characterising difference and identity might correlate with the diversity of personal components to which judgements of similarity and difference can be applied. Ally this to typical West African village settings (in which everyone seems to be related to everyone else in several ways), and to a diversity of situations (which call for the same people to do all sorts of different things with one another – what used, following Gluckman, to be called multiplex social relationships), and it may be reasonable to suppose that such complexity of sociality needs to be handled without undue recourse to the grey areas between identity and difference.

Identity between two people, therefore, would derive from a particular component of personhood that became relevant because of a certain situation in which (minimally) two people (or perhaps not only the living but also the dead, gods and animals) discovered an identity. Identity was called forth transiently in the course of activity. From this perspective certain things are not possible: difference and identity cannot be fixed apart from the situations under which criteria of identity are relevant. This may be a truism, but in the context of the composite and corporate design of the person I have been discussing, it means that the whole person is not subjected to identity claims by another. It appears that only twins are potentially identical in terms of their componential make-up, and it may be significant that twins are always differentiated in West African societies.

Several other features of reported West African sociality are reconcilable with an account of the person in composite terms. Seen processually, the composite-ness of the person invites particular kinds of attempts at human regulation of its internal relationships: by assembly, mutual adjustment and dispersal or reallocation. Numerous accounts seem to attest to attempts, often by means of 'ritual', to modify internal personal relationships and, especially, to deal with the dissolution of the corporate person by the inheritance, special emplacement (in ancestral reliquaries and shrines) or expulsion from the space of the living of differentiated components of the dead. The changing composition of the person is attested not only in periodic rituals of passage or of curing, but also in the externality of naming (by reference to times, places, group membership and so on) and in the multiplicity and changeability of personal names during a lifetime.

At this point, I conclude briefly before leaving my epitomisation of a 'traditional' West African person, and the reports of sociality consistent with it, in order to ask: what was incompatible with this 'natural kind' of person? My summary and elaboration of West Africanist ethnography started from a material contrast between Europe and West Africa that suggested a crucial role for relationships between people unmediated by land; it continued deductively to examine the elaboration of this concern with relationships between people. Although the material contrast clearly involves conceiving Africa as some kind of contrasted counterpart to Europe, it would be difficult to reconcile the specific features of West African personhood as the merely negative products of European positive self-knowledge. This is not to say that features of West African personhood did not forcibly, and selectively, impress themselves upon researchers because they differed from what Europeans normally understood to be, say, slavery, conception or kinship. These features clearly challenged the observers' suppositions familiar from everyday or specialised anthropological parlance; therefore, they had to be described in vocabulary that expressed divergence from conventional expectations or by a modified descriptive lexicon. The consistency between the propositions I have synthesised is attributable neither to the unfettered operation of the European imagination nor to reported West African realities, but to a historical dialectic between the two that calls attention to itself by inviting the discovery and modification of the suppositions with which it starts out, and thereby changing the terms of European imagination and reported West African realities themselves. However, European ethnographers did consistently construe their counter-imaginings as evidence for a precedent state of affairs that was disappearing in the face of global religions, politics and economics – in short as a traditional West African condition. Furthermore, this precedent condition became the key focus of anthropological scholarship.

Identity, Ethnicity and the Person

I have been, very literally, using the term identity in a way which is presumably not what is usually meant by someone's identity – who they, or some defining other, think they are. That is part of my point. At least in Chamba, I cannot think of a term which translates with our sense of identity. However, there are numerous other terms, crucial to the style of construction I am calling 'modern', which also do not translate easily into Chamba nor, I imagine, into hundreds of other West African languages. Prominent among these are ethnicity and nation. These terms form a second 'conceptual cluster', definable in their current usage only in terms of one another. Their current prominence derives from situations in which their relationships may become mutually charged in an irreversible fashion. Ethnicities, it seems, can more readily be made than unmade under present circumstances. Chamba have been called into being by a set of circumstances such that, whatever the vagaries surrounding exact criteria of inclusion in Chamba-ness, it is difficult to envisage a near future in which this label will become a less salient category of identity.

Current ethnic identities were not called into being from nothing. Great, historically specific labour went into the outcome, and that outcome could have been different (some people could have been left out, others included; the ethnic crystallisation might conceivably have occurred around a different term...) Nonetheless, Chamba became the ethnic term (especially in Nigeria) and, once established, plenty of historical justification – that is to say antecedent usage – can be found for it. It could hardly be otherwise; a set of salient differences cannot plausibly be conjured from thin air, especially when they involve a collective construct (tribe or ethnicity) that by definition has historical moorings. That there is a redefinition of history around this ethnic term, involving the elaboration of a collective memory, needs no amplification. No ethnic or national identity is impugned by noting that it arises historically and is represented as the culmination of a historical process – none is impugned because none is exceptional – notwithstanding that some got there sooner, some have made greater investment in the outcome, and some have gained more unchallenged purchase upon people's loyalties.

To return to identity. Its current usage is recent, although it is an old word apparently derived from Indo-Germanic pronominal bases I and DE (*Oxford Etymological Dictionary of the English Language*). Originally, identity meant simply sameness, the nominal form of *identitatis*, from the roots *id* and *dem* – a present state of enduring sameness (a sort of this-thatness between things). In relation to the person, we may ask: the same as what? Presumably, the same as the person previously. For institutional purposes, individual identity is proved by an identity card, identity disc, fingerprints or voice patterns, social security number or whatever.

Personal identity involves an integration of memory which allows people to demonstrate that they are the continuation of a previously existing state of awareness. The philosophical controversy over relationships between memory and identity draws attention to the commotion always found around the weaker points of a way of world-making. Such unresolvable activity is manifest around cognate elements of the terms ethnicity, nation, and indeed race. A variant of the same problem is involved in each case: whether memory is evidence for the existence of an entity, or whether its existence is the precondition of its memory. The queries chase one another in circles: I am an individual by virtue of my memories; but only by having been an individual (of the sort my memories are supposed to demonstrate) can I lay claim to continuity of existence, which is the condition of these memories in fact being mine (see Warnock 1987). To the extent that ethnicity, tribe, nation and race are narrated in similarly bounded terms, the same conundrum must apply.

This movement in focus along the semantic range of the meaning of 'identity', from sameness to a unique difference, demonstrable by something being essentially the same only as itself at a previous moment, is symptomatic of the presuppositions shared by terms such as identity, ethnicity, tribe, nation and race. Stretching an analogy, we might say that the West African notion of the person – under the description offered here – is reminiscent of the identikit photograph, which allows the resemblance of a unique individual to be constructed from a set of parts which could be recombined to make up someone else. At least in English, one may ask whether the semantic history of identity has been motivated by its resemblance to other terms with connotations of uniqueness, ideation or boundedness, although these are of Greek derivation (idiom and idiosyncrasy; idea; ideology). Whatever the case, a word that once stressed the 'very same' (as something else) has come to be synonymous with 'unique' (identical only to itself). A conundrum of defending bounded sameness over time comes to apply to personal identity, Chamba identity, or Nigerian identity – to which correspond modes of recollection of a past to which a present has become identical – at least under some privileged descriptions. I am not suggesting that this was a mode of recollection unknown in West Africa. I noted earlier how, under systems of positional succession, the present incumbent of an office becomes identical to his predecessor, so that, for instance, the foundational history of a chiefdom may be told by the present chief in the first person, albeit that the history refers to events a century earlier. Generally, however, the older sense of identity seems to fit the traditional West African notion of 'oneness' between personal elements better than the newer sense of identity as 'uniqueness'.

Modernity and Identity

My typification of a modern style of identity is largely implicit in the foregoing. I shall treat modernity as the problem that results from the insertion of post-colonial states into a system of global internationality put in place after the Second World War. The experience of colonialism was the condition for this insertion, just as the supercession of the colonial powers was the condition for the international norm of the nation state to become globalised. The post-colonial state was bequeathed various devices of government from the colonial period, varying from very general techniques to highly specific institutions: maps, lists, censuses, judiciary and legislative arrangements, military and police forces, the commodification of land and so on. In relation to legal and economic systems of the state, the individual was called to respond in terms of an understanding of identity as something bounded and unique, especially in so far as it determined rights and, in practice more importantly, defined obligations.

The post-colonial West African state thus created a political space into which were interpellated subject citizens. Creating bounded nations of bounded personal identities simultaneously realised a third ideally bounded subject, the tribe or ethnic group, within this political space. Identity, ethnicity and nation crystallised as a cluster in West Africa, drawing on such similar presuppositions as that the self-evidence of each was underlined by its analogy to the other two. Language difference, in particular, was politicised in this matrix because of the indissociable relationship it could seem to enjoy with the essences of personal identity, ethnicity and nationality.

Much has been and remains to be written about issues over which I am skimming rapidly. My present interest concerns the four basic entities involved in textual accounts of the movement from tradition to modernity; entities commonly 'structured like': an individual self, an ethnicity, a nation state and a global system. To each corresponds a position of privilege within types of account: (auto-)biographical, tribal historical, national historiographical and the various accounts of the broadest context of these three. Although the transition between tradition and modernity, and the problem of relating the entities structured as I have suggested, are very common features of the textualisation of West African societies, quite how such accounts work in detail cannot be known in advance of the facts. Particular identities entrain specific problems of narrative to which solutions must be essayed.

Bali-Nyonga Identity: Whence Chamba-ness?

Bali-Nyonga is the most populous of five chiefdoms in the Bamenda Grassfields of the North West Province of Cameroon which, by dint of their assertion that their founders were of Chamba origin, have come to be known as Bali-Chamba chiefdoms.[4] The mounted Bali-Chamba raiders reached the Grassfields towards the end of the first quarter of the nineteenth century as part of a diaspora of Chamba-Leko (the eastern Chamba language) speakers from their homelands around the current Nigeria-Cameroon border, some five hundred kilometres to the north

(Fardon 1988). Events in Chambaland prior to the final exodus of the raiders have been the subject of competing interpretations, encouraged by the scant evidence available. The definitive departure of most Chamba raiders coincided with intensification of Fulani *jihad* in Adamawa (the eastern extension of the Sokoto caliphate) involving the establishment of Fulani lamidates within and around Chambaland, one of which took the name Tchamba. The ancestors of the Bali-Chamba were not the only raiders active in the early nineteenth century. Those whom we know to have been operating in Chambaland and in the plains below the River Benue entertained fluctuating and tactical relationships of alliance with the Fulani jihadists. One of these Benue Chamba chiefdoms, Donga, briefly concerns us later. It is likely that the future Bali-Chamba, who are recalled as being united under a leader called Gawolbe, also entertained relationships of periodic co-operation with the Fulani, although their expansion took them ahead, and eventually beyond the range, of Fulani state-building prior to the imposition of colonial rule. In very general terms, local free-booters, like Chamba and their allies, were probably useful to competing Fulani factions during the early nineteenth century when the impact of *jihad* was first felt. However, as raiding consolidated into a movement of conquest, the support of erstwhile allies became dispensable, and many of them came under pressure themselves to submit to Fulani overlordship. By the time colonisation of Chambaland occurred, the interests of Chamba and Fulani as categories (though not necessarily as individuals) were defined by antipathy – and in general terms have so remained.

Grassfields traditions recall two waves of raids by Chamba and their allies. These intrusions were eventually halted at a battle near Bafu Fundong, called Kolm (in variant spellings). The defeated Chamba, whose hero leader Gawolbe was killed, then split into several factions. The faction that eventually founded Bali-Nyonga seems to have contained a minority of the core Chamba and their close allies recruited before the sweep across the Grassfields. It seems that the succession was contested, and the ancestors of Bali-Nyonga may have set off under a female leader to settle on the borders of Bamum. Here they incorporated a large group of people called Bati, whose numerical preponderance may have caused the group to abandon the Chamba Leko language in favour of a Bantoid language called Mungakka, related to the language of Bamum. Settling near its present site, Bali-Nyonga engaged in a number of – what are now seen as –

internecine wars during the 1860s with another of the Chamba states, Bali-Kumbat which (like three other smaller kingdoms) retained Chamba Leko as its language. By force of arms, a position of influence was established in the Grassfields by Bali-Nyonga before it became the focus of German interest after 1889 with the arrival of the German explorer Eugen Zintgraff. Bali-Nyonga briefly became the brokers of German interests in the Grassfields, and Mungakka expanded in importance.

I want to register some problems that were to face later historians of Bali-Nyonga by virtue of events prior to the end of German colonialism, as well as some telling anachronisms, in my brief account. The chiefdom of Bali-Nyonga was to take a leading role in the definition of Chamba-ness in the Grassfields, yet most Bali-Nyonga did not speak a Chamba language, although Chamba Leko survived as a court language. The composition of the chiefdom had become extremely mixed, so that a minority could argue descent either from Chamba or from their adherents picked up outside the Grassfields. In terms of language, descent, culture and organisation, Bali-Nyonga was a Grassfields chiefdom and might well have established an historical account of itself as a Grassfields successor state, albeit one that had frequently been the scourge of its neighbours. However, this did not happen. Even pre-colonially, the leaders of Bali-Nyonga seem to have been concerned to retain their 'Chamba' status, for instance by petitioning help from other Bali to reconstitute 'Chamba' cults.

Why then did they make such efforts? Moreover, and here is the anachronism: what identity were they claiming when they stressed their northern, immigrant 'origins'? Despite the terms I have used above, it clearly could not have been a Chamba identity in any simple sense. Although the origins of the term Chamba are not beyond dispute, we do know that 'Chamba' is not a Chamba term. Neither Chamba language has a {ch}; the cognates of Chamba are *Sama* or *Samba*. Since Chamba is not of Fulani origin either (their term for Chamba retains an initial {s}), it seems most likely to have been a Hausa traders' term, adopted and textualised by Europeans via their translators. Given the complexities of interpretation – often via intermediary languages – and given also that we have to work from published reminiscences with unknown relationships to any utterances which they purport to record, quite what particular Bali were saying to particular Germans is difficult to guess. In any case, the term Chamba is notably *not* prominent in early German sources.

What Bali were calling *one another* around the turn of the last century is yet more difficult to guess. Given their rather frantic history of relocation, splitting, recruitment and dispute during the nineteenth century, it is readily understandable that collectivising terms would be in a fluid state. *Ba'ni* (singular *Ya'ni*) might refer to all the inhabitants of the five Bali states, or it might distinguish the longer-term adherents of these polities and their predecessors.[5] *Ndagan* could be used to designate elements whose origins lay outside the Grassfields; this term is probably cognate with Daka (a term which contrasts situationally with *Sama* in Chambaland). Nowadays, *Ndagan* is sometimes taken to be synonymous with Chamba; however, the remaining clan names in Bali-Nyonga suggest that *Ndagan* included peoples who, were they in the north, would now belong to ethnic groups distinct from Chamba (e.g., Pere, Bata). *Sama* (the likely cognate of Chamba) was used as a royal clan name and as the term for a class of royal appointees (encharged with the *lela* martial ritual) who contrasted loosely with *Ndagana* (the custodians of *voma* harvest ritual). Between themselves, and when it suited them, the five Bali chiefdoms could refer to one another by locational terms (each of which had a composite form, Bali-something, as well as a non-composite form without the common term).

Early German sources tended to use the term Bali and to note that the Bali came from the north, or southern Adamawa, but located this place more precisely by reference to known extant Fulani chiefdoms.[6] Nonetheless, the pieces of a jigsaw of Chamba diaspora had begun to be put together. For instance, Zintgraff's first voyage took him from Bali-Nyonga to Takum (now in Nigeria) where he assured himself that the rulers of the two chiefdoms shared descent from the movement under Gawolbe, as well as a common language. However, Benue Chamba were generally known as Dinyi (or some variant), so the relationship was based on common origin from a raiding movement rather than on the common ethnic term Chamba.

There were moments in its history when Bali-Nyonga could have equally, or probably more plausibly set in train arguments for an ethnic identity other than it did. So why, and when – eventually – Chamba? Minimally, Bali seem to have been telling Zintgraff and subsequent German interlocutors that they were from the north, and therefore distinct from the Grassfielders among whom they dwelt. In a variety of ways, northern origins may have been prestigious. In Bamenda we find the odd specta-

cle (from a Chambaland perspective) of 'Chamba' claiming kinship with Fulani (the 1961 *Chamba National Almanac* has a caption to a photograph of a Fulani and a Bali observating that they
are of 'common stock'). However, Fulani and *Ba'ni* were both
northern raiders, and to liken *Ba'ni* to Fulani might suggest their
special suitability as intermediaries in the regulation of their
northern Kamerun colony – for whom the Germans, at least in the
person of Zintgraff, were looking at that time. Prominent among
the Fulani lamidates to the north of the Grassfields, which the
Germans were yet to conquer, was one called Tibati, which in turn
had been founded from Tchamba (the lamidate founded in
Chambaland) by Hamman Sambo.[7] The term Chamba linked connotations of northern power and Fulani-ness, while simultaneously differentiating the Bali from their neighbours in a fashion
which may have corresponded to German perceptions (or Bali
perceptions of German perceptions) of the exceptional character
of the Bali.

The precise period at which the Bali chiefdoms became defin-
itively 'Chamba' in their own accounts is unclear. My sense from
readily accessible documentation is that, once the term became
available, there was a two-stage crystallisation of a sense of collective Chamba-ness, involving all five of the Bali chiefdoms,
around the earliest and latest years of the British administration.
One thread running through the period (see Chilver 1963, 1967)
concerned Bali-Nyonga local hegemony, and what a contemporary local writer dubs 'Baliphobia' (Nyamndi 1988). Military
exploits both before and after the arrival of the Germans, and various German and British ratifications of its position, had enabled
Bali-Nyonga to assume formal administrative control over a relatively widespread population. By virtue of active resistance, both
on the ground and in the courts, this position was gradually erod-
ed from the later German period onwards. Numerous enquiries
were pursued and reports written[8] with a view to clarifying the situation. Bali-Nyonga became adept at handling the succession of
consultations which required them to account for themselves historically. The more general efflorescence of Grassfields historical
studies[9] argues against over-emphasising the point, but the embat-
tled position of privilege that Bali-Nyonga had attained must have
added immediate point to their historicising efforts.

Early British reports show that the Chamba connection had
become conventional wisdom for District Officers – and presumably for Bali also.[10] The majority Chamba populations of the

north were either in Nigeria or the northern Cameroons Mandate
(a very small minority was in French Cameroon). Ethnographic
developments in these British-administered territories were to
have an impact on 'Chambaisation' in ways that could hardly
have been foreseen. The Government Anthropologist C.K. Meek
spent six weeks of 1927 in Donga (the most significant of the
Chamba chiefdoms below the Benue in Nigeria). His published
account (1931) makes evident the skein of resemblances among
the dispersed and varied Chamba in Nigeria. As an assistant,
Meek employed the services of a young man who went on to
become Gara of Donga in 1931. Mallam Bitemya Sambo Garbosa
II's own book on Chamba history and the Donga chiefs (privately published in Hausa) was the fruit of a long process of research.
Garbosa tells us that he wrote a first draft of his book in 1923,
renewing his efforts after working with Meek to complete a further draft in 1932–3. The private publication of the two volumes,
which include details of his visit to Bamenda in 1954, probably
occurred in 1956. How widely earlier versions of the book circulated I do not know, but it was available to Bali commentators on
publication if not earlier.[11]

The scholar/administrator M.D.W. Jeffreys[12] not only published materials on Bali history collected by himself (e.g., on
Bali-Kumbat in 1957) but in a 1962 article synthesised previous
sources. Prominent among these sources is a text transcribed by
Isaac Fielding Pefok in 1933 (see Jeffreys 1962b) from the testimony of Tita Nji ('son' of Galega I, d.1901) at the instigation of
Fonyonga II in 'the vernacular' (i.e., Mungakka).[13] Among the
many interests of this text is the addition of five chiefs to the Bali
regnal list prior to the generally accepted hero-leader Gawolbe
(Jeffreys 1962a: 185). Jeffreys (who accepts the integrity of the
additional five chiefs whom he incorporates into his own dating)
reports (1962a: 192–3) that a meeting of the Fon's council was
specially convened in November 1960 to discuss the discovery
of the chiefs, about whom they previously had known nothing.
The oldest men were 'intransigent in their refusal to accept
Tita Nji's account as Bali tradition'. Tita Nji not only added five
unknown fons but supplied them with a history. A first Gawolbe
settled in Tchad from Syria and conquered the Fulani; four generations later a second Gawolbe, who had quarrelled with and killed
Sama (a half-brother by their common father Gangsin and a
Fulani woman), led the incursions into Bamenda. Gawolbe II died
at the battle of Kolm and transformed into a bull elephant; fol-

THE PERSON, ETHNICITY AND THE PROBLEM OF 'IDENTITY'   35

lowing this the confederation dispersed to form the present Bali chiefdoms.

Jeffreys (1962a, Appendix C) notes the formation in 1960 of a Bali Historical Society, while deploring some of the more speculative attempts to reconstruct Bali origins. Renewed interest in history had immediate local antecedents in conflagration over land issues (the 'Widekum Riots' of 1952, see note 8), and the visit of Garbosa II of Donga to Bali in 1954 as well as the broader implications of impending reunification with Cameroon. The Bali Historical Society became the focus of Phyllis Kaberry and Sally Chilver's initial investigations of Bali-Nyonga history. As they tell us in their published account of the political system of Bali-Nyonga (1961), their visit in the previous year was only of twenty days but:

> occurred during a period when the new intelligentsia and the traditional office-holders were seriously discussing the traditional system of government and its significance for local and national elective party government. We had the collaboration of the History Committee of Bali-Nyonga under the presidence of Mfon Galega II. Regular meetings were held in which important men, conversant with the history and government of Bali-Nyonga, thrashed out the questions we put to them and arrived at agreed answers which were translated to us by Councillor Alfred W. Daiga (the Mfon's secretary). (Kaberry and Chilver 1961: 355)

Sally Chilver's two-part report (1964) – unpublished but greatly cited in regional literature – was submitted to the Bali Historical Society after her second period of research in 1963. A pan-Chamba Union was formed but seems to have come to little, beyond a well produced 1961 Almanac. However, Bali-Chamba history came on apace. Part of the impetus derived from publications edited by the anthropologist Edwin Ardener and published in Buea by the Government Printer, making them readily available to local schools. Two volumes in the series consisted of a résumé of Bamenda history and tradition based on Kaberry and Chilver's researches (Chilver 1966; Chilver and Kaberry 1968). The success of this venture[14] was noted by the Secretary of State for Primary Education and Social Welfare in his Foreword to a shorter volume – Sally Chilver's translation and synopsis (1966) of the parts of Zintgraff's writings (Zintgraff 1895) relevant to Bamenda history. Roughly between 1960 and 1968, the readily accessible material at the disposal of local historians increased exponentially[15] and school history projects flourished (Chilver personal communication). Published accounts for the early 1970s are less numerous but this may represent only the result of the vagaries of my access to sources. From the later 1970s fresh initiatives are evident in the publication by 'a group of Bali-Nyonga youths' of a series of historically oriented brochures.[16]

Perhaps little of practical significance can be claimed for a Chamba identity that crossed national, provincial and state boundaries.[17] But the sense of a Chamba-ness that included peoples in North Cameroon, Northern Nigeria, Nigeria below the Benue, and the North West Province of Cameroon had clearly become an established fact – at least in the imagination – by this time (see note 9). Chamba identity fits the overall scheme of larger-scale ethnic identities emerging in West Africa during the twentieth century. It had, though, been a work of great effort – and of no great likelihood from a late-nineteenth-century commentator's point of view. Had colonisation not occurred when it did, there is little reason to suppose that Bali-Nyonga would have 'become' Chamba. Given another century, the claim to common origin with the other four Bali chiefdoms (had Mubako survived in all of them) might have been dropped, or retained in a fashion as perplexing to putative ethnographer/historians of the early twenty-first century as the common claim to Tikar origins (on the part of many other Grassfields chiefdoms) has been to ethnographers of the twentieth century. Of course, the Chamba-ness of Bali-Nyonga is a very selective appropriation of the past. Descendants of some of the raiders from outside the Grassfields would probably – had they stayed where they were – have become elements of the Chamba of the homelands (themselves defined through an historical process). It is difficult both to put the case more strongly and to decide whose representation of whom the 'Chamba-ness' of Bali-Nyonga is. My earlier question about African realities and European representations ceases to make sense. At best we can describe the work as comprising interrelating historically situated suppositions, and the tendencies towards a particular outcome. The retrojection of entities (here, the Chamba) into the narrative of a period (the nineteenth century and earlier) when they clearly did not exist is virtually impossible to resist given the conventions for putting collective 'actors' into a comprehensible history.

Bali-Nyonga: Narrating Modernity

To pursue the question of identity further, I shall refer in greater detail to two locally produced volumes of Bali history. Both were published in 1988: Ndifontah B. Nyamndi's *The Bali-Chamba of Cameroon: a Political History* and the collectively authored account *An Introduction to the Study of Bali-Nyonga: a Tribute to His Royal Highness Galega II, Traditional Ruler of Bali-Nyonga from 1940–85* (Titanji et al. 1988). The death of Galega II prompted both publications, since the first is apparently a history that outgrew the possibility of placing it in the second. This skewing in my sources may fit all too easily with the argument I want to make.

The insertion of Bali-Chamba identity into modernity, by which I mean strictly a narrative task of writing history evaluatively, is achieved in particular via the representation of the individuality of Grassfields rulers. This is striking to an observer more familiar with Chambaland, where this is rarely the case. Reasons for the emphasis are all too obvious: Grassfields chiefdoms in general attribute great centrality to their fons, and Bali-Nyonga has been portrayed as an extreme of this tendency; German accounts, particularly Zintgraff's travelogue (locally accessible as Chilver 1966), tend to stress the personal relationships between the German explorer and the African king. The variant of indirect rule practised by the British consolidated the political functions of chiefship; many of the writers of Bali history presumably absorbed a 'Kings and Queens' account of British history as part of their education. Finally, as we have seen, the occasions for the production of the literature are themselves likely to skew representations in favour of chiefly centrality.

The Bali-Chamba story recounted in these books concerns origins, dispersal and reunification. Northern, Chamba origins are conflated with stereotyped Fulani characteristics. Bali-Chamba are portrayed as the racial inheritors of the martial virtues of the Chamba, 'a tall, negroid people with a distinctly imperious bearing' and an 'inherent love for independence' (Nyamndi 1988: 1, 4–5). Defeated at Bafu Fundong, the united Bali-Chamba dispersed to engage in local conflicts until the meeting between Zintgraff and Galega. Both sources note that Bali-Chamba people looked Zintgraff straight in the eye, something he had not met elsewhere in Africa, and that the two leaders subsequently made a blood pact.[18] Zintgraff brought Bali into the wider world, a clear theme, dated exactly to 16 January 1889 (Gwanfogbe in Titanji et al. 1988: 23) and recognised in the Bali the martial virtues they now feel in themselves – as it were externally and objectively.

Most of the German colonial period, the transition between British administration and reunification with Cameroon, occurred within the reigns of two Bali-Nyonga fons: Fonyonga II (1901–40), son of Galega I (mid-1850s to 1901) and his son Galega II (1940–85). Their descent line is traced from the leader of the Chamba alliance, Gawolbe. In the accounts, the rulers make the transition to modernity. I present Galega II, the 'Fon of a new age' (Nyamndi 1988: 139), through a brief collage of our sources. He was sent to school because his father had enthusiastically supported education since the earliest establishment of a German missionary school. Fonyonga II had learned to read and write at the age of forty-five (Ibid. 115). The future Galega II eventually became a pharmacy dispenser. Although he never attended secondary school he left a son with a Ph.D. to succeed him (Ndangam in Titanji et al. 1988: 63).

> The idea of development appears to have been uppermost in the new Fon's mind as seen by the fact that a few months after his accession to the throne he organised the Bali Development Committee in 1941 to plan streets for Bali town and to open up roads in the area.[19] Two years later in 1943 he founded the Bali Improvement Union (BIU) to foster the education of capable young men. The organisation launched a scholarship scheme from which a good number of young people were able to do higher education abroad in Europe and the U.S. (Nwana in Titanji et al. 1988: 72)

> In the mid 40's V.S. Galega II became the Chairman of Bali Area Rural Council. When later on the Gah of Bali Gham assisted him as Vice-Chairman of Bali Council the idea of an association for the Chamba family occurred to him. He contacted the other Chamba Fons in the North West Province and the *Chamba Wat-Coon* (Pan Chamba Association) was formed to preserve the rich cultural heritage of Bali Chamba. The five Fons of the Chamba group met frequently and exchanged visits especially during the *Lela* festival. (Ndangam in Titanji et al. 1988: 47)

> He was born in a grass-roofed palace. He died in a modern one that contrasts sharply with the old one in magnificence. The painful etiquette by which people entered the palace bare-footed got discarded in one stroke of reform. (Ndangam in Titanji et al. 1988: 62)

> His *private world* [he had 35 wives and over 200 children] ... reveals an ordinary human being with extraordinary responsibilities and obligations (Ibid. 61, my emphasis)

To his wives he insisted on three things: The first, based on economic consideration was that they should learn a traditional craft appropriate to women
and keep themselves busy. Most of his wives learnt how to weave grass-trays
(*Kukad*). Secondly he insisted on their keeping themselves and their premis-
es clean, an idea, no doubt ingrained in his life-style from his medical pro-
fession. Thirdly he got all his wives actively engaged in the learning of Bali
culture. He organised cultural classes for his wives and children and got
experts ... to teach them the *Mubako*, the original language of the Balis as
well as the *Lela* songs and dance. These private classes clearly yielded positive fruits as could be seen by the role played by the Fon's wives at the *Lela*
dances especially in the production of *Lela* music. (Ibid.)

Galega II was the first Fon to clothe his wives in North West Province and
went around to encourage his colleagues to do the same. It is said that Galega
II, a close friend to the Fon of Bafut, Achirimbi II, forced the latter's wives
to be clothed by providing the first dresses to them. (Nwana in Titanji et al.
1988: 73)

Galega II seems to have recognised in himself the qualities his
obituarists also note. When British settlement of the 'Widekum
Riots' (see note 8) awarded Bali compensation of £9,000, the sum
was astutely transvalued through investment in a modern, pipe-
borne water supply for Bali town (Gwanfogbe in Titanji et al.
1988: 38). Galega II was a British-nominated representative to the
Regional House of Assembly for Eastern Nigeria, a proponent of
unification with Cameroon rather than Nigeria, and actively
involved in the leadership of the single Cameroonian political
party in his region following Independence.

I leave the final word on Bali-Chamba ethnicity in the modern
world to one of our authors:

ideally [a] consolidated kingdom remained the dream of many Bali. But
practically it seemed so unfeasible in geographical terms as to be completely out of this world. Yet on closer examination the prospect is not all that far-
fetched either. After all there are many components of that unity, and
common territory is only one of them. (Nyamndi 1988: 154–5)

Conclusion

Basil Davidson (1992) has recently argued that Africans have
been alienated from their own history by Europeans. Evidently he
intends a greater theme than my narrow example can contest. In
Bali-Nyonga the seizure of history as argument has been part of
the sense of transition to modernity (measured also in airstrips,
cash crops, doctorates and priesthoods, involvement in national

affairs, town planning, educational institutions, church buildings and so on). If the history has not been entirely of their own making, then it has not obviously been entirely of European making either. The opposition simply fails to capture even such subtleties as I have been able to glean from extant records. Entities structured as individuals, ethnicities, nations and a wider context, perhaps a global one, may be a common terminus but this is hardly to suggest that other entities (Africa or Europe) can be portrayed in any simple way as the agencies responsible for this outcome. One is struck rather by the way in which professional anthropologists and local historians, both accepting bounded identities as a norm, find different problems. To oversimplify: while the anthropologist tends to construe what fails to fit as indicative of a preceding situation, the local historian has to interpret it as precursive of modernity, and a possible future. As remarkable, though, are the complex connections between these projects.

A note of reflexivity (historical rather than personal) may be an appropriate way to end. As a postgraduate student, looking to do fieldwork in Nigeria or Cameroon – the specialisations of my anthropology department – I read C.K. Meek's chapter on the Chamba and chose fieldwork in Chambaland on account of the extraordinarily varied forms of social organisation he described. Meek had collaborated with Garbosa, and I was given a copy of Garbosa's book by the Chamba Chief of Ganye on my arrival in Nigeria. Earlier Garbosa took some responsibility for galvanising interest in history among Bali chiefs, and it was from the meetings of the Bali Historical Committee that Phyllis Kaberry and Sally Chilver composed their early accounts of Bali-Nyonga history. Phyllis, one of my teachers, arranged for me to have access to Sally's handwritten reports to the Bali Historical Society and then to meet her. Putting together a synthesising account of different Chamba communities seemed an 'obvious' task, the step that had to be taken before anything else could be done. Chamba intelligentsia in the homelands consistently reinforced my sense of purpose by defining what they thought I was doing in pan-Chamba terms. Looking back it is far from clear whether I decided to write a pan-Chamba account or whether the feasibility of that account was lying in wait to kidnap a likely passing author. Skipping ahead almost twenty years, I find myself reading Nyamndi's account of Bali history, which draws upon my own doctorate and many of the resources for writing Grassfields history that are locally available in the Phyllis

Kaberry Resource Centre founded in memory of her pioneering work.

Event rich in fact and recollection, to borrow Edwin Ardener's phrase, Bali-Nyonga history has involved a skein of collaborative moves, themselves compounded of academic careers, political trajectories and theoretical proclivities – both Cameroonian and European. Quite who is writing whom, and in terms of what, becomes increasingly difficult to decide, quite apart from the steps (some of them now lost) by which we got 'here'. In retracing these steps I have tried to offer one interpretation of the sense of modernity, and some sense of the context in which a historiographic tradition has revolved around the intellectual and practical formulation and insertion of identity.

Notes

* The two halves of this paper were written with a single argument in mind but originally delivered to different audiences. The first was presented to the 'Identity in Africa' seminar at the University of Bayreuth in February 1993. An earlier version of the second half made up the bulk of a paper for a seminar on 'Modernity and Communication' at the University of Manchester the following month. The stimulation of these invitations is traced in the themes I try to articulate here. Thanks are due to Janos Reisz for his invitation to Bayreuth, and for the focus on identity; commentators at Manchester provided numerous suggestions of which I have availed myself.

1. See Douglas and Hull, 1992 for reprints of Goodman's 'Seven Strictures on Similarity' and 'The new Riddle of Induction', and especially the emendation of Goodman's argument to apply to 'human kinds' by Ian Hacking in that volume.

2. This owes much to Goody (1971) (as developed by e.g., Terray 1972, Meillassoux 1981) and the related arguments of Kopytoff (1987). Counter-examples have been produced (e.g., Hopkins 1973; Law 1976, 1978), but the generalisations hold over a remarkably wide range of societies.

3. See Fardon and Furniss, 1993 for discussion of the tropes of 'dearth' and 'plenty', and Palmié (n.d.) for other instantiations of the idea of frontier.

4. Between 1976 and 1990 I spent roughly three years researching among Chamba, but my experience of Bamenda occupied only ten weeks – in 1984, during research funded by the Economic and Social Research Council. Even then, I was not based in Bali-Nyonga, and I do not have a command of Chamba Leko (the minority language of Chambaland). While passing acquaintance with the local scene in Bamenda, as well as a more

thorough-going immersion in the history and culture of Chambaland, have been helpful to writing this paper, my discussion is historiographic: reliant upon previous writings and devoid of further ethnographic specification. My argument would be greatly enhanced were I able to go beyond the texts at my disposal, for instance to know how written opinions relate to local oral debates. As in every previous foray into Bali-Chamba affairs, I am indebted to Sally Chilver for her advice, encouragement and guidance both personally and through her publications.

5. The derivation of this term is problematic. Raiders from the north, of whatever ethnicity, were called Bale, Tibale, Tibar, Tipala or Tibana in the Grassfields. Chilver and Kaberry (1965; 1968) examined the records of recaptives (collected in Sierra Leone by Koelle) in which cognate terms appear as names for their original captors, and have noted that this name was known to a British parliamentary commission by the mid-nineteenth century. Whether this term derives from, or is the source of, Bali cannot be decided as things stand. Although some commentators claim Bali to be a European misrendering of Bare, {r} or {l} are substitutable in Chamba Leko dialects, and Mubako favours {l} (for instance what Bali call *lela* would be *lera* in most Chamba Leko chiefdoms). Moreover, the singular of *Ba'ni* is reported to be *Ya'ni*, whereas Chamba Leko generally form plurals through the addition of suffixes. One of Chilver's sources (Fokunggan Sambum, recorded in 1963) claims *Ba'ni* to be a Bati word (personal communication).

6. The cartographer Moisel, basing his report on information derived from Ernst and Dorsch of the Basel Mission in 1907, claimed that the original Chamba homeland was unknown but they were once settled around Koncha (a Fulani lamidate). Keller's 1969 account brings the Bali from Garoua, another lamidate, and suggests a Mubako derivation for the name. The ethnographer Frobenius published two accounts of his 1911 researches in Chambaland. The first, in 1913, remarks the relationship between Chamba and the chiefdoms below the Benue (notably Donga), while the second (1925) stresses the relationship between Chamba and Bali to the exclusion of the Benue connection. Strümpell's wordlists show clear appreciation of the linguistic relation between Chamba Leko and Mubako. Although Ankermann's account of the *lela* ceremony is based on observations in 1907–8, he does not explore the historical precedents of Bali; neither does the missionary Vielhauer in his account of the *voma* festivals in 1910 (Baumann and Vajda 1959). For general discussion of early German sources see Kaberry and Chilver 1968: 355–8.

7. This resemblance of terms, especially once Barth's early reference was taken up, seems to have caused confusion between Chamba, Tchamba and Hamman Sambo (for instance Jeffreys 1962a represents Hamman Sambo's exploits as evidence of Chamba expansion).

8. Chilver (1967) provides a vivid account of the establishment of the Zintgraff-Galega axis. Despite the relative decline of Bali fortunes under later German rule, 1905 is the date crucial to later disputes, since it was then that Fonyonga II's control over thirty-one villages, predominantly south of Bali, was promulgated (Ibid. 499). Further groups were added in 1906 and 1907 but not retained when reversal of this policy ensued by the end of the German period. Rumblings of discontent continued, beginning when land claims against Bali-Nyonga were refused by Hunt in 1921, a position that was ratified by Goodliffe's enquiry and report in 1949. Further unsuccessful legal action ensued in 1952, followed closely by rioting (the 'Widekum Riots') which claimed fifteen lives and caused considerable damage. The Manson Report of 1953 (reproduced in Nyamndi 1988, Appendix Four) ratified the existing position and awarded compensation to Bali. However, the issue did not go away. Copies of Goodliffe's report, appended to letters to the State Governor and Head of State from the Bali Fon in October 1977, were circulating in bound form when I visited in 1984, as the Fon attempted to repudiate another land demand. By 1977 the Fon had conceded that the Bali had conquered land in Bamenda but argued, via the by-then established Chamba connection, that the Bali had themselves been dispossessed in Northern Cameroon and were not, for that reason, either inciting their Chamba 'kith and kin' to join them in North West Province, or themselves intending to launch land claims in the North. Extensive Chamba ethnicity, at least rhetorically, had become a serviceable device in argument.

9. Njoya's historical work on Bamum is an obvious early instance (see Tardits 1980).

10. Hunt, in 1925, notes 'The Bali clan belong to the Chamba-Leko tribe and originally came from Tschamba' (para. 7). Hawkesworth's 1926 Assessment has the Chamba divide in Ngaoundéré to form the Bali tribe 'via the Tikar route' or to follow the 'Jukun route' to Donga (para. 16).

11. M.D.W. Jeffreys (1962a: 172) notes that he had a translation of Garbosa's work made by a member of the Veterinary Department in Bamenda; its date is not given.

12. Jeffreys was in charge of Bamenda Division between 1936 and 1945.

13. Sally Chilver, who has also translated this text, suggests it may have circulated in several versions as a manuscript copied by school teachers from the original in 'Church Bali' (i.e., the Mungaka of the Basel Mission orthography) dictated to Pefok by Tita Nji II, the grandson of Galega I, in the mid-1930s. Jeffreys appears to have confused Tita Nji II with his eponymous father, who was son of Galega I and known to Zintgraff.

14. More recently, Paul Nkwi and Jean-Pierre Warnier have written an account explicitly designed to succeed Kaberry and Chilver's volume (1982: 4).

15. Phyllis Kaberry and Sally Chilver produced numerous publications around this time and both took pains to assure their published and unpublished accounts were available locally (e.g. Fohtung 1992 [1962]).

16. The first of these, 'The *lela* festival' (16 pp., locally cyclostyled and bound), appeared in 1978. In the following year a record of *lela* music was issued in France on the Arion label, recorded by Dr Errol Leighton. The third 'attempt', as the series is described, largely consisted of a collection of personal names. Apparently distinct from this series is a 'Portrait of Their Royal Highnesses' (i.e., the fons of Bali-Nyonga) compiled by Augustine F. Ndangam and Dr Elias Nwana, who together motivated much of the effort of the overall historical initiative. (Dr Nwana kindly put me abreast of this research as it stood in 1984.)

17. The Chamba National Union in Cameroon, formed in 1958, apparently 'died a natural death' because the five chiefs could not agree about 'precedence, always reading into it a retrospective legitimization of power that went back as far as Gawolbe's succession' (Nyamndi 1988: 156). Over the years the Nigerian Chamba Union has sporadically issued calendars, and relationships have been maintained between the more important chiefs.

18. Zintgraff seems to have been rather profligate in making blood pacts, as the excerpts in Chilver, 1966 attest.
    Editors' note. From Zintgraff's account and also from Sally Chilver's researches (personal communication) it appears that it was the envoy of the Bali Fon, sent out to welcome the explorer, who looked directly into Zintgraff's eyes. This envoy was of Bati (i.e., Bamileke) origin.

19. For an analysis of town planning as a ritual of competitive moderniation see Richards, 1992.

CHAPTER TWO

Political Relationships on the Eastern Marches of Adamawa in the Late Nineteenth Century:
A Problem of Interpretation*

Philip Burnham

Introduction

The emergence of African history as a discipline, in contrast to European imperial history of Africa, is still quite a recent phenomenon. It dates to the 1950s and was closely linked with the political trends that led to the demise of colonial rule (see Vansina, Mauny & Thomas 1964). These developments also coincided with a growing interest, within the discipline of social anthropology, in linking historical and anthropological perspectives as a corrective to the excessively static models of society which had been characteristic of functionalist anthropology between the two world wars.

Such a linkage, however, posed a number of intellectual challenges, both theoretical and methodological, to which the disciplines of history and anthropology have responded, with more or less success, in the intervening decades. For those of us who have worked on such problems in Cameroon and in adjacent states such as Nigeria and the Central African Republic, the fine example set by Sally Chilver, working during much of the time in close association with Phyllis Kaberry, has been of fundamental importance in setting standards and showing the way. On a personal plane, we have always been able to count on Sally's unstinting help and advice in pursuing our research interests.

Sally and Phyllis, in their joint research in the Cameroon Grassfields, effectively breached the disciplinary barriers separating history and anthropology, laying the basis for a rich harvest of data which illuminated both the historical development of Grassfields societies in the pre-colonial era and the transformations of these societies during the colonial period and after Cameroonian Independence. Sally's erudition and broad knowledge of the archival sources, combined with her fieldwork experience in the Grassfields chiefdoms, enabled her to develop a multi-faceted method of historical research which had few equals in the 1960s.

I was one to benefit from Sally and Phyllis's advice and moral support from the late 1960s onward although, through a quirk of fate, I wound up going to the 'far east' of francophone Cameroon rather than to south-western Cameroon as I had originally planned. Eastern Cameroon was largely *terra incognita* for anthropologists and historians in the 1960s; I remember a south-ern Cameroonian friend who commiserated with me when he heard that I would not be working in his part of the country, and who remarked that I was going to a region 'without history'.

In the event I got more history than I had bargained for, and this raised many of the methodological and theoretical problems of the relationship between history and anthropology. For one thing, the region was blessed with comparatively rich archival sources from the late nineteenth century, as it had been the setting, for better or for worse, of one of the major episodes in the colonial scramble for Africa. Likewise, from the nineteenth century onwards, this region was the borderland between the Islamic West African world of the Fulbe states of Adamawa and a Central African world that was effectively beyond the reach of Islam during the pre-colonial period.

At the time of my first field research in eastern Cameroon, one of the very few published historical works for the area was an article by Catherine Coquery-Vidrovitch (1965) entitled 'De Brazza à Gentil: la Politique Française en Haute-Sangha à la Fin du XIXᵉ Siècle'. This article concentrated on historical events of the proto-colonial period in the Haute-Sangha region of what is today the western Central African Republic – an area immediately adjacent to and closely bound up with eastern Cameroon. In her work, Coquery-Vidrovitch emphasised the richness of the archival materials relating to the exploration of the Haute-Sangha region and their value both for the historian and anthropologist. To provide a glimpse of the quality of the available materials, she chose to focus on a small selection. First, there was the collection of personal letters in the Bibliothèque Nationale in Paris from the Commissioner General of the Congo, Pierre Savorgnan de Brazza, to his subordinates Charles de Chavannes and Albert Dolisie concerning de Brazza's mission of exploration to the Haute-Sangha in 1891–94. Secondly, there were two reports of a mission to the Ouham River undertaken in 1894–95 by François Clozel, another of de Brazza's collaborators, and now housed in the Centre des Archives d'Outre Mer (henceforth CAOM) in Aix-en-Provence. (Much of this material has now become more easily accessible, thanks to its publication in Elisabeth Rabut's 1989 work *Brazza Commissaire Général: le Congo Français 1886–1897*.) Although Coquery-Vidrovitch presented her article very much as a preliminary work, she indicated (1965: 26, my translation) that her aim was to

... show how by using essentially European archival documents, and in spite of an absence of local written sources or research on oral history relating to the subject, the historian can establish a more or less satisfactory picture of a particular African region, people or succession of events at the beginning of the colonial period proper.

Much as one must applaud Coquery-Vidrovitch's groundbreaking research in the French colonial archives, I fear that this sanguine view of the unproblematic exploitability of such colonial documents has not been borne out by my own work over the years in eastern Cameroon and the western Central African Republic. Unfortunately, Coquery-Vidrovitch does not seem to have been able to correct for some of the major built-in biases in the colonial documents, and her writing has often presented an inaccurate portrayal of the political structures and interrelations of the Fulbe and Gbaya peoples in the Haute-Sangha basin in the proto-colonial period. Although I will take the opportunity here to correct some of these misinterpretations, my discussion will also touch on other questions. On one hand, there is the interesting question raised by Coquery-Vidrovitch of the significance of the 'politique musulmane' (political policy toward Moslem peoples) adopted by de Brazza and his collaborators in the early days of exploration. This important building-block of French colonial policy can be shown to have had many historical repercussions, and a proper understanding of this policy can contribute significantly to the historiography of this period. On the other hand, and more generally, there is the question of the proper relationship between history and anthropology in the interpretation of social changes during the key proto-colonial period of African history. It is my contention that, for this crucial period during which the social and political structures of African peoples were experiencing the first direct effects of European colonial contact and were undergoing exceptionally rapid change, there can be no justification for maintaining the disciplinary distinctions of method that have tended to separate history from anthropology; the fullest possible armoury of methods is required.

The Historical Background

The historical context within which the first contacts between European explorers and the peoples of the Haute-Sangha region took place was the 'scramble for Africa' – more specifically the events which French authors refer to as the 'race to Chad'. With the British Royal Niger Company effectively in control of the Niger-Benue route to Yola, the capital of Adamawa, and the Germans in southern Cameroon also turning their attention to the Adamawa hinterland of their new colony, the French colonial powers in the Congo (a term which at that date encompassed present-day Gabon, Congo and parts of the Central African Republic) were anxious to establish their claim to their own colonial hinterland up to Lake Chad and beyond. Their eventual aim was to link up with their colonial possessions in North and West Africa, thereby blocking both British and German colonial expansion (Rabut 1989: 440–2). The mastermind of this grand geopolitical design was de Brazza, who by the beginning of the 1890s had been appointed Commissioner General of the Congo on the basis of his outstanding record of exploration of the region from 1875 onwards.

By 1890, two principal routes were envisaged as offering access to the interior from the coastal zones. One followed the Oubangui affluent of the Congo River to Bangui and beyond, and it was via this route that several major French explorations, including those of Crampel, Dybowski, Liotard, Maistre, Marchand and Gentil were launched. The other route, which de Brazza himself came to prefer, was via the Sangha affluent of the Congo, which penetrated the hinterland directly northwards and promised to provide a more direct access to Lake Chad. De Brazza also preferred the Sangha route because it gave direct access to the southern states of Adamawa, such as Ngaoundéré and Boubanjidda, and thus offered the possibility of nipping in the bud German designs on these Fulbe states, while at the same time opening up a competing southerly route for the Adamawa trade to that of Yola on the British-controlled Benue (see Rabut 1989: 168).

The first French effort to penetrate the Haute-Sangha met with failure. An expedition under the leadership of Alfred Fourneau pushed as far north as the village of N'Zaoure (also known as Zaouro Koussio or Kouisso), where it was attacked during the night of 11 May 1891 by a large force and suffered substantial losses. Following this reversal, de Brazza resolved to take over the exploration of the Haute-Sangha himself and in November 1891 set out on the riverboat *Courbet*, eventually founding an expedition base at Bania in January 1892. De Brazza's stated purpose at this time was not so much to punish those who had attacked Fourneau as to establish peaceful relationships with the peoples of this region in order to promote trade and to extend French political influence into this potentially important area. Nonetheless, a strong force was kept close at hand, to be called upon when needed.[1]

Upon his arrival in the Haute-Sangha, he immediately sought contact with the Gbaya of this region (then known to the French as 'N'dri' or 'N'dere'), whose territory he understood to extend to the north-west and to be in contact with 'Foulhas' (i.e., Fulbe) who had conquered the country from the west. Further north there were said to be more Fulbe, mixed with Hausa populations, who were in communication with the upper Benue valley and Yola, the capital of Adamawa.[2] These reports were soon confirmed when de Brazza received a visit in February 1892 from the Sarkin Fada, one of the titled courtiers of Lamido Abbo, ruler of the Fulbe state of Ngaoundéré, who delivered a letter from the Lamido enquiring about de Brazza's intentions in the area.[3] There ensued an exchange of correspondence between de Brazza and the ruler of Ngaoundéré in which de Brazza emphasised that, as Governor of the French colony of the Congo, he came with only peaceful intentions, that he had no plans to encroach on Adamawa, that he dissociated himself from the actions of the Europeans to the west (i.e., the Germans in Cameroon) who were reported to be selling firearms to the 'idolatrous' tribes of that region, and that France had a long history of friendly relationships with Moslem peoples such as the Fulbe.[4] De Brazza's intelligence concerning the political situation in the Fulbe states of Adamawa was soon further enhanced by his encounter with the French explorer Louis Mizon on 7 April 1892 on route southwards via Ngaoundéré from Yola, which he had reached by ascending the Niger and Benue Rivers (Mizon 1895).

As de Brazza's knowledge of the political situation in the Haute-Sangha basin improved during 1892, he became increasingly drawn to the idea of extending French influence in this region through a close alliance with the Fulbe of Ngaoundéré.

> Whatever the prevailing opinions concerning the expansion of Moslem civilisation among savage peoples, it is an indisputable fact that there exists a series of populations to the west of the Sangha river and north of the French Congo where the Moslem element has already infiltrated itself and who are (therefore) fated to evolve towards a more advanced social level under this influence. This is an established fact which cannot be undone. Were we to try to react against it, we would only reawaken ideas of resistance and fanaticism. But we can exercise an influence on this process that is favourable to our aims by developing our relations with the Fulbe and Hausa, who seem to me to display a certain spirit of tolerance, and by encouraging their expansion to the detriment of the (Moslem) peoples further east who seem to be more fanatic.[5] (My translation.)

De Brazza's plan to lend support to Fulbe political interests in the Haute-Sangha was soon put into action through a series of military operations during July and August 1892 in which French forces allied themselves with warriors under the command of N'Gouachobo, an influential vassal war-leader who represented Fulbe interests in the lower Mambere valley, to undertake the repression of the Gbaya war-leader Bafio and his followers who were opposing the extension of Fulbe rule in this region.[6] Alongside such military operations, de Brazza pursued a policy of supporting Hausa commerce in ivory, kola nuts and cattle through the improvement and policing of trade routes, the circulation of Maria-Theresa thalers as a trade currency and the encouragement of the growth of Hausa trading settlements at Nola, Gaza and Berberati in an effort to redirect the Adamawa trade southwards, away from Yola in the north.[7] Much of this effort was achieved relatively peacefully during the period 1892–94, although in addition to the repression of Bafio just mentioned there were other major military operations against the war leader Massiepa and his followers in May 1893 and again in February 1894.[8]

By early 1894, French control over the Haute-Sangha was well established, with a string of posts guarding the trade route from Nola in the south to the important trading centre at Kounde in the north. De Brazza maintained high hopes for this region, whose healthy climate and suitability for cattle husbandry gave him cause to envisage eventual colonisation by European settlers.[9] However, just as one of de Brazza's lieutenants, François Clozel, was preparing a new exploration northwards from the Haute-Sangha toward Lake Chad, news arrived of the signing in Berlin of the Franco-German Treaty of 4 February 1894 (Rabut 1989: 170). This fixed the frontier between German Cameroon and the French Congo at approximately the location of the present-day boundary between Cameroon and the Central African Republic. De Brazza's grand designs on Adamawa were therefore blocked, and the strategic interest of the Haute-Sangha region for the French disappeared virtually overnight.

The 'Politique musulmane' of de Brazza and His Associates

As is apparent even from the brief historical synopsis given above, de Brazza and his lieutenants pursued a markedly pro-Moslem policy in their relationships with the Fulbe states of Adamawa during the period 1892–94. This was, of course, just one facet of the broader French colonial design at the end of the nineteenth century which, at its grandest, envisaged the extension of French control over an immense territory, stretching from the Congo, through Lake Chad and the Sahara, on to West and North Africa – an area largely inhabited by Moslem peoples.

De Brazza, in his efforts to counteract British and German influences in Adamawa, sought to capitalise on the considerable French colonial experience of dealing with and administering Moslem populations in North and West Africa via this 'politique musulmane'. His use of Moslem Senegalese *tirailleurs*, literate in Arabic and speaking the Fula language, as intermediaries and interpreters was a consciously formulated strategy, later amplified by the recruitment of Algerian Moslem teachers to staff outposts in the Haute-Sangha.[10] Likewise, the presence from the outset of Alphonse Goujon in de Brazza's exploration party was due largely to Goujon's long experience of Moslem society in Algeria and his excellent knowledge of Arabic (see Broc 1988: 165). The later addition in 1894 of François Clozel to the Haute-Sangha exploration effort may also be interpreted in this light, since Clozel had skills as an Arabic language specialist and Islamicist (Broc 1988: 80–1) and had first-hand knowledge of the Moslem kingdoms of Baguirmi and Adamawa, obtained on the recently returned Maistre expedition (Maistre 1933).

As de Brazza and his expedition entered into progressively closer relationships with the Fulbe state at Ngaoundéré and its ruler Lamido Abbo, de Brazza formed a plan to establish a Fulbe-administered French protectorate over Ngaoundéré and its sphere of influence in the Haute-Sangha. His aim was to govern this large area beyond the present reach of French colonial administration so as to enhance French trade relationships with this region without incurring the substantial costs of direct rule. In discussing his plans for a protectorate, de Brazza emphasised that the French legal code should be applied only to Europeans in this region, so as (my translation) 'not to render sterile in advance any efforts of use to (our) colonial rule'.[11]

As we have seen above, at the outset of their relationships with the Fulbe the French tried to ingratiate themselves with Ngaoundéré by raiding Gbaya and other 'savage' groups who continued to oppose attempts by the Fulbe and their vassals to extend their dominions. De Brazza characterised the Fulbe as forming a 'nobility' at the top of a governmental system which was comparable to that of the European Middle Ages. In this way, the French were inclined to portray the political situation in the Fulbe-controlled areas of the Haute Sangha as having been 'in equilibrium' for a decade or more prior to the French arrival,[12] thereby classifying opponents of Fulbe rule as renegades who were recalcitrant to political progress. At the same time, this interpretation of the political situation gave additional justification to the French to undertake punitive expeditions against a leader such as Bafio, whom they presumed to be implicated in the attack on the Fourneau expedition. It also served to legitimate their plan for a French-supported Fulbe protectorate in Adamawa on the grounds of the greater 'civilisation' of the Fulbe in comparison to 'savage' and 'cannibalistic' pagans such as the Gbaya and Yangere.[13] Unfortunately, Coquery-Vidrovitch (1965: 30–2; 1972: 201 et passim) accepted this equilibrium view of the political situation in the Haute-Sangha, which led her to misinterpret the nature of Gbaya-Fulbe political relationships.

At this time, the fact that slave-raiding formed the principal basis of the economy of the Ngaoundéré state was systematically glossed over by de Brazza (despite his awareness of its large scale), especially in his letters to the Under-Secretary of State at the French Ministry of Colonies. Instead, de Brazza laid emphasis on the scope for trade in ivory, and eventually in cattle. As mentioned above, it is significant that de Brazza argued for the necessity of ensuring that the French code was not applied within the proposed Fulbe protectorate since, among other issues, the question of the continued Fulbe slave-raiding and trading would otherwise immediately have become awkward.

Following the 1894 Treaty of Berlin, which decisively thwarted French designs on Adamawa, French policy toward Ngaoundéré and the other Fulbe states of Adamawa altered fundamentally. There was a rapid diminishing of French interest in the Haute-Sangha, since the dream of a French-supported Fulbe protectorate over this area had now faded.[14] De Brazza returned to the coast, leaving his subordinate Alphonse Goujon in charge. The events which followed, which Coquery-Vidrovitch (1965: 29–36) has interpreted simply as resulting from the personal failings of Goujon, a man whom she portrayed as a small-minded and inhuman authoritarian, carried away by his new responsibilities, can instead be seen to flow logically from the contradictions inherent in de Brazza's 'politique musulmane' and the aborted protectorate scheme. Coquery-Vidrovitch appears not to have appreciated the extent to which de Brazza's 'politique musulmane' was an expedient, which could be discarded (along with the pro-Fulbe policy more generally) as soon as it had outlived its usefulness.

De Brazza himself acknowledged, in his handing-over instructions to Goujon in September 1894, that the new colonial frontier was likely to promote conflict between the French and the Fulbe:

> We must also envision the tense situation that may emerge between us and the Fulbe of the political class resulting from the nature of their eastwards incursions – the character of which, given the situation of the country, we can no longer hope to modify or to direct in a manner favourable to our influence.[15]

In other words, whereas the annual slave-raiding activities of the Ngaoundéré state and its Gbaya tributaries to the north and northeast of the Haute-Sangha had been winked at by de Brazza and his associates before 1894 when the protectorate was still on the cards, these same activities were to be viewed in a different light when it became a question of the Fulbe of Ngaoundéré, now under German control, sending raiding forces into French territory. Such raiding now had to be stopped, and it is clear from his reports that Goujon interpreted his military repression against the Fulbe slave-raiding forces in this light.[16]

While I certainly hold no brief to defend Goujon or the military repression that was a prominent feature of the proto-colonial period in this region, Coquery-Vidrovitch is surely mistaken in interpreting Goujon's military actions from 1894 to 1896 as representing a significant departure from those that had preceded them under de Brazza's command. True, Goujon now directed his principal efforts against the Fulbe rather than against the Gbaya opponents of the Fulbe. However, de Brazza had fully condoned, even roundly praised Goujon's earlier military exploits against the Gbaya, Dzimou and Kaka (also known as Mkako),[17] although he took care not to participate directly in these military operations. He preferred a two-pronged approach to dealing with the native populations. As Commissioner General he travelled with a relatively small, lightly armed party to conclude treaties and other negotiations in which the French interest in peaceful trade relationships was emphasised, while a larger and more heavily armed military force (commanded by subordinates like Goujon or Decoeur) was kept ready a few days' march away.[18]

De Brazza's personal letters clearly describe this double game, acknowledging that the French presence did not work in the interests of various native peoples and indicating, in his official letters to the Under-Secretary of State at the Ministry of the Colonies, that he had tended to obfuscate the more unpalatable aspects of his colonial endeavours (my translation):

> In the period of repression that we must now embark upon, one must keep in mind such eventualities [i.e., the risk of large groupings of native peoples opposing French penetration]. Keep this in mind in [planning] the replenishment of munitions ... Once one begins, one cannot know where this will lead [and] it is not a question of playing for the gallery ... Keep in mind that the situation which I describe to the Department [i.e., the Ministry of Colonies] is perhaps a bit optimistic and that I do not broach the [question of] the general interest of the native peoples ...[19]

Despite Coquery-Vidrovitch's indications to the contrary, Goujon's military repressions against the Fulbe and their allies between 1894 and 1896 were not of significantly greater scale than those which Goujon and others had carried out under de

Brazza's direct orders against Bafio and Massiepa, opponents of the Ngaoundéré Fulbe, in 1892, 1893 and 1894. However, in view of the new colonial frontier between German Cameroon and the Haute-Sangha, they were now more likely to attract international attention and have more far-reaching effects; de Brazza was therefore careful to distance himself from Goujon's actions and to have Goujon transferred.[20]

Along with the letters of de Brazza, Coquery-Vidrovitch also made extensive use of the two reports by François Clozel concerning his mission to the Ouham River in 1894–95, referred to above. In interpreting Clozel's observations, we are again confronted with a notably pro-Moslem attitude and another variant of the French grand design to link up their Equatorial and West African colonies on the basis of a 'politique musulmane'. Clozel had prepared for his proposed 1894 mission to Adamawa, Baguirmi and Lake Chad by securing, through the good offices of the French Consul at Cairo, a letter of introduction to the Mahdist leader Rabah, conqueror of Baguirmi and Bornu, from his former protector, the ex-Governor-General of the Sudan Zubir Pasha (Coquery-Vidrovitch 1965: 34). At the same time, Clozel and Emile Gentil hatched a scheme to restore the deposed chief of Baguirmi to his throne by providing French military support against Rabah, thereby establishing a strong French presence in Chad while at the same time 'repairing the faults committed by the present administration of the Haute-Sangha [i.e., Goujon] vis-à-vis the Fulbe' (my translation).[21]

However, de Brazza did not approve the plan, and Clozel's mission was limited to an exploration of the previously unknown region to the north-east of the Haute-Sangha, extending up to the Ouham River. As Coquery-Vidrovitch indicated, Clozel's trip did yield invaluable data on the populations of this region, some of which are reported in what is probably the earliest published ethnography on the Gbaya (Clozel 1896). However, it was on the basis of Clozel's work in particular that Coquery-Vidrovitch develops her erroneous picture of Gbaya-Fulbe political relationships as having reached a state of equilibrium by the proto-colonial period.

Fulbe-Gbaya Political Relationships in the Proto-colonial Period

As Coquery-Vidrovitch (1965: 27; 1972: 202) interprets de Brazza's and Clozel's accounts of the political situation in the Haute-Sangha during the period 1892–96, this was a borderland between two cultures, the Gbaya and the Fulbe, which had long been separated by a 'wall of misunderstanding'. However, within the last decade prior to the arrival of the French there had been a *rapprochement* between the two peoples in response to two external pressures: the threat of 'the powerful empire of Rabah' to the north and the arrival of the Whites from the south. Through their contact with the Fulbe, the Gbaya had developed a more cohesive political organisation. Although still based on the patrilineal clan, this organisation also consisted of a set of titled offices, borrowed from the Fulbe, and some of the incumbents of these offices had received a certain veneer of Islam and familiarity with Fulbe political culture through having spent a period of enforced residence at Ngaoundéré (Coquery-Vidrovitch 1965: 28–31; 1972: 204–5). Coquery-Vidrovitch (1965: 28–9, my translation) speaks of this as 'a remarkable organisation which permitted Clozel to traverse Gbaya territory in a state of security guaranteed by Gbaya chiefs'. She omits to mention that Clozel himself contributed to this 'security' by executing some recalcitrant Gbaya chiefs (see Rabut 1989: 171).

Although the basis of the economy of the Fulbe state was slave-raiding, Coquery-Vidrovitch argues that by this period the Gbaya were no longer subject to these attacks (1965: 28–30; 1972: 204–5). Strong Gbaya resistance to earlier raids convinced the Fulbe that it was more advantageous for them to direct their raids against populations further east. The Gbaya were therefore only required to provide free passage and foodstuffs to the annual Fulbe slaving column. Another important factor in the politico-economic structure of this region in the early 1890s was the presence of numerous 'Hausa' traders (in fact drawn from a wide range of Moslem trading peoples) who organised commerce within the Haute-Sangha region, serving in some cases as representatives of the Fulbe lamido of Ngaoundéré and as disseminators of Islam *vis-à-vis* the Gbaya and other non-Moslem populations.

While many of the elements in the picture that Coquery-Vidrovitch paints are based on fact, it is the interpretation of those facts which is at issue. To begin with, however, it is necessary to reject totally Coquery-Vidrovitch's claims concerning the roles of Rabah and of the Whites in driving the Fulbe and Gbaya into each other's arms. This grossly anachronistic interpretation neglects the fact that by 1891–92 when de Brazza and his men first approached the Haute-Sangha (let alone by a decade earlier as Clozel and Coquery-Vidrovitch argue!), neither the Fulbe of Ngaoundéré nor the Gbaya and the other peoples of the Haute-Sangha had any knowledge whatsoever either of the presence of Rabah and his troops, who were then far to the north-east, or of the French, who prior to 1891 had remained far to the south. Once again, we encounter an example of the fascination of French explorers such as Clozel with a sweeping view of Moslem political affairs across Africa, which owed much to their preoccupation with the French colonial 'politique musulmane'.

As for the supposed political equilibrium between the Fulbe and the non-Moslem peoples of the Haute-Sangha, the ethnographic and historical research carried out over the last twenty-five years by myself and my close collaborator, Elisabeth Copet-Rougier, has established that a much more dynamic and fluid interpretation is appropriate. To begin with, the equilibrium interpretation cannot account for the well established fact that many Gbaya, Mkako and other groups had not submitted to Fulbe overlordship and continued to mount spirited resistance to Fulbe incursions. It was these groups, such as that under the leadership of Bafio, which became subject to French military repression on behalf of the Fulbe, as we have seen above. As I have argued in an earlier publication (Burnham 1980b: 63), it is likely that the scale of the political groupings under such leaders who organised resistance to the Fulbe had itself been enhanced by the Fulbe threat. On the other hand, there was also, among Gbaya and other groups of the Haute-Sangha that submitted to Fulbe overlordship, clear evidence of the emergence of a more complex and centralised, multi-ethnic chiefdom structure, as Elisabeth Copet-Rougier (1987) and I (Burnham 1980a; Burnham, Copet-Rougier & Noss 1986) have documented in the Bertoua and Kounde chieftaincies. However, these emergent structures did not depend on external threats from Rabah or the French, but rather on complex exploitative and redistributive relations of slave-raiding, trading and tribute.

In order to conceptualise more adequately the range of social organisational forms and their patterns of transformation operating within the Haute-Sangha region during the proto-colonial period, it is useful to conceive of a global structure containing a centre, a middle and a periphery (see Burnham 1980b). At the centre of the system was the Ngaoundéré state with its slave-raiding system and allied Hausa trading apparatus. At the peripheries were the groups resisting Fulbe attack, where leadership roles might be enhanced if continued military opposition proved successful. In the intervening structural position was a diversity of social forms that has been well described by Copet-Rougier (1987: 346, my translation) as follows:

> the historiography of these societies reveals ... the diversity of social configurations which they may display: here, some clans localised into tribal groups or perhaps chieftaincies; there, scattered multi-clan hamlets with no tribal structure; elsewhere, a dominant clan surrounded by clan segments which [together] defend a defined territory. No one of these structures is more typical than another. They are the transitory results of contingent processes.

To appreciate such ever-shifting patterns of political development, it is necessary to work from a model of historical transformation derived by systematic confrontation of the historical documents, both written and oral, with ethnographically based social organisational analysis. Working with this array of tools, the African historian can make a more adequate evaluation of the complex social changes that characterised the crucial proto-colonial period.

Conclusion

Despite the peripheral position today of the borderland between Cameroon and the Central African Republic, in relation to the modern centres of population and power in these two countries, we have seen that this area is one of the better served in the region with archival sources from the proto-colonial period. This situation offers both considerable potential and substantial challenges, particularly as regards the opportunities presented to us for developing relatively detailed historical pictures of the politically uncentralised peoples of this region, such as the Gbaya, the Yangere and the Mkako, before they had been fundamentally transformed by colonial conquest.

Yet, as we have seen, the availability of the relative wealth of documentation provided by de Brazza and his associates can lay a number of methodological traps for the unwary historian or anthropologist who is not prepared to utilise the fullest possible range of analytical methods to elucidate the social processes and events of this period. When written documents are to hand there is a great temptation to place excessive reliance on their veracity or objectivity. Even where, as Coquery-Vidrovitch has often done, the material in these documents is critically evaluated on the basis of her assessments of the motivations and ethnocentric biases of the European observers, a purely documentary approach is not likely, *pace* Coquery-Vidrovitch (1965: 26), to permit a largely satisfactory historical picture to be drawn. What is clearly lacking here is the possibility of a systematic confrontation or 'triangulation' of sources from different perspectives and, in particular, a lack of any reference to accounts or models of social and political organisation based on indigenous sources.

Coquery-Vidrovitch may well respond, and with some justification, that her 1965 article was only a modest, armchair-based effort, intended simply to alert other workers to the potential of these archival sources. This justification is less convincing, however, if applied to the relevant passages of her major 1972 book on the concessionary company regime in the Congo. Here (1972: 201–9), for example, she repeats her arguments about 'the precarious equilibrium' established in the late pre-colonial period between the Gbaya and the Fulbe and the role, both of Rabah and of the arrival of the Europeans in the Haute-Sangha, in destroying this purported equilibrium. Moreover, although this is not the place to elaborate on the issue, she goes on to compound her misinterpretation of these proto-colonial political events by linking them directly with the emergence, some three decades later, of the Karnu rebellion in the same region (see Burnham and Christensen 1983).

It is of course not the case that the construction of models of political organisation based on indigenous sources for the proto-colonial period is an unproblematic endeavour or that, once constructed, such models are in themselves historical panaceas. The oral traditions that can be collected among such fluid and acephalous groups are typically very sketchy indeed, and they must be supplemented by other techniques. These include toponymic and other cartographic methods as well as analysis of the organisational potentials of indigenous and borrowed social forms, such as village structures and larger-scale settlement patterns, political title systems and other such conceptions and classifications of power, forms of tribute and reciprocity, modes of servitude and other structures of hierarchy and subordination.

All these sources of data, each of which is subject to its own particular problems of interpretation, can be combined to enrich, reorient, and sometimes even overturn the historical picture presented in the contemporary European documents.

While methodological arguments will doubtless continue over the proper dosage (and possible side-effects) of oral tradition, archaeology, historical linguistics, or geographical, ecological and social organisational models in the writing of African history, when dealing with the proto-colonial period for which all such data and techniques are at our disposal, there is surely no convincing reason not to make the fullest possible use of them all – without reference to disciplinary boundaries. This is a lesson that the work of Sally Chilver, in close collaboration with Phyllis Kaberry over many years, has taught younger generations of researchers in Cameroon, to their lasting benefit.

Notes

* I would also like to acknowledge, in the fullest terms, the close collaboration of Elisabeth Copet-Rougier in much of the research on which this article is based (see Burnham, Copet-Rougier & Noss 1986; Copet-Rougier 1987). At the same time, I take sole responsibility for the views expressed in this article.

1. Letter from de Brazza reprinted in Rabut 1989: 189–90.

2. Ibid. 194–6.

3. Ibid. 203–9.

4. Letter from de Brazza to Abou ben Aïssa, 26 April 1892 reprinted in Rabut 1989: 200–2.

5. Letter from de Brazza to the Sous-Secrétaire d'Etat aux Colonies, Gaza, 23 May 1892. CAOM, Gabon-Congo, III 13d. Reprinted in Rabut 1989: 203–9.

6. Letter from de Brazza reprinted in Rabut 1989: 220–4.

7. Ibid. 239–4 and 244–6.

8. Ibid. 239–44. See also ibid. 170.

9. Ibid. 227–36.

10. Ibid. 248–54 and 203–9.

11. Personal letter from de Brazza to Dolisie, Bania, 11 July 1892. Bibliothèque Nationale, Paris, Manuscript Department, Nouvelles Acquisitions Françaises, 12807. See also letter from de Brazza to Dolisie, Libreville, 24 March 1892. CAOM, AEF, 2 B 116, no. 5, pp. 5–7. Reprinted in Rabut 1989: 341–3.

12. Letter from de Brazza to the Sous-Secrétaire d'Etat aux Colonies, Gaza, 23 May 1892. CAOM, Gabon-Congo, III 13d. Reprinted in Rabut 1989: 203–9. Also, report from Clozel to the Ministre des Colonies, Langrune-sur-mer, 25 August 1895. CAOM, Gabon-Congo III, 15. Reprinted in Rabut 1989: 254–63.

13. See Clozel report, footnote 12.

14. Letter of instructions from de Brazza to Goujon, Bania, 15 September 1894. CAOM, Afrique Supplément. Reprinted in Rabut 1989: 248–54.

15. See de Brazza letter, footnote 14. See also letter from de Brazza to the Sous-Secrétaire d'Etat aux Colonies, Libreville, 7 May 1896. CAOM, Gabon-Congo, IV 11. Reprinted in Rabut 1989: 443–5.

16. General report on the expedition of 1896 from Goujon to de Brazza, Nola, 23 December 1896. CAOM, Gabon-Congo IV 13. Letter from Goujon to de Brazza, Nola, 16 July 1895. CAOM, Gabon-Congo IV 13.

17. Personal letter from de Brazza to Dolisie, Bania, 1 September 1892. Bibliothèque Nationale, Paris, Manuscript Department, Nouvelles Acquisitions Françaises, 24040. Reprinted in Rabut 1989: 225–7.

18. Letter from de Brazza to the Sous-Secrétaire d'Etat aux Colonies, Brazzaville, 25 November 1891. CAOM, Gabon-Congo, III 13d. Reprinted in Rabut 1989: 189–90. See also personal letter from de Brazza to Dolisie, Bania, 11 July 1892. Bibliothèque Nationale, Paris, Manuscript Department, Nouvelles Acquisitions Françaises, 12807. See also letter from de Brazza to the Sous-Secrétaire d'Etat aux Colonies, Bania, 1 September 1892. CAOM, Gabon-Congo, III 13d. Reprinted in Rabut 1989: 220–4.

19. Personal letter from de Brazza to Dolisie, Bania, 11 July 1892. Bibliothèque Nationale, Paris, Manuscript Department, Nouvelles Acquisitions Françaises, 12807.

20. Letter from de Brazza to the Ministre des Colonies, Libreville, 21 April 1896. CAOM, Gabon-Congo, IV 13a. Reprinted in Rabut 1989: 264–6. See also letter from de Brazza to the Sous-Secrétaire d'Etat aux Colonies, Libreville, 19 September 1896. CAOM, Gabon-Congo, IV 13. Reprinted in Rabut 1989: 445–6.

21. Report from Clozel to the Ministre des Colonies, Langrune-sur-mer, 25 August 1895. CAOM, Gabon-Congo III, 15. Reprinted in Rabut 1989: 254–63.

CHAPTER THREE

Mythic Transformation and Historical Continuity:
the Duala of Cameroon and German Colonialism, 1884–1914

Ralph A. Austen

In a ground-breaking paper E.M. Chilver (1967) presented us with a picture of German rule in Cameroon from the perspective of a crucial local community, the Bali-Nyonga of the Grassfields.[1] This paper shifts the study of the same historical era to that region of the Cameroon coast Littoral from (and against) which German forays into the Grassfields were organised.

Although the Duala people and their two major rulers, 'Kings' Bell and Akwa, were already well known before the colonial era as middlemen in the Atlantic trade, their thirty years under German domination occupy a special, almost mythic, place in historical memory. There are three somewhat contradictory sources for the special power of this experience. The first is a Faustian myth of the German *Sonderweg* (exceptional historical path), rooted in the role of Germany as the dynamic yet dark centre of modern European development, and underscored by the exceptionality of an African colonialism distinguished from the 'ordinary' rule of Britain and France. Secondly there is the myth of extreme oppression, based upon the catastrophic climax of German rule in Douala, a struggle over urban land expropriation which concluded with the execution of the leading local chief, Rudolph Duala Manga Bell, for high treason. Finally there is the Golden Age myth, cultivated among the Duala with adult experience spanning the German and subsequent French mandate periods, which contrasts the prominence and prosperity achieved during the former era with the relative obscurity which followed.

I refer to these representations of the Duala-German relationship as myths not because they are completely untrue (all can be supported with extensive evidence) but rather because the only way in which their various truths can be reconciled is to recognise both an ambiguity and a banality in colonial history which the myths themselves obscure. Nonetheless, one cannot simply dismiss such one-sided and inflated representations of an important era in the past. They not only draw some of us to give particular attention to this aspect of the past but also illuminate more general contradictions in the ongoing confrontation between Africa and Europe.

The present paper concentrates upon the political aspects of the Duala-German colonial encounter, stopping short of the final encounter over expropriation.[2] German regimes throughout Africa differed from those of Britain and France in two important characteristics: first, the lack of an historical model for the administration of overseas territories; and second, the very active involvement of the metropolitan parliament, the Reichstag, in colonial affairs. Both of these peculiarities can be traced to the sudden manner in which Germany entered the ranks of the European Great Powers. No further explanation is needed for the lack of colonial experience but the Reichstag role, which became figuratively and literally fatal for the Duala, requires some comment.

This unusual level of legislative colonial concern did not derive from the substantive interest in Africa among German strategic or economic interest groups but was rather an artifact of the general position of the Reichstag in the Wilhelmian state. This national body was elected, from its inception, by universal male suffrage and thus represented a wide range of sophisticated ideological positions; however, the conservative Prince Otto von Bismarck had designed the new political system to deprive the legislature of real control over the most critical realms of government. The Reichstag thus devoted a disproportionate amount of its considerable energies to those matters (including the colonies) left fully under its jurisdiction, partly as a device for eventually widening such jurisdiction (Hausen 1970: 50–51).

German Administration: Defining a Colonial Entity

For Germany to rule the Duala,[3] it was necessary to establish both the organisational basis of political domination and its relationship to wider territorial control. The German achievement of such a definition required an often painful passage through a series of unplanned stages: first, retreat to a modified version of the previous British consular system, then a more formal government limited to the Littoral, third, a disorderly advance into the interior, and finally a 'reformed' regime which culminated in the crisis of Duala expropriation.

Neo-Consular Rule: 1884–85

Had the goals of colonial expansion been evident at the time of Cameroon's annexation, a model for ruling the new territory might quickly have suggested itself to the Germans. However, it immediately became evident that both the Berlin Government and the Hamburg merchant firms already active on the coast were clear only about what they wanted to avoid when a local government was established.

Bismarck's idea of colonial administration was a 'British' method of delegating the whole affair to interested merchants, thus saving the Reich both budgetary and political costs. However, the commercial firms in question, Woermann and Jantzen & Thormählen, steadfastly refused to accept such a burden. Instead they and Bismarck tacitly agreed that, at least in the short run, German needs could be met by a permanently stationed official with powers similar to that of the earlier peripatetic British consul (Rudin 1938: 32, 39, 120–26; Jaeck 1960: 81–83). However, events on the ground quickly made this period much shorter than anticipated.

The unfurling of the imperial banner not only failed to overcome any of the long-standing Duala political divisions which had led to colonial annexation in the first place, but added to them a far more explosive issue: the polarisation of local forces around Anglo-German rivalry. At an international level, Britain never challenged Germany's claims to the Wouri estuary. However, the Foreign Office did attempt for a time to retain the Baptist settlement at Victoria and also solicited new 'protectorate' treaties with rulers in the West Cameroon hinterland. Within Douala British merchants also continued to outnumber representatives of German firms. Efforts to replace the ineffectual consular Court of Equity with a German-dominated Cameroons Council met with a British boycott, amidst rumours of plots by merchants and Baptist missionaries to undo the new colonial arrangements. The German Imperial West African Commissioner, Gustav Nachtigal, emulated his British predecessors by departing from Douala soon after signing the annexation agreements, but he did leave behind a makeshift permanent representation in the person of his deputy, the physician Max Buchner (Rudin 1938: 43–55; Ardener 1968: 25–31, 41–5).

Under such circumstances, it is not surprising that those Duala segments dissatisfied with both the continued ascendancy of the Bell chiefdom and the new arrangements made with Germany should undertake violent action. The centre of this dissent was Bonaberi ('Hickory'), the Duala quarter located across the Wouri River from the main town and theoretically subordinate to Bell. One of King Ndumbé Lobé Bell's major motives in seeking European protection was to prevent the kind of defections which had been attempted in the 1870s and early 1880s by segments of his following, including Bonaberi. However, Kum a Mbapé (Lock Priso), the Bonaberi ruler, was the only significant Duala chief not to have signed a German protectorate treaty in July 1884. Believing (probably with some local European encouragement) that he would have the support of the British, Kum attacked and burnt Belltown in December 1884. This effort was supported by the ruler and inhabitants of Bonapriso (Joss), a subordinate community which had been at the centre of earlier internecine Bell politics and subsequent Akwa-Bell warfare.

Buchner reacted to these events by calling in the small naval squadron which had been patrolling West Africa to back up German interests in the volatile scramble process. Gunners and marines from the ships quickly suppressed the revolt by destroying both Bonaberi and Bonapriso. The fighting cost one German and twenty-five African lives. In Duala terms this was a major war and one which ended any efforts at military challenge to European rule. For the Germans, the rebellion demonstrated the need to move beyond the methods of informal empire. The ineffectual Buchner immediately surrendered local authority to Admiral Knorr, commander of the West African squadron, who remained in charge until July 1885, when the first colonial Governor, Julius Freiherr von Soden, arrived at Douala.

Restricted Formal Administration: 1885 – c.1900

In principle, Soden and his immediate successors possessed the full accoutrements of a colonial state: a civil bureaucracy, a military force, and at least the beginnings of a modern transport link between the coast and the interior in the form of several small steam vessels. The new order was physically represented by its quarters on the Joss Plateau, confiscated for Government use from the rebels of December 1884. However, even after the collapse of Bismarck's 'British' model and the departure from power of Bismarck himself, the Reich was not committed to large-scale political investment in its colonies. The European administrative staff thus remained small; military organisation grew slowly and was based mainly on African recruits (first, foreign *Polizeitruppen*, and only after 1895 a Cameroonian *Schutztruppe*); mechanised travel and effective administration remained limited to the coast and adjacent Littoral river system.

This apparatus was sufficient to inhibit the Duala from any direct contestation of German rule, but was kept very busy asserting its authority over small inland rulers, especially along the Wouri, Abo and Sanaga Rivers. Modest as it was in territorial extent, the conquest of the Littoral also incurred political costs in the Reichstag. Deputies of the liberal and socialist left made considerable capital out of the scandals surrounding a mutiny by Dahomean police conscripts and the extreme mistreatment of inland chiefs and villagers (Rüger 1968: 91–147).

Although these campaigns had the long-term goal of making the interior more accessible to direct European trade, from a political perspective they offered the Duala support against peoples they had never been able to overcome on their own. Thus the Duala refused to take sides with either the Dahomean mutineers or any of the recalcitrant inland rulers. The Germans, in turn, formalised this relationship by delegating official powers to chiefs who accepted their authority, which meant primarily the Duala. Although no official representative or judicial body brought together government officials, European merchants, missionaries and African chiefs, the small scale of the colonial bureaucracy and the fact that it was centred in Douala meant that much of the political style of the earlier consular regime survived on an informal basis.[4]

The Puttkamer Era, circa 1897–1907

The most radical shift in the administrative status of Douala occurred under the aegis of the one colonial governor who would embody all the mythic qualities of German rule, Jesco von Puttkamer. Although Puttkamer had begun his colonial career at Douala as *Kanzler* (second in command) under Governor von Soden from 1885 to 1887, and presided over a restricted coastal regime during the first years of his own lengthy governorship, he began even before his second tour in Cameroon to formulate several projects which would dramatically shift the focus of Cameroon development: first, the establishment of large-scale European plantations in the area of Mount Cameroon; second, the granting of vast north-west and south Cameroon forest zones to parastatal concession companies, and finally the extension of political control over the densely populated savannah regions of the Grassfields and Adamawa. None of these policies worked out in the way that Puttkamer and his allies had planned, but their combined permanent effect was to shift the focus of German policy away from the coast. This process of interior expansion gained additional strength from the single uncontested success of Puttkamer's concessionary policy, the private construction between 1906 and 1911 of Cameroon's first full-size railway, the Nordbahn, from Bonaberi via the Mungo valley to Nkongsamba.

The most obvious political change in the Littoral resulting from this inland expansion was the abandonment of Douala as the colonial capital. In 1901 Puttkamer transferred his headquarters to Buea on the side of Mount Cameroon, for health as well as bureaucratic reasons. In administrative terms Douala and its surroundings were thus reduced to the status of a territorial subunit and placed under the supervision of a *Bezirksamtmann*, the German equivalent of the classic District Commissioner or *Commandant du Cercle*.

However, as the port of entry for an ever-expanding commerce, and in particular the starting point of Cameroon's two railway lines, Douala actually gained in urban stature during this period. To meet the demands of this new role, the German administration began to intervene more directly in Duala society, first undertaking a campaign to modernise streets and housing in the main indigenous quarters of the city, then introducing direct taxation, and finally expropriating land required by the new railway installations.[5]

Metropolitan political involvement in Cameroon affairs reached its peak during the Puttkamer era, mainly around the land, labour and trade controversies aroused by plantations and concession companies. However, the strains of urban development in Douala also produced conflicts which culminated in 1906 with special judicial hearings in Cameroon and the calling of both Puttkamer and the *Bezirksamtmann*, Eduard von Brauchitsch, before a Colonial Office investigator in Berlin. It is difficult to determine the relative weight of these various issues (along with the official charge of forging a pass for his *demi-mondaine* mistress) in the ultimate dismissal of Puttkamer from his governorship (1906). However, when the Duala side of the urban questions is discussed below, it is important to keep in mind the general political context of these local affairs.

The Era of 'Reform': 1907–1914

The years of German colonial administration immediately preceding its termination by the First World War are generally cited as a period when, under the leadership of Colonial Secretary Bernhard Dernburg, the irresponsible policies of figures such as Puttkamer gave way to more rational development, which paid special attention to the interests of the African 'native' (Smith 1978: 183–219). This period receives only brief treatment here, not because it is insignificant but precisely because its importance for the Duala requires lengthier examination in later sectors of the essay.

In so far as the post-Puttkamer administration concentrated on strictly economic issues, the Duala did benefit. Further railway construction gave greater value to all activity in Douala and the new emphasis on indigenous, rather than expatriate, plantation agriculture allowed the regime to recognise a major new dimension of Duala commercial enterprise. The governor who immediately succeeded Puttkamer, Theodor Seitz (1907–11), also proposed political reforms that would give Douala the status of a self-governing municipality, in which both Africans and Europeans enjoyed rights of representation. However, this plan met with opposition from both the Colonial Office and the all-European Cameroon Government Council which had been introduced by Berlin decree in 1904.[6] For the Duala, therefore, the political legacy of the reform era was not improvement but rather the expropriation crisis in which all power within the local administration was to be abandoned in a desperate play for both Reichstag and interior Cameroon support.

Segmentary Politics and Colonial Chiefdom

The continuing and growing importance of the small Duala population in German colonial politics can be traced to a combination of the peculiarities of German rule in Africa and the specific circumstances of Cameroon. It is the German element in this situation which explains the rather ambiguous role assigned to Duala rulers in the new colonial state as well as the ability of these rulers to bring their local grievances to the attention of the Reichstag.

In any case it would have been difficult, even under a more articulated British-style indirect rule system, for colonial administrators to find a place for the coastal middlemen chiefs. The authority of Duala 'kings' never rested upon any visible state apparatus, which might have been co-opted, but rather on control over networks of inland trade, which colonialism sought to dissolve. As it turned out, the Duala retained more of their pre-colonial influence in the era of European rule than did the coastal middleman states of Nigeria (Wolpe 1983). In terms of colonial geopolitics, this persistence can be explained by the difficulty of extending European administration into the more populous inland regions of Cameroon, as well as to the continuation of Douala, even after the interior was effectively penetrated, as the major commercial centre of the territory.

From Segmentation to Formal Jurisdiction

The mini-war between the Germans and Bonaberi-Joss in December 1884 represented the last eruption of classical Duala segmentary politics, in which the potential hegemony of one faction (in this case Bell) was countered by the defection of its own subordinate units. With their military actions of 1884 and the subsequent installation of a colonial state apparatus, the Germans not only insured themselves against further armed Duala resistance but also determined that intra-Duala competition would no longer reach such levels of violence or complexity.

However, given the budgetary constraints under which it operated, the colonial regime could not substitute its own bureaucratic agents for the African chiefs it had now pacified. The politics of the Littoral during the first decades of German government thus centred around the negotiation of a role for local rulers which would be both self-supporting and consistent with the goals of European domination.

The most immediate and continuous issue in these negotiations remained the question of financial support. The income of Duala rulers in the pre-colonial period had come principally from their inland trading enterprises and the comey (tribute) paid to them on the coast by European merchants. Given their goal of eliminating the middleman trading role of the Duala, the Germans had to find other sources of revenue for the chiefs such as salaries, court fees and fines, and a share of tax revenues.

As a general policy the Germans did not follow the British practice of paying salaries to recognised chiefs. However, the major Duala authorities did receive such compensation on the basis of their previous comey rights, which had been guaranteed in the 1884 protection treaty.[7]

Establishing the political role, as well as the income, of chiefs through judicial functions held a special appeal for German colonial bureaucrats, almost all of whom had qualified for their positions by legal studies in preparation for the state Assessor examination. However, during most of the administration of the first German governor, von Soden, the organisation of Duala political authority still followed the 'informal empire' model of the consular-era Court of Equity. Soden had initially attempted to set up yet another version of this constantly reformulated body, in which representatives of the chiefs as well as the merchant houses would regularly meet. The records indicate that the procedures degenerated into *ad hoc* and frustrating intervention of the administration into local quarrels.[8] As already noted, the European merchants had no formal role in government for the first two decades of German rule; when this situation changed with the establishment of a territorial *Gouvernmentsrat* (government council), the remedy was more legislative than judicial, and Africans were excluded.

The German Government decided in 1890 to recognise officially the distinct judicial powers of Duala chiefs, and they followed this two years later by creating a second level of *Eingeborenen-Schiedsgerichte* (Native Appeal Courts) which were eventually extended throughout the Littoral. The chiefs' courts were only empowered to deal with civil and criminal cases involving very limited sums, fines or periods of imprisonment, while appeal courts could both retry such cases and serve as the court of first instance for any other matters not involving penalties of more than two years' imprisonment or death. The *Schiedsgerichte* were required to keep records for the inspection of the German administration, to which, in turn, further judicial appeal was allowed (Ruppel 1912: 853–4).

Native courts of this kind not only constituted the most formal public function which the German regime was to grant Duala and other Littoral chiefs, but also provided additional income through the sharing of fees and fines. Officially, the most lucrative form of this compensation, that accruing to the *Schiedsgerichte*, went not to chiefs but to individuals named by the governor as court members. However, these nominees were always linked to particular chiefdoms within the appeal courts' jurisdiction, and their relative weight within a given court was perceived as a major political issue.

Direct taxation was not introduced by the Germans into Cameroon until 1903, and until 1907 the new tax regulations applied only to the Douala district. From the beginning, the Douala district administration experienced great difficulty in tax collection despite offering chiefs five to ten percent of the revenue.[9] Rather than strengthening the position of the chiefs, this measure proved so unpopular with their people that it ultimately entered the agenda of major political disputes between African and European authorities.

The tax collection problems are symptomatic of more general contradictions in the new conception of Duala rulership. The German goal had been to transform the chiefs from factional leaders into the depoliticised instruments of low-cost colonial administration. However, by the very act of creating an authority more powerful than anything which had been known previously, the European regime raised the political stakes involved in occupying even a circumscribed chiefly office. The Duala rulers thus experienced not only the general dilemma of colonial intermediacy – being caught between European demands and African resistance – but also an enlarged, if less direct, reconstitution of their earlier segmentary conflicts.

Segmentary Politics with a German Accent: Akwa vs. Bell, 1885–1911

The establishment of German rule in Douala was accompanied, and in part caused, by the express willingness of both leading indigenous rulers, Ndumbé Lobé Bell and Dika Mpondo Akwa, to give up full autonomy in return for a more orderly settlement of the endless political conflicts. The Bell faction can be seen as the more immediate beneficiary of this change, since their successes in the palm-product trade during the 1880s had been threatened by rebellious subordinates. However, the Akwa chiefs made the same requests for European intervention and proved more uniformly willing to sign the German annexation treaty. Yet by the early 1900s Bell ascendancy had become so obvious that the Akwas launched a series of protests which culminated in the first explosive eruption of Duala and German politics into one another's realms.

The German-Akwa conflicts contributed as much to the mythologisation of this era as did the later execution of the Bell ruler. The Akwas even have their own martyr, Mpondo Dika, the self-styled Prince who spent most of this period in Germany and later died mysteriously while interned by the Germans in Northern Cameroon. The main antagonist of the Akwas was no less than Governor von Puttkamer, for whose subsequent deposition the Duala took credit.

To understand these developments in fuller historical terms it is necessary, first of all, to recognise in them a continuity of earlier Duala politics, which the Germans neither consciously cultivated nor had the power to overcome. The disturbance which sent this process into a new orbit was the rise of the Bells, which itself emerged less from the logic of Duala tradition or European colonial policy than from the contingencies of personality and unplanned economic change.

Personality factors are always the easiest to introduce into a political narrative and in the Duala-German case they provide critical, if not sufficient, explanations for the rise of Bell over Akwa. European accounts of Douala during the decades immediately preceding and following colonial annexation are almost uniform in praising Ndumbé Lobé Bell and his British-educated heir-apparent, Manga. Dika Mpondo Akwa, on the other hand, was generally despised by Europeans, and his son Mpondo, a generation younger than Manga, was to become the target of

European scorn and even ridicule in both Douala and Germany (Austen 1986: 217–21). Bell immediately received a higher compensation than Akwa, as a result of his greater pre-colonial commercial success. On the other hand, German censuses of Douala indicated that the Akwa faction represented a far larger portion of the local population.[10]

The Bells suffered a setback during the administration of the first German Governor, von Soden, who favoured the Akwas and exiled Manga Bell to Togo for two years. Soden was very annoyed at complaints raised in Germany by Alfred Bell, a nephew of the ruler sent abroad for European education (Austen 1986: 216–17). The governor was also influenced by his official interpreter, David Meetom (Mwange Ngondo), himself a secondary Akwa chief. The exile of Manga was never tied to any specific issues; Soden simply called him a 'bad influence' responsible for generally uncooperative Bell attitudes towards the Government.[11]

It is possible, however, to see policy considerations behind the shifting fortunes of the two Duala factions. Soden was committed to European commercial penetration of the area north-west of Douala which constituted the main Bell trading zone. The governor linked his proposals for eliminating the entire Bell chiefdom directly to a project of the Jantzen & Thormählen commercial firm and the explorer, Eugen Zintgraff, involving plantations and a trading station on the Mungo River.[12]

The long-term ascendancy of the Bells dates from the moment of Soden's departure in 1890. While in exile Manga Bell had established a good relationship with the German commissioner of Togo, Eugen von Zimmerer, who then took over the governorship of Cameroon. Apparently chastened by his punishment, Manga subsequently took care to cultivate all the important German officials in the Littoral, including Karl Leist (notorious for inciting the Dahomean *Polizeisoldat* mutiny), Seitz (during the period when that later governor served under Puttkamer in Douala) and especially the long-tenured Douala *Bezirksamtmann*, von Brauchitsch.[13] Meanwhile in 1894 the Akwa-based government interpreter, Meetom, was detected in gross abuses of his powers and eventually shot while fleeing German justice.[14]

Under Zimmerer's governorship the Germans also gave up their efforts to penetrate the interior via the Mungo River, thus returning this waterway to unchallenged Bell influence. Instead, the Europeans undertook a conquest of the Sanaga route to the south-east, establishing their trading firms at Edea. At first this policy opened up new commercial opportunities for the entire Duala merchant community. However, the closing of the Sanaga in 1895 to all African coastal traders hurt the Akwa in particular, since this was a region where they had much stronger pre-colonial ties than the Bells [15](Kaeselitz 1968: 21–5).

Despite the advantages gained (or regained) by the Bells in the early 1890s, German policy in this period did not envisage privileging one Duala faction over the other. The system of native appeal courts established between 1892 and 1897 sought rather to balance Bell and Akwa within Douala (each took turns in providing the president of the local court) and to define the various inland regions as political entities under German control and separate from the Duala.

The special role of the Bells became apparent, however, when Ndumbé Lobé ('King Bell') died in December 1897, and the status of Manga as his successor had to be defined. Seitz immediately determined that Manga would inherit his father's comey compensation as a 'salary' (at a slightly reduced level). A similar status (but at still lower rates of compensation) was then granted to the three other principal Duala chiefs.[16] However, a few months later Seitz took the even more radical step of assigning to Manga a new and lucrative appeal jurisdiction over the entire non-Duala Littoral.[17] The distinction which this measure created between Bell and Akwa became apparent within the same year when Mpondo Dika (the beneficiary of several years' study in Germany) was threatened with exile by Seitz for claiming comparable authority among the Abo.[18] Moreover, at Manga Ndumbe Bell's death in 1908 the same jurisdiction was transferred to his son, Duala Manga Bell, a contemporary of Mpondo.[19]

The formalisation of Bell ascendancy coincided with the shift in the German colonial focus from the coast to the interior. For all Duala this was a stressful period, when they seemed to be losing influence within Cameroon while confronting an intensified European interference in their immediate urban realm. In this new context both Bell and Akwa rulers found it necessary to assert their position through direct appeals to the metropolitan German Government.

The major occurrences in Duala-German political relationships during the first decade of the twentieth century have been very fully chronicled by Adolf Rüger. The present account will not, therefore, provide a detailed narrative but rather an outline of events and an analysis of their relevance to understanding the redefinition of authority in the Littoral. Again, attention has to be paid to the contingency of personalities, but these now played out their roles in a context not only of Duala segmentary rivalries but also of the systemic imperatives of urban modernisation and the structure of domestic Wilhelmian politics.

The political story of this era may be summed up as follows: in 1902–3 Manga Bell and Dika Akwa personally presented complaints and requests to the colonial authorities in Germany; between 1903 and 1906 the Douala *Bezirksamt* undertook extensive street, sanitation and housing renovations in the city; in 1905 the Akwa chiefs despatched a list of twenty-four complaints to Berlin, for which act they were twice put on trial and convicted; in 1911 Mpondo returned to Douala and was himself arrested for illicit commercial-political activity.[20]

The journeys of Bell and Akwa to Germany reveal ongoing parity between them: both were accompanied by sons educated in Germany; moreover their basic complaints (against government tolls, brutalities by local officials, remoteness from the governor in Buea, restrictions on Sanaga trade, loss of elephant-hunting rights) were the same. However, financial problems prevented Dika Akwa from arranging his departure as quickly as Manga Bell and so he was received later and more casually by the Berlin authorities. Moreover, Dika's complaints included the favouritism shown to Bell.[21]

Despite strong initial objections by Puttkamer, some of these grievances were actually dealt with both for the Duala as a whole and for Manga personally. To the Duala leaders this success indicated that appeals in the metropolis could have some affect. However, it is unlikely that they took into account the broader political circumstances which made even such minimal victories possible; the journeys to Berlin coincided with the first major attacks in the Reichstag and the *Kolonialrat* (Colonial Advisory Council) against the plantations and concession companies comprising the '*System Puttkamer*' (Gründer 1982: 141–8).

The key figure in efforts begun in 1903 to modernise Douala was not Puttkamer but Brauchitsch, who because of his role in both urban and agricultural improvements remains a legendary figure in Duala oral memory. However, the records of his actions in Douala indicate that he strayed well beyond the bounds of correct German administrative deportment. In the investigation of Akwa charges against him Brauchitsch made very inconsistent statements, finally confessing partiality towards Manga Bell, brutality towards the Akwas, and the purchase of a young Duala woman for sexual purposes.[22]

The fond Duala memory of Brauchitsch can be justified by his energetic pursuit of a clearly very difficult task. In order to meet its new commercial role, Douala essentially needed streets with proper drainage. However, the elevated river-bank settlements which constituted Bell, Akwa and Deido 'towns' are divided from one another by swampy depressions, so that the construction of a continuous road system required considerable labour. The *Bezirksamt* had only limited funds to pay for such work and spent all of it on the first stage of construction in the Bell sector of Bonanjo, leaving nothing over for the more difficult efforts within the larger Akwa sector and across the lowland boundary zones. The project also called for the removal without compensation of many houses and fruit-bearing trees from the path of the roadways.

Of the twenty-four complaints in the Akwa petition of 1905, only five referred directly to the modernisation project. While it is impossible to assess the relative importance of this petition in contributing to Puttkamer's ousting from Cameroon, it is clear that the Reichstag gave it considerable attention.[23] The Akwa chiefs succeeded in having their 1905 condemnation for libel and defamation against the Cameroon administration reviewed in the following year by a German judge not connected with the local regime. However, the result was only a second conviction with a somewhat milder prison sentence. Moreover, the other Duala chiefs, particularly Manga Bell, emphatically distanced themselves from the Akwa complaints, thus further strengthening Bell hegemony in the Littoral.

The final effort at recovering Akwa authority came from Mpondo Akwa, who remained in Germany after 1906 and used his time there to plan a large-scale trading venture. Following his return to Cameroon in 1911, Mpondo attempted to raise money in Douala and the Littoral hinterland for what appeared to be as much a political as a commercial undertaking. These activities were the grounds for his arrest by the Germans, who then exiled him to Northern Cameroon until his death during the First World War.[24] Mpondo, whom Seitz describes as 'the very caricature of a human being', seems to have embodied the mythic aspects of Duala-German relationships in both tragic and comic forms. A contemporary German music-hall routine featured 'Prinz Akwa', a monocled black dandy usually accompanied by a white female 'Cousinchen'. The latter was easily identified by those in the know as Puttkamer's mistress, whose false claim to aristocracy had been the official reason for the governor's dismissal.[25]

If the Bells managed early colonial politics so as to achieve an unprecedented ascendancy, it was the Akwas who played upon the widest possibilities of the German presence. Up to 1911 it still looked as if the Bell approach was more realistic, particularly because it was built upon a real, if also modest, transformation of the Duala economic base through extensive cocoa plantations. Yet, as the land expropriation crisis of 1910–14 was to show, not even playing by the apparent colonial rules could assure a smooth relationship with the new European regime.

The preceding narrative of Duala-German relationships has not indicated the over-riding international forces which brought about the imperialist partition of Africa in the first place and, in the case of the dispute over Douala urban land, introduced the factor of the First World War, which undoubtedly accounts for the drastic punishment meted out to Duala Manga Bell. The links between global and local historical processes are difficult to explain even in academic terms, and for those experiencing them on the ground – whether Africans or Europeans – they are most easily understood by translation into myth. The German colonial regime would thus affect the most serious transformation of the Duala middleman position once the myths about the original colonial encounter transformed themselves into cataclysmic politics. However, this catastrophe only engendered still further myths about the powers of both colonisers and colonised to bring about changes in African existence.

For Cameroon, these beliefs remain coloured by the German encounter but perhaps, despite the undeniable particuliarities of the *Sonderweg*, this experience is only a more dramatic version of the illusions, disappointments and brutalities encountered throughout modern African history.

Notes

1. My own contribution to the volume in which this essay appeared, and most of my subsequent work, owes a huge debt to Sally Chilver who, at a critical moment of doctoral research, urged me to study Indirect Rule by going out

to do fieldwork in Africa rather than 'poking around in the remains of a lot of second-rate minds in Britain'.

2. I have dealt with economic issues as well as the urban expropriation crisis in previous publications, see especially Austen (1977).

3. Note that 'Duala' is used to refer to the ethnic group, 'Douala' to the city.

4. A valuable personal account of German administration in this period is given in Seitz 1929a and b.

5 Douala *Bezirksamt* proclamation on Nordbahn railroad expropriation, 25 January 1907 and ff., Archives Nationales du Cameroun, Fonds Allemandes (hereafter ANC/FA) 1230 'Enteignung von eingeborenen Besitz in Bonaberi und Bonasoma' (these measures are to be distinguished from the later and more general expropriation of Duala urban land).

6. Buea-Berlin correspondence, 25 December 1907–11 November 1911, Deutsches Zentralarchiv, Potsdam (hereafter RKA) 4279: 4–46; Seitz 1929, vol. 2: 54–8 and 92.

7. Rüger 1968: 188–9; RKA 3823, *passim.*

8. Soden report of 17 July 1885 meeting with chiefs, ANC/FA 333: 3–7 *et passim.*

9. See Douala *Bezirksamt* annual reports, for 1904–08, ANC/FA 397: 912, 859.

10. See the census by Nachtigal of 12 November 1888 in RKA 4208: 399 and of Zimmerer in 1894 in ANC/FA 333: 245–50.

11. Soden to Berlin, 6 November 1888, 28 March 1889, ANC/FA 333: 65 and 92–3.

12. Soden to Berlin, 24 March 1889, Berlin to Soden, 29 June 1889, ANC/FA 333: 88–91 and 114. Soden's letter of 6 November 1888 cited above was written on stationery of the Zintgraff expedition; see more on Zintgraff in Chilver 1967.

13. Leist to Governor, 28 August 1891 ANC/FA court records.

14. ANC/FA Court Files 1894/1 no. 167; ANC/FA 942: 61 ff.

15. Rudi Kaeselitz, 'Kolonialeroberung und Widerstandskampf in Südkamerun (1884–1907)'.

16. Seitz to Governor, 6 January 1898, Colonial Department Decree, 22 September 1898, RKA 3824: 16–7 and 23.

17. Seitz to Governor, 29 March 1898, ANC/FA 208: 12; Brauchitsch memo, 5 May 1906, RKA 3823: 101–2.

18. Seitz correspondence, 27 July–17 August 1898, ANC/FA 23K.

19. B*ezirksamtmann* Röhm to Governor, 14 March 1909, ANC/FA 43.

20. Rüger 1968: 196–219; Austen 1986: 217 ff.

21. Dobritz to Berlin, 18 January 1906, RKA 4435: 40.

22. Germany, *Verhandlungen des Reichstags* (hereafter RT), vol. 222 (1905/06): 3387–3420; ibid. vol. 241 (1907): 1832–69.

23. In addition to the two white papers on the petitions cited above, see RT 214 (1906): 630–75, RT 216: 2137–2171, *passim*.

24. Rüger 1968: 216–19; Austen 1977: 493–4; for a time some Akwas believed that Mpondo was not really dead and would some day return, like Barbarossa, to lead his people back to glory (interview, Albert Mpondo Dika, Akwa/Douala, 28 June 1970).

25. Kobler 1956: 134–5; see also the interview with Mpondo reported in Hamburg *Nachrichten*, 11 June 1907, Hamburger Staatsarchiv.

CHAPTER FOUR

Imperialisms at the Century's End:
Moghamo Relationships with Bali-Nyonga and Germany 1889–1908

Robert O'Neil

Introduction to Moghamo

The Moghamo[1] occupy a transitional zone between the forests of the upper Cross River basin and the Bamenda Grassfields of North-West Cameroon. A small number of Moghamo villages lie clustered around Widekum at the base of the main approach to the Grassfields. For generations the market here has been an inland port, linking the forest and the Grassfields. Regional exchange flourished and Efik and Duala agents were followed by successive German and British traders and administrators.

The earliest census attempt by British officers estimated the Moghamo population at 10,453 (Sharwood-Smith 1924: 65). At the end of the nineteenth century, the area may have had a population density of thirty to forty people per square mile. It was this relatively dense population that attracted first slavers and, later, coastal labour recruiters (Nkwi and Warnier 1982: 39). When the German explorer Eugen Zintgraff arrived in 1889, the Moghamo were living in scattered, polygamous, patrilineal and extended family homesteads, several of which joined to form villages under a fon and a council of senior village heads.

The Moghamo practice agriculture. They subsist on plantains, cocoyams, yams, bananas and palm-oil from the lower forests, and maize, beans, sweet potatoes, groundnuts and vegetables from the upper areas. The men control surpluses in palm-oil and kernels, groves of kola-nut trees and raffia-wine bushes. In upper Moghamo pigs and other small livestock are raised. In later colonial times, robusta and arabica coffee, as well as some cocoa, were introduced as cash crops. In the late nineteenth and early twentieth centuries a typical household might have two acres of farmland where women cultivated cocoyams, yams, beans, groundnuts, maize, spinach, pumpkins and plantains. In a village with access to the forest, each adult male had an average of nineteen oil-palm trees (Sharwood-Smith 1925: 65). The tapping of palm-wine was one of the principal occupations of the men: 'In many villages the drinking of water is almost unknown' (Ibid. 63). Senior men carried a raffia bag and a cow-horn drinking cup as status insignia. Zintgraff noted in 1889 that 'everything was done here to the accompaniment of feasting and singing' (Chilver 1966: 1).

By the end of the nineteenth century lineage leadership of autonomous village settlements was moving from a loose association of segmented lineage settlements towards political consolidation. Internal factors influenced the process of consolidation: especially population growth and a lack of vacant land which led to conflicts over political, economic and ritual control of settlements. External pressure came in the form of early nineteenth-century attacks by intrusive northern raiders, the Chamba, and by contacts with Western mercantile capitalism through Efik and Duala trade networks to the south and west.

The Bali-Nyonga

Twenty-one kilometres east of the Moghamo village of Batibo lies the main settlement of the Bali-Nyonga,[2] whose ruling dynasty originated from a raiding band dominated by the Chamba of the middle Benue. Many of the warriors were mounted, dressed in long gowns and armed with bows and arrows. Warrior bands were accompanied by war-priests who carried sacred spears, and played two-note flutes and under-arm drums. Their women and children moved with them. These were regional rather than tribal movements, multi-ethnic in composition, comprising groups of different Chamba, Bata, Bachama and Pere. They incorporated elements of groups through which they passed, including Buti, Tikar, Kutep and even Fulani (Fardon 1988: 87–8).

The devastation brought by raiding parties is remembered in apocalyptic terms (Ibid. 88). Searching for food, fodder, captives and slaves, they drove inhabitants from their villages and burned what they did not need. They passed by the present Bamenda Station to Bafreng, Mankon, Bafut and Meta'. Finally they reached the site of the present Bali-Town, at that time inhabited by Moghamo, went west to attack Batibo (Aighui), then Enyoh, down the escarpment into the Banyang forest and finally to Bafu Fundong near Dschang, where they were defeated and their leader, Gawolbe, killed. With his death, in the 1830s, the group broke up into seven bands.

One band, the Bali-Muti, raided Moghamo for slaves before going north. The Moghamo called this group 'Bangchu' or 'red-mouthed ones' from their habit of chewing kola. From their camp at Kifom (near the site of the present day Cameroon Protestant College) they conquered or drove into flight villages that included Mengen and 'Baku', the latter a Ngemba group also known as Mbutu. They raided Moghamo, attacked Aighui and drove the Enyoh people down into the Banyang forest. The Bali-Muti finally left the area but a small group called the Konntan stayed behind at Kifom. They continued to raid the countryside for a few years until they faced an alliance of the Bali-Nyonga and the people of Moghamo and Meta' villages who had been displaced. The Bali-Nyonga, had settled on the southern border of Bamum, had incorporated a group of Bati allies and were now attacked by the expanding power of Bamum. After crossing the Nun with other retreating groups, their leader, Nyongpasi or Fon Nyonga I, encamped first at Bafreng. The subsequent raiding into Moghamo forced some Moghamo villages to flee to the hills and forests until starvation forced them to return (see Sharwood-Smith 1925: 54–5; Kaberry and Chilver 1961: 358ff; Russell 1980: 20ff; Chilver 1967: 479ff; Fardon 1988: 87–8).

Whole areas between Ambo and Aighui in Moghamo were depopulated along with a strip along the escarpment ridge at Lower Ashong. Koelle interviewed 'Tando' of 'Njin', or Njen, a village today administered by Ashong. Tando said he had been captured by Bali raiders. The 'Tebana had burnt all the towns of the country so that people sought refuge in the woods' (Nkwi and Warnier 1982: 116–7). Those years of conquest and harassment were vividly recalled by Moghamo informants, although specific incidents have given way to memories of an extended period of raids and counter-raids. Displacement in that time and Bali-

Nyonga entrenchment during the German colonial period have been the source of boundary disputes up to the present day.

Having lost their horses, and cut off from replenishment, the Bali-Nyonga began to change their policy. In the late 1850s Fon Galega I became leader. He took control of an important Meta' market, and began to rely more on trade to sustain his people and less on raiding the surrounding country (Sharwood-Smith 1925: 10–11). He also moved his war camp to a more permanent site at Ntanka, a place formerly occupied by Moghamo people, probably of Mengen village (Soh 1983: 12–15). After beating off an attack by the rival Bali-Kumbat, Fon Galega I continued to raid outlying villages for slaves to work at his new settlement or to be exchanged for guns and powder. The population of Bali increased, swelled by an influx of new refugees and captives (Russell 1980: 25; Kaberry and Chilver 1961: 360). It was the Bali-Nyonga settlement, under the leadership of Fon Galega I, that Eugen Zintgraff and his party were to enter in January 1889.

The Arrival of the First Germans

In 1889 the Fon of Bali-Nyonga entered into an alliance that was seen as an opportunity to overcome Bafut and Mankon rivals and further expand his influence. The relationship between Moghamo village leadership and the Bali-Nyonga after 1889 was determined by the favourable impression made by Fon Galega I and Bali on the German explorer Eugen Zintgraff. Zintgraff's subsequent friendship with the Bali-Nyonga was to influence the role of the Bali in regional economic and political activity for the next twenty-five years.

Zintgraff's plan was to lay out a line of stations from the coast to the 'high plateau' along a secure road. In so doing he hoped to divert trade from routes that ran north to the Benue and west to Calabar and redirect it towards German traders at the Duala coast. Zintgraff's vision of a secure road and the exploitation of human and natural resources along its route became bound up with the fortunes of the Bali-Nyonga. The Governor turned down Zintgraff's plan but, following a direct appeal to Bismarck, permission was granted.

The first recorded European expedition to the Western Grassfields set off in December 1888. By the time its party reached the Banyang area, Zintgraff was the only European in a group composed of one hundred Lagosian and seventy-five Liberian Vai carriers. The interpreter and guide was Muyenga, a slave of King Manga Bell of Douala. Muyenga is thought to have been part of a refugee group from Bamum that had settled in Fon Galega's new settlement before ending up as a slave in Douala. Muyenga led the party up the escarpment along a trade route that rivalled one which ran through markets and settlements at Widekum and Aighui (Batibo) and on to Bali. In Banyang the party clashed with Chief Defang from whom Zintgraff took hostages and captive slaves of Grassfields origin.

According to Pa Neaka, an informant at Ashong, Zintgraff's party emerged from the forest at Enwen. The Fon of Ashong sent palm-wine and kola nuts to the strangers along with escorts to bring Zintgraff to the site of the old Ashong palace; a place called 'Ngakuruchuchen', that is 'the palace near the mouth of the forest'. Informants say that the old palace was also a marketplace. Muyenga had guided Zintgraff to a trade-friend of the Bali-Nyonga, Fon Enoh of Ashong. When such a large party, led by a European, arrived at Ashong the news passed quickly to surrounding villages. Zintgraff was given a house near the Ashong marketplace. On the 13 January many of the surrounding village heads came to Ashong, some of them to attempt to persuade the Ashong village leaders to kill Zintgraff and sell his party into slavery. On 14 January a band of two hundred armed men arrived from an unidentified village, perhaps Pinyin (Chilver 1966: 2). According to Zintgraff, despite the arrival of such a large group, all remained peaceful.

The Fon of Bali-Nyonga had heard of Zintgraff's arrival and sent many people to meet him but they were afraid to approach him. Pa Abraham Tituwan of Bali-Nyonga heard the story of Zintgraff's arrival from his father, Ngoh Sama, a servant to Fon Galega. The news was that an unknown 'thing' had come to Ashong with a skin that was red like fire. Ngoh Sama went for a closer look and returned to tell the Fon. Galega then ordered a drink called *fuga* to be prepared; maize and groundnuts, ground and mixed with water. The mixture was then put into a calabash of corn-beer. Ngoh Sama was instructed to take it to Zintgraff. If the white man drank, they would know that he was really a man. Ngoh Sama did as he was told, and according to the story, Zintgraff drank, proving that he was a man and not an animal. When Bali-Nyonga heard what had happened, Ngoh Sama was ordered to go back to Ashong with a group and return with

Zintgraff. The Fon sent a gift of 'three elephant feet and yams' along with an invitation to visit Bali-Nyonga. When Ngoh Sama met Zintgraff the second time he was carrying the Fon's spear, the *Fongseh*. After an exchange of gifts and a 'blood pact' with Fon Enoh of Ashong, the German-led party left for Bali-Nyonga. When Zintgraff arrived on 16 January 1889 a horn was blown to announce the presence of a stranger in the village. The Fon ordered that food be prepared for Zintgraff and his party. After Zintgraff had eaten a little, the Fon led him outside the palace and showed him to the people. To quiet their fears the Fon held Zintgraff by the hand and then turned to tell the people that he was human and not fire because his body was cold like that of a human being. The shrewd Fon Galega did not fear Zintgraff but thought that he was a slave-dealer because of the numbers of captives trailing behind his party. He was intent on keeping Zintgraff at Bali to prevent him from making contact with rival kingdoms in the region.

By the year 1889 Fon Galega I was perhaps in his late fifties with 'an erect and powerfully built' figure (Jeffreys 1962: 185). He had successfully consolidated his local position, increased his armament with muskets, beaten off an attack by Bali-Kumbat and subjected a number of villages, including those of Moghamo-speakers. He had also extended his sphere of influence to Ashong and southward into the Banyang forest, west towards Aighui and Widekum, and eastwards to the northern Bamileke groups (Kaberry and Chilver 1961: 361). He told the Germans that, prior to their arrival, he had had influence over at least seventy-two villages, a claim reduced in 1904 to thirty-two (Jeffreys 1962: 185). Phyllis Kaberry observed that Bali-Nyonga suzerainty had been confused by 'European conceptions of feudal relations'. Nonetheless, Bali-Nyonga did have tributaries whose status was defined by the surrender of flags and certain prized game. Beyond the tributaries 'lay a discontinuous ring of satellites and allies whose relationships with the Bali-Nyonga shifted between acceptance of Bali leadership and trade friendship' (Chilver and Kaberry 1968: 13).

When the German expedition arrived in 1889, the population of Bali was about six thousand. The total population of neighbouring tributary villages was estimated at fifteen thousand. It was essentially a township-state because the population farmed outside and returned to the Bali settlement, rather than forming new villages in farming areas. From Bali the Fon exercised control over conquered groups and had ties of friendship with the larger Moghamo villages to the west such as Ashong, Bessi, and possibly Guzang where there was an important market. The Fon's army was well organised into warfare and slave-raiding units and he was able to muster about two thousand warriors armed with muskets to impress Zintgraff on his arrival. Bafut and Mankon were Fon Galega's more powerful neighbours, and his rivals for the control of regional trade in ivory and palm-oil, with a population that supplied women, labour and slaves.

With a combination of shrewdness and aggression, Fon Galega strengthened his new kingdom. In 1891 he was to tell a German officer training the Bali troops that he now preferred diplomacy because 'war and violence scare men like goats that are frightened by a leopard and run off into the bush' (Hutter 1902: 339). Despite protests of a new statesmanship by Fon Galega, Hutter witnessed a war-party in action, providing a description that brings to life the constant fear of attack that occupied Moghamo villagers outside the Bali-Nyonga conquest zone.

> Heads of men killed during war constitute the principal booty; women and children are taken away as captives... Warriors assemble... they march at night... attack at daybreak... the tactic is surprise... They hurl themselves forward... spear or gun in hand. Their war cries, the thundering sounds of large elephant tusks [horns], the firing of guns, the strange whizzing of spears, the crackling of burning roofs of grass throwing up flaming pieces into the air, the rustling of collapsing banana plants, the cries of dying people whom the victors behead as they fall... It is terrifying... To this is added the bleating of frightened sheep and goats. Fowls fly off over the flames. Women and children shout ... over which shines the tropical sun from a deep blue sky. ... The Bali do not torture or martyr prisoners. (Hutter 1902: 357/8)

The Germans were to join the Bali Fon in an alliance which the latter saw as an opportunity to weaken and divide Bafut and Mankon and further expand his influence (Dillon 1990: 14). Zintgraff assured Galega that he would return to establish a station at Bali-Nyonga after he had explored the north. His expedition continued northwards, was refused transit to Adamawa, and had returned to Bali-Nyonga by mid-November 1889. On Christmas Eve 1889 Zintgraff left for the coast, where he prepared a report for the Chancellor in which he argued for a protected route to the interior through Bali. The interior was 'to be served by the route as being rich in palm products, ivory, hitherto flowing mainly into the British sphere, and as a source of manpower' (Chilver 1967: 484). In addition, to satisfy critics of the cost of such a proposal, he suggested a cheaper alternative: the unification of the Grassfields people under Fon Galega 'subject to German overrule'.

In 1890 Zintgraff organised a combined research and commercial expedition. This group of 375 people, including representatives of the firm of Jantzen & Thormählen, reached Bali-Nyonga on 25 December 1890. During this stay a combined Bali-German force was routed by Bafut and Mankon. Four Germans, 170 carriers, and hundreds of Bali-Nyonga, along with allies from Ashong and other villages, were killed (Chilver 1966: 29–31; Sharwood-Smith 1925: 62). Leaving a force at Bali, Zintgraff returned to the coast. He asked for arms and training officers, and for permission to use local labour to construct a road to Bali-Nyonga.

In August 1891 he was back at Bali-Nyonga negotiating a treaty of protection with Fon Galega, who became recognised as 'the paramount chief of the surrounding tribes of the northern Kamerun hinterland'. Captain Franz Hutter provided the Bali-Nyonga with M-71 breech-loading rifles and ammunition while he began to train a unit of Bali-Nyonga warriors he called the *Bali-Truppe* (Russell 1980: 80). The balance of regional power was upset not only by the treaty with the Germans but also by the introduction of repeating rifles and military tactics. Captain Hutter remained at Bali in May 1892 while Zintgraff went off to establish a station along the road in the forest at Tinto. Under Hutter the *Bali-Truppe* and smaller allied groups were encouraged to attack hostile Moghamo groups west of Ashong (Bamessong). The leader of an Ashong contingent, the eldest son of Fon Enoh of Ashong, was called 'Commander'. He is remembered for his role in attacks by the Bali-Nyonga on the Moghamo villages of Kurlabei, Ambo and Aighui. Hutter wrote that after these attacks and ambushes warriors were rewarded with a fathom of cloth for the head of each male they killed. Captive women and children became personal spoils (Chilver 1967: 488).

Not everyone was impressed with the Bali-Nyonga. Road-builder G. Böckner reported that the Bali depended solely on German support and were at odds with all their neighbours (1893: 7–9). *Rittmeister* von Stetten wrote that the Bali had little natural wealth and were in fact being set up as middlemen (1893: 33ff). Contrary to expectations, he saw little ivory in local markets, and considered it unlikely that they could divert what trade there was.

In the meantime, Eugen Zintgraff resigned and was forbidden to return to Kamerun for two years. In January 1893 the Bali station was closed. Hutter, escorted by his *Bali-Truppe* left for the coast. He dismissed his men at Tinto, leaving them in possession of weapons that were to become a cause of anxiety for the German government in Kamerun until the German expulsion in 1915 during the First World War.

Labour Recruitment

Although Zintgraff's Bali station was now closed, labour recruitment from the Grassfields for coastal plantations began to take place. Zintgraff returned to Kamerun in 1896 as a plantation manager at Victoria in the employ of Dr Max Esser. Esser was convinced that the only exploitable resource which justified the maintenance of a road to the Western Grassfields was the recruitment of labour and, together with Zintgraff, he set out to visit Fon Galega in search of plantation labourers. With Zintgraff's help he persuaded Fon Galega to become a recruiter for his plantations. In return for sending to the coast several hundred men each year, Galega would receive a head-tax for each one on departure and return. In addition, every Bali-Nyonga recruit had the right to take five others from 'subject tribes' with him without payment (Chilver 1967: 492; Russell 1980: 22).

Esser's company was the West Afrikanische-Pflanzungsgesellschaft Victoria (WAPV). Between June 1897 and April 1899 several hundred recruits of Bali and 'allied and subject tribes' reached the plantations. Many of these workers were from Moghamo villages. The mortality rate was very high. As the plantations expanded, the demand for labour increased. To satisfy their quota the Bali-Nyonga depended on men of Moghamo and other groups such as the Meta', rather than the core Bali-Nyonga. Just as such areas had represented a pool of potential slaves in pre-colonial times, they now became the object of forced labour recruitment with the backing of the Germans (Dillon 1990: 14,270). To this end they used the warriors trained by Hutter and armed with M-71 rifles to attack Moghamo villages. In 1899 Fon Galega was expected to meet a plantation levy of one thousand men. He was allowed a free hand and used whatever means he could to meet WAPV demands

(Russell 1980: 82). More than any other factor at the time, the recruitment of labour from 'vassal' villages in Moghamo and elsewhere contributed to an enduring enmity to Bali-Nyonga. What was envisaged on one hand by Fon Galega as a kingdom prospering through shrewd diplomacy and trade, and on the other hand by Zintgraff as a streamlined intermediary for colonial administration, could not survive the role of labour recruiter. Even 'trade-friends' became victims, although at first some village leaders, e.g., 'Commander' of Ashong, were able to profit from the recruiting arrangements (Chilver 1967: 483–4).

One battle occurred at Kurlabei in Moghamo over the refusal by Fon Acha of Batibo to send any more workers to Bali-Nyonga. Instead of men, Acha sent Galega a stone and said he was not going to send any more people to Bali-Nyonga. This story may conflate a series of incidents, but it illustrates the vigorous response which such labour recruitment could provoke. The Bali-Nyonga came with their *Bali-Truppe* and warriors from allied Moghamo villages, Bessi, Guzang and Ashong. The force attacked Batibo and then moved against Ambo, Kurlabei and Effah. The 'rebellious vassals' were defeated. Yet it was not long before the Moghamo villages who were allied with Bali-Nyonga were forced into a different posture. The more intensified recruitment led to increased opposition from Moghamo village leaders.

Hans Ramsay, manager of the North-West Kamerun Company (GNK), visited Bali-Nyonga and the surrounding area in 1900. He had already established an outpost factory at Widekum to tap the palm-oil belt. At Bali-Nyonga he was well received but concluded that Zintgraff had overestimated the position of the Bali-Nyonga. They had, he thought, achieved their present position mainly through the 'finesse and wisdom' of Fon Galega. He considered the Bali-Nyonga to be pillars of support for the Germans, but at the same time he saw them as an obstacle to further penetration of the interior. Despite his misgivings, he planned to open an outpost at Bali-Nyonga for the recruitment of labour (Ramsay 1901: 26). Before he could act, the WAPV opened a post on land given to them by the Fon. On his visit Ramsay had been met by Fonte, the personal servant of Fon Galega, because the Fon was seriously ill. The death of Galega I in 1901 ended an era in which German participation in Western Grassfields political and economic life was effected through explorers, recruiting agents and client agreements with local leaders, principally the Fon of Bali-Nyonga.

German Military Expedition

In April 1901 Lt. Strümpell set out for Bali-Nyonga with two European officers and fifty African soldiers. His task was to secure the road for a larger force under Lt Pavel. At Bali-Nyonga Fon Galega died on 24 May 1901, and Tita Gwenjang was made Fon Nyonga II (Jeffreys 1962c: 185, fn.63; Sharwood-Smith 1925; Chilver 1967: 494).

In November 1901 Pavel led two companies from Tinto to Bali-Nyonga. These arrived on 14 and 15 December respectively, and immediately reopened the station that had been closed with the departure of Hutter in 1893. The 'firepower' of Pavel's units were impressive, as shown by his reports of action in Bangwa and later Bafut (Pavel 1902: 90–2).

Pavel's force combined with companies that arrived from Kontcha and Ossidinge to attack first Bafut and then, on 20 and 21 December, Mankon. Paul Mzeka (1990: 78ff) describes the German punitive patrols. 'Five months after the Vijin (Pavel's party), a far more savage gang led by a Lt. Houben, and comprising about forty soldiers and a large contingent of Bali and Babungo carriers, arrived Nto' Nso' stealthily in the night… in the evening of the following day, they set the palace ablaze…' Pavel's officers set up a new camp at Bafreng, before moving in 1902 to a new site at Mendankwe. Thus began the direct German administration of the Bamenda Grassfields. When the Military Station at Bamenda (Mendankwe) was opened, the Kamerun Government's immediate goal was to facilitate the regular supply of manpower to coastal plantations (Nkwi and Warnier 1982: 214). For the Moghamo, the opening of the *Bezirk* meant an increase in the demand for human resources, a demand that already exceeded the apparent available supply. German commercial interests, namely the WAPV and the GNK, had already come into a conflict of interest in Bali-Nyonga over labour. In addition, the Station was to make its own demands for workers in local development.

The Zintgraff-Esser WAPV agreement with Fon Galega in 1896 to supply workers for the Victoria cocoa plantations was challenged by Ramsay, the General Manager of the GNK. The GNK had been granted an exclusive monopoly concession area, and so started a factory near Ossidinge on the Cross River, served by two steamers (Mullendorf 1902: 70–92). The factory needed a supply of workers to clear the area around the Cross River 'beach' (Chilver 1967: 495) and porters to carry palm products, ivory, valuable timber and wild rubber from the interior (Rudin 1938: 290). Ramsay discovered that the concession was not as exclusive as it had been made out to be; at Bali he found the Fon acting as recruiting agent for the WAPV. The WAPV and other Kamerun plantation interests had been encouraged between 1898 and 1901 by the initial supply of labourers arriving at the coast from Bali-Nyonga (Mullendorf 1902: 70–92; Chilver 1967: 495). From the beginnings of the Kamerun colony the Germans realised that the exploitation of Kamerun depended on a local labour supply. Labour was critical to interests on the coast. The coastal peoples refused to work on plantations and the practice of contracting labour from 'Cape Verde to the Congo' could not be continued (Mullendorf 1902; Rudin 1938: 346). Workers from the Grassfields were considered to be better suited to plantation work. Unfortunately, dysentery flourished on the slopes of Mount Cameroon, and many of those who arrived from Bali-Nyonga died. A 1901 report stated that between twenty-five and fifty percent perished. The District Officer of Ossidinge claimed that fifty percent never returned home after their contracts expired. While making efforts to maintain more healthy working conditions, the WAPV investment was so precariously dependent on the labour source that they were not too concerned with the morality of the forms of compulsion used by local recruiters, such as the Fon of Bali-Nyonga, to fill their quotas. In 1902 one went so far as to say that 'the Bali are more or less eager to hire for the plantations'. Despite GNK objection, the Government acknowledged the special contract between the WAPV and the Fon of Bali-Nyonga when new regulations and permits were issued to recruiters in 1902.

Bamenda Station

The opening of the Station at Bamenda in 1902 added a third interest to the contest for labour: the GNK sought porters and labourers, the WAPV recruited plantation workers, and now the Government made its own demands for messengers, labour for road-building, porters for expeditions and workers to help build the new station.

By 1902 the prestige of the Bali-Nyonga had fallen in the estimation of the Germans. They were mistrusted by the administration because of their brazen use of the Hutter-armed Bali irregulars. They also threatened German trading interests by becoming traders themselves. The Bali-Nyonga used the irregulars armed with M-71 rifles to form armed trading parties that extended Bali-Nyonga influence as far south as Kumba. Perhaps most disturbing for the colonial administration, and of course for victims in Moghamo, was the active use of the same armed bands for slave-raiding.

Trading parties reached the Kumba area in the south-west with a limited quantity of goods to trade (usually wild rubber collected on the way and small amounts of ivory) but they did have slaves for sale. The profit in slave-dealing was substantial at the turn of the century. A male slave sold on the Kumba market in 1900 to Duala or Mbonge traders might bring thirty bales of striped or blue cloth (Chilver 1967: 496). The Bamenda Station was therefore faced with the Bali-Nyonga as rival traders, despite the fact that the road to the interior had been built to bypass such indigenous middlemen. They were also using questionable tactics to recruit labour for the WAPV and engaging in slave-dealing, a practice that had been forbidden in Kamerun.

Slavery

Coinciding with the founding of the Bamenda Station, a decree was issued on 21 February 1902 which forbade 'the sale or exchange of domestic slaves or any form of slavery'. However, slave-dealing continued at Bali-Nyonga until the 1920s (see Chilver 1967: 497 fn. 46; Ruppel 1912: 846; Skolaster 1924: 303–4; Wirz 1973: 193ff). Not only were Bali-Nyonga raiding parties capturing 'recruits', they were also retaining slaves in Bali. In addition to selling slaves, some portion of the labour presented to the WAPV consisted of domestic or purchased slaves. A slave recruit was supposed to hand over part of his earnings to the Fon (Chilver 1967: 497).

Informants at Anong in Moghamo told the story of Simon Peter Nguti whom, they said, had been captured as a small boy by the Bali-Nyonga. He had gone with friends to crush palm-oil nuts. Bali-Nyonga men caught him since 'he had wounds on his legs and was unable to run away like the other children'. He was taken to Bali where he remained for some years until he was sent as a labourer to a WAPV plantation. There he fell ill and was nursed back to health by a missionary priest. He later went to school, and when the Germans left he became Catechist of Sasse (O'Neil 1991: 16–7). Jeffreys interviewed an informant from Tabesob in Nso' who had been taken with three others by Bali-Nyonga kidnappers acting as road workers. Nso' is at least five days' journey from Bali. They were taken to Bali-Nyonga where the informant remained a domestic slave for seven years until 1913, when he was sent to the WAPV as a labourer. He was released by the British and used as a porter to carry supplies for their troops moving from the Cross River against Bamenda. (Jeffreys 1962c: 167–8). Sixtus Azumambom of Tedze, in Ngie country, described how Bali-Nyonga slave traders took his father away early in the 1900s: 'Bali slave traders came to the big men of the quarter and demanded a slave. They gave a small boy [his father] otherwise there would be war. The boy, later known as Pius Gabinga, stayed at Bali-Nyonga with Fon Galega. When there was no more slave trade he was sent to school at the Basel Mission. Later he followed his class teacher, a white, to Kumba.'

The Moghamo relied on local intelligence and the use of 'talking drums' to warn of impending raids. Nonetheless, the depletion of village population through labour demands and slave-raiding threatened each lineage, their farms, and the very existence of the village. Villages that benefited from access to important trade routes and markets were being overpowered by the Bali-Nyonga, as were German interests. Men who did go to the plantations often did not return. These were critical years for Moghamo lineage leaders. In the meantime, Bali-Nyonga continued to raid neighbouring villages 'burning and carrying people into captivity' (Duncan 1921: 6).

The District military officers distrusted the Bali-Nyonga. Much was left to an officer's personal judgement; they were given wide latitude in the exercise of their powers and were subject to little supervision. Two events took place after 1902 that changed perceptions of the Bali-Nyonga. One was the settlement of the Basel Mission at Bali under Pastor Ernst in 1903, the other was the conduct of the Bali-Nyonga during the Anyang rebellion of 1904.

The Basel Mission

On 17 March 1903 the Basel Missionary Society opened a new mission on a site in Bali given by the Fon. In the same year was opened a *Volksschule*, a vernacular school with a three-year course. It was to be followed by a *Knabenschule* which taught a two-year course (Keller 1969: 26–9). Instruction was in Mungakka, the language of Bali-Nyonga, followed by German in the *Knabenschule*. The missionary Ernst soon established a good relationship with the Fon, becoming an advisor who stood between him and the administration at the Bamenda Station. While Ernst lived, royal patronage was assiduous, although schooling was considered as a type of *corvée*. At times the Fon supervised the round-up of school-age children, and even pursued runaways. Most of the children were not native to Bali-Nyonga, but from subject villages. One Moghamo informant said that many of the pupils came from Bafuchu and Meta'. By 1905 the Bali school had three classes and 181 pupils. By 1906 a 450 seat church was completed, but as yet no one had been baptised. The German *Knabenschule* opened in 1907 with a class of 130 of the brightest pupils from the vernacular school. At the same time, a school for girls was established. On 27 March 1907 all of Fon Nyonga's so-called 'sub-chiefs', including many Moghamo village heads, assembled at the Bali-Nyonga market with 283 prospective pupils for the Bali schools. One hundred and sixty were chosen for the vernacular school. The *Knabenschule* was also to serve as a catechist- and teacher-training centre.

Finally, after years of preparation, the Reverend Ernst baptised thirty-two school-children at Bali-Nyonga church on Sunday, 20 November 1908. It was the first recorded baptism in the Bamenda Grassfields. Shortly afterwards, Ernst died while on home leave in Germany (Chilver 1967: 498). This was a great loss for the mission and the Bali-Nyonga people, since he had been instrumental in restoring the prestige of the Bali-Nyonga with the German administration between 1902 and 1908 (Chilver 1967: 503).

The Cross River Rebellion

The second event to work in Bali-Nyonga's favour was a rebellion in Anyang country. Count Pückler-Limburg, the first civil administrator for Ossidinge, was murdered while on tour in January 1904 (Rudin 1938: 313). A District Officer, von Knobloch, left Bamenda Station with the 2nd Company of five officers and 120 men to meet with Colonel Müller's forces at the Cross River (1904: 698–702). The uprising was put down in six months and the villages that had taken part were looted and destroyed with the inhabitants fleeing to the bush. The Kamerun Government had feared an uprising after news of the Herero and Boxer troubles. Once more, superior firepower assured light casualties for the Germans. In the Anyang campaign a single European died (of malaria) along with forty-two of their African soldiers. The Anyang lost two hundred who died and two hundred more who were taken prisoner (Rudin 1938: 310). While the Bamenda Station was undermanned, Grassfields groups tried to reassert themselves. Bali-Nyonga remained loyal, 'steady, obedient and helpful' (Chilver 1967: 498). Also, when the 2nd Company returned, Bali-Nyonga supplied soldiers of the *Bali-Truppe* to help punish those villages that had fallen away. For this Bali-Nyonga was rewarded.

Moghamo Subjected to Bali Nyonga

The German officer von Knobloch attempted to determine which groups were the legitimate subjects of the Fon of Bali-Nyonga. On 15 July 1904 he recommended that Pinyin (a neighbouring village east of Ashong) be placed under Bali. When this was reported to Fon Nyonga, the latter added seventeen additional villages to his list, including Enyoh, Bessi and Kuruku. Bali supporters among the missionaries had told Knobloch that areas claimed by Bali-Nyonga had broken away because they felt that the Government no longer supported the Bali-Nyonga Fon. In a letter dated 19 November 1904 the Governor signified an 'agreement with the policy [of recognising Bali-Nyonga] in so far as careful enquiry proved that a state of dependence had previously existed' (Russell 1980: 82).

Some areas refused submission to Bali-Nyonga and were 'pacified' early in 1905. According to informants, they refused to supply food and workers through the Fon of Bali-Nyonga and so were raided. In March and April 1905, patrols assisted by Bali auxiliaries attacked southern Moghamo villages. Captain Glauning, the new head of the Bamenda Station, reported in March that 'the pacification of the population of this district has not ceased to make progress'. He noted that the villages that had refused supplies paid penalties which included ivory, and that 'they will behave' (DKB 1905: 557–8). Punitive raids extended beyond the Moghamo area previously subdued by the former Hutter irregulars, and extended as far as the south-eastern edge of Bamileke. The Bali-Nyonga impressed Glauning with their ability to put as many as one thousand irregulars at the service of the Germans (DKB 1906: 353–5).

Although Zintgraff's treaty with the Bali-Nyonga had been approved by the German Foreign Office, it was only on 15 June 1905 that Captain Glauning formally installed Fon Nyonga as paramount chief of 'thirty-one tribes'. This was proclaimed, according to Ernst, in the presence of forty-seven 'chiefs'. Some Moghamo village heads later claimed they did not understand what was happening, thinking only that the Fon of Bali-Nyonga was to act as a mediator with the Germans (Chilver 1967: 499).

Increased labour recruitment for plantations, road-building, work at the Bamenda Station, carriers for food, maintenance of area paths and rest houses, in addition to claims for tribute and workers at Bali under a paramountcy, became intolerable in Moghamo and led to open rebellion. Anong, Batibo, Enyoh, Bunji and Ambo were among the villages that took part in an uprising in the early months of 1906 that 'seriously harassed some parts of the district', above all the regions of the Bali-Nyonga and along the road between Bali and Tinto. The villages were 'energetically punished'. They had to submit to forced labour, the delivery of ivory and some livestock once their 'tenacious resistance' was broken (DKB 1906: fn.15).

However, conditions did not improve. On 13 April 1907 the whole region, bounded to the south by Kuruku and extending to the Nigerian border, was declared impassable to all except those with written authority from the Bamenda Station. In April and May Captain Glauning attacked Ashong, Bali-Nyonga's former trade-friend, before moving against Bamumbu to the east of

Ashong. In each case villages were punished because of their insubordination to Bali-Nyonga (Podevin 1916).

In addition to Moghamo 'vassals' there were others, referred to as 'the five towns', which were villages driven away from Bali-Nyonga and then forcibly resettled on former village sites by then within Bali conquest land. In some documents they are called 'slave settlements' but they seem to have been settled and recognised as sub-chiefdoms, fealty being demanded by the Fon. Bunji was one such, and its people were constantly at odds with Bali-Nyonga. Along with Guzang, Bunji was punished in 1907 or 1908 for not sending workers to Bali. Local informants said that their village head was killed at this time by the Germans (Podevin 1916).

Moghamo Rebellions

Village authorities in Moghamo were left with little choice but to unite their meagre resources to resist further demands from recruiters and the Military Station at Bamenda. They had been plundered of their most valuable resource – their able-bodied population – and harassed by armed Bali irregulars, as well as being cut off from participation in trade and associated sources of wealth – slaves, ivory and other resources. For example, the small village of Bunji claimed in 1916 that ninety-six of its people had been 'lost' to the Bali over a period of years (Podevin 1916).

The rebelliousness of the Moghamo demanded more and more attention by the Station in the form of military patrols. Questions were raised about the wisdom of supporting Bali-Nyonga claims in return for the dubious advantage of using the Fon as an administrative intermediary. Villages were punished for refusing to send more people to Bali-Nyonga or to supply porters for the Germans, and for refusing to acknowledge the paramountcy of Bali-Nyonga. After the death of Glauning in 1908, his successors undertook enquiries and found that the punished villages had been exhausted of their human resources and should be allowed to 'rest' (Chilver 1967: 502).

Evaluations and impressions of the past have changed over the past seventy-five years. The testimony of people interviewed by the British between 1916 and 1922, of witnesses at enquiries of 1948 and 1952, and the stories of elder Moghamo and Bali-Nyonga informants of the 1980s reflect minds intending to justify current attitudes and courses of action, rather than to point out the intolerable injustices inflicted on the Moghamo.

After 1916 British officers attempted to assess the extent of Bali-Nyonga paramountcy. They reviewed Moghamo claims to pre-German autonomy and for the restoration of ancestral land. Both before and after the Bali-Widekum War of 1952, witnesses revived stories of the mid-nineteenth century arrival of the Bali-Nyonga and their settlement on the land of villages of 'Widekum' origin, including Moghamo-speakers. In 1984 passions were still roused over boundaries fixed between Moghamo and Bali-Nyonga which reduced Moghamo farmland. Elder informants recalled stories of nineteenth-century Bali-Nyonga raiding and the later seizure of their land with German assistance. If Moghamo villages resisted it was 'because they refused to be under Bali', a reference to being treated by the Germans as 'vassals' of the Fon of Bali-Nyonga. While all the above perceptions are truthful, they do not tell the whole story about the contemporary conditions between Moghamo and Bali-Nyonga. Testimony about the period fails to emphasis the havoc caused by the extraction of labour. The energy of informants is often directed to the preservation of a nineteenth-century Moghamo that was never under Bali-Nyonga paramountcy. The issue of Bali-Nyonga's involvement in the recruitment of labour for coastal plantations and other Kamerun labour demands is often overlooked. Such involvement led to open rebellion, a closure of the region to travellers, and a lasting, although sometimes ill-defined, bitterness towards Bali-Nyonga.

This course was set in 1896 when Fon Galega I, with the persuasive Zintgraff at his side, concluded a labour recruiting agreement with the WAPV. Fon Galega was given a free hand and so utilised the traditional *Basoge*, or warrior raiding and trading parties, already trained in the use of rifles and tactics by Hutter in 1891–93. Deployment of these German-supported raiders turned even old Moghamo trade-friends against the Bali-Nyonga. Their tactics and the clandestine demands of Bali-Nyonga itself led to a depletion of Moghamo village manpower and critically undermined the political and economic authority of its village leadership.

When Captain Glauning (known locally as 'Grauni') was killed on 5 March 1908, the Kamerun administration began to realise that serious problems were being caused by their client Bali-Nyonga's insatiable demand for labour 'recruits'. The administration concluded that special care needed to be taken with villages of the interior, including those of Moghamo. They were not to be called upon to supply more workers than their communities could endure. The recruitment from such villages of so many workers so 'that native farms were neglected, family life suffered, and too few people [were] left behind to gather and transport local produce,' came under scrutiny (Rudin 1938: 324).

Notes

1. Sometimes spelled 'Mogamo'. On the use herein of 'Moghamo', readers are referred to Ngwa (1979) for current usage and to O'Neil (1987) for further historical information.

2. Moghamo informants referred to this composite group as 'Bali' or 'Kura-Tibab'. Koelle's informants called them 'Tebana'. The term 'Bali' is possibly derived from the term *ba'ni* in the Mungaaka language spoken by the Bali-Nyonga (Fardon 1988: 206).

CHAPTER FIVE

Nso' Military Organisation and Warfare in the Nineteenth and Twentieth Centuries

Verkijika G. Fanso and Bongfen Chem-Langhêê

Military organisation in West Africa, as Robert S. Smith observed, 'exhibited a bewildering variety of types, ranging from the village war clubs of the Kom and the age-grades of the Ibo to the elaborate military hierarchies of the Hausa-Fulani, the Oyo and the Dahomeans' (1976: 73–4). In this paper we focus on the military organisation of Nso' which seems to have embraced a number of these different types of organisation. In the nineteenth and twentieth centuries the Nso' fought major offensive and defensive wars, as well as engaging in frontier incidents at local village level. These types of conflict only partly overlap with Warnier's threefold classification, which comprises competitive wars of honour between local communities, wars of capture undertaken with the objective of taking captives for internal use only, and predatory wars for the purpose of acquiring captives for the long-distance slave markets (Warnier 1989: 12–13). The wars which Nso' fought in the nineteenth and early twentieth centuries include the Noni wars of expansion against Din, Dom, Djottin, Lasin, Mbinon and Ŋkor; wars against Bamum around the 1830s to avenge the murder of Yee Ne', a Nso' princess, and around 1886 in which the Bamum monarch was slain; the Nsungli wars in the mid-nineteenth century; and the German war of 1906 (Mbiba 1991). The material presented in this paper suggests that Nso' military organisation after around 1825 departs from

Warnier's model and perhaps suggests yet another item to add to Smith's list of types.

Nso' on the Arrival of the Germans

At the beginning of this century the Germans were imposing their rule on the Western Grassfields. They heard exaggerated stories about the might and military exploits of Nso' whose inhabitants were described as warmongers and gruesome slavers. The first German to arrive in the kingdom in 1902 observed some nine-hundred skull-trophies of war enemies hanging from the walls of the war lodges in the capital Kimbo'.[1] The Germans discovered that Nso' had not only inflicted two major defeats on the neighbouring kingdom of Bamum, but had slain and decapitated its paramount in or around 1886. Fon Sangge of Babungo described the Nso' ruler to the cartographer Max Moisel in 1907 as 'the powerful Bansso chief'.[2] Two years earlier, a German report had stated that all attempts to secure the peaceful submission of Nso' had been unsuccessful.[3] This is consistent with an anecdote wide-spread in Nso' and neighbouring groups. On being invited to make an act of submission on pain of military sanction, the Fon of Nso' is said to have replied, while pouring a handful of *saar* (finger millet – *Eleusina corocana*) through his fingers, that his people were as uncountable as this and that he had nothing to fear.[4]

In 1905 the main sources of intelligence available to the Germans were Bali, Babungo and Bamum, all with particular axes to grind. Even if the story of the nine hundred skull-trophies is genuine, we do not know the time-scale for that accumulation. As for the 'frightfulness' of the Nso', we have no evidence that they engaged in regular 'wars of capture', as did the Bamum, Vute, Chamba and Fulbe, though Nso' may also have succumbed to the temptation of raiding for slaves. One suspects that the German claim that the Nso' were 'much-feared slavers' was designed to neutralise opposition in the Reichstag to heavy colonial military expenditure. It appears that, save for the Wimbum, Nso' was held in good repute by its neighbours to the south and west, in contrast to Bamum, Bali-Kumbat and Kom.

Military Organisation

The power of Nso' was based not solely on its comparatively large population or superior weaponry, but also on its flexible military organisation. For, 'success in battle depends more on leadership and organisation ... than on weapons.' (Smith 1976: 73). The military organisation of Nso' was centred in *manjoŋ*, a network of military and hunting societies open to all males of fighting age. Before the nineteenth century, while the palace was still at Kovvifəm, *manjoŋ* was organised under a single *taamanjoŋ*[5] (leader of *manjoŋ*), its most senior officer, appointed by and answerable to the Fon. Each village had its *manjoŋ* club under a local leader. When the capital moved to Kimbo' the head of *manjoŋ* acquired the new title of *mfoome*, although the term *taamanjoŋ* continued to be used by many as synonymous with *mfoome*.

Oral traditions state that while at Kovvifəm the kingdom was frequently attacked not only by its immediate Nsungli and Bamum neighbours but also, from the eighteenth century, by more formidable Adamawa raiders, locally known as *bara' nyam* (lit. 'advanced people of horses'), or as *Balinyoy* (perhaps in reference to Ba'ni).[6] The prime purpose of these wars was to loot and to acquire captives for the slave markets. In one such raid on Kovvifəm, which we tentatively date before the end of the eighteenth century, these raiders not only sacked the settlement and took away many captives and loot, but also forced the Fon to take refuge at Taavisa, some eight kilometres to the west, where he later died and was buried. As a result of these devastating raids, Kovvifəm was eventually abandoned and the Palace moved to Kimbo'.

The evacuation of Kovvifəm ended neither the hostilities with Nsungli and Bamum neighbours nor the constant menace from the north and north-east where the Wollarbe Fulbe were now establishing forward raiding-posts. The desire to provide better defence against these enemies, to consolidate the new capital, to reduce losses in wars, to continue to grow and expand, and always to keep part of the fighting force in reserve called for the reorganisation of the military system. Two sectors were established: Ba' and Gham, with part of the capital and villages to the south and west of the palace belonging to Ba', and those to the north belonging to Gham. Each sector had its headquarters within the palace precincts, and was headed by a *mfoome* – *Mfoome Ba'* and *Mfoome Gham* respectively. The overall head of the state-wide *manjoŋ* was the Fon of Nso'.

The division of *manjoŋ* into Ba' and Gham sectors was gradually reinforced by a network of old and new fraternities, located in the capital and different villages of the kingdom. Some of these were existing lineage societies which were drawn into a palace-centred system. These fraternities included, among others with a diversity of names, *njoŋ, mfu', anyaaŋ, nshoro', jwim, mekoŋ, mekuv, kweebiri, saamba* and *ŋgwa'*. *Njoŋ* was the fraternity named after the generic term *manjoŋ*, the first and original military society; it was the drinking or meeting club of *manjoŋ*. Each village had its own *njoŋ* led either by a *tavnjoŋ* or a village *mfoome*. In Kiyan it was known as *ŋge'* and under the leadership of *mfoome, ŋgwaaŋ* and *lavŋge*; in Ŋkar it was known as *yaawan*. The *njoŋ* lodges in the capital and in the villages were often used for weekly meetings by other groups lacking their own club-houses.

Mfu' was the most senior of the fraternities, and the most important wing of *manjoŋ*. The esoteries of *mfu'* are said to have been acquired from Bamum during one of the early Nso'-Bamum encounters. According to *Mfoome* John Ngo, Nso' warriors entered the *mfu'* house at Yar, beyond Mbokam, and found *nyam mfu'* (bull-roarer) and *kifu ke mfu'* (medicine and secrets) and took both. Those courageous enough to drink the medicine soon discovered its potency: it 'made the heart strong', and rendered men brave to go forth, fight and capture enemies. The concoction of the medicine was soon learned from the Bamum and the *mfu'* institution was brought and introduced in Nso' as the 'strong arm' of *manjoŋ*.

These fraternities also had distinctive military functions. *Nshoro'* followed *mfu'* (some say it emerged from *mfu'*). Permission to introduce such groups was granted by the Fon, as was the case for *mfu'*. *Kweebiri* was reputed to have important medicine for curing wounds sustained during war or hunting. *Mekoŋ* was a fraternity of people who were good with the spear (*koŋ*). *Mekoŋ* fraternities were found mostly in villages which did not have *nshoro'*, although a few villages had both. *Saamba*, a war-like dance society, was obtained in the early part of the twentieth century from a group on the Ndop Plain. A village which lacked any of the major *manjoŋ* fraternities consoled itself with *saamba*. Unlike the other *manjoŋ* fraternities, women participated in *saamba* dances, although they were barred from membership. *Ngwa'* existed for adolescents learning how to use weapons by hunting together to catch small game for the Palace.[7] Many of the junior fraternities, such as *mekuv*, *meshev*, *saamba* and *mekoŋ*, were organised at the level of the lineage rather than the village.

In this way the military establishment was organised from the centre, through the sector, to the village. Each village, particularly those on the borders, had its *manjoŋ* and its related fraternities to defend it against sudden attack before help could be obtained from the wider sector and the state. Each village had its own local titled war-leaders, such as the village *mfoome* and his deputy *ŋgwaaŋ*, as well as a group of noted warriors called *anyaaŋ* who took the initiative in war, planned it and acted as scouts, reporting possible invasions to the centre. The *anyaaŋ*, drawn from all the villages of each sector, held periodic meetings at their head-quarters in Kimbo' under the leadership of the sector *mfoome*. This group is said to have constituted the governing body over all Nso' *manjoŋ*; it acted as a war council on the battlefield.[8]

The local senior officials of *manjoŋ*, i.e., the *mfoome* and his assistant *ŋgwaaŋ*,[9] from each village held weekly meetings of *manjoŋ kaavi* (so called since they were usually held on *Kaavi*, the market day in Kimbo' and the last day in the Nso' eight-day week) with their sector *mfoome*. During such meetings, border security and other developments in the villages were discussed, and directives and news from the Palace and the sector dissemi-nated. *Manjoŋ* officials held office for life *ceteris paribus* and their titles were not necessarily inherited by their descendants.

Mfoome Ba' and Mfoome Gham

Since the 1830s Nso' military organisation has been divided into Ba' and Gham under the leadership of the two most senior *manjoŋ* officials, *Mfoome* Ba' and *Mfoome* Gham. These two state officials, both commoners, were appointed by the Fon in respect of their valour and character and were directly answer-able to him. The titles were conferred for life, and could only be revoked for acts of felony, in which case the man stripped of the title would be exiled for life. While *Mfoome* Ba' was reputed to be a distant descendant of the family of the great councillor,

Shuufaay Ndzəəndzəv (see below), *Mfoome* Gham was always a retainer or ex-residential member of *ŋweroŋ*, the regulatory society (Chilver and Kaberry 1967: 103). These two state *amfoome* alone of the entire kingdom had the privilege of clashing their cutlasses with the Fon during the maleri dance, a victory celebration staged at the beginning of each dry season.[10] In fact, the eponym of *Mfoome* Ba' and *Mfoome* Gham was *fon koŋ* (lit. king of the spear).

Each *mfoome* received from the Fon a *mfiŋ mo'on* (single gong, also known as *ŋgem li'*). The late *Mfoome* Ba', John Ŋgo, stated that any man going to war swore on the *ŋgem li'* that he would fight until victory was won even if his *mfoome* was killed, and that if he tried to run away the spear that killed his *mfoome* should also kill him.[11] *Ŋgem li'* is actually termed *ŋgem kili'* (*kili'* = oath), i.e., the gong for oath-taking. The present *Mfoome* Ba' has two *ŋgem li'* in his keeping, one used by his predecessor in office (John Ŋgo) and another given by the Fon after his elevation. Each *Mfoome* also received a *ciciwar* (white flag) which they carried to war, and also displayed during the *maleri* dance. The first *Mfoome* Ba', Bamfon, established the tradition of wearing a *wav atavnjoŋ* (baldric of leader of *manjoŋ*) for warfare and *maleri*.

Warfare in the Nineteenth and Twentieth Centuries

The Nso' Fon usually declared war, after consulting with his council, by inviting the *Mfoome* of the sector in whose direction the group to be attacked lay to clap cutlasses with him, and requesting the *Mfoome* to bring to him the skulls of the enemy leaders. If a *Mfoome* and his assistants wished war to be declared against a particular group, they would first inform the Fon and discuss the matter with him. The Fon would in turn discuss the matter with his war council. If it was agreed, he would invite the Mfoome, the two would clap their cutlasses and so the war would be declared. Henceforward, the conduct of war was left wholly in the hands of *Mfoome* and his assistants. *Mfoome* would quietly send messengers to his village *amfoome* to summon their fighters, and directly to renowned combatants asking them to prepare for war. If war was not immediate, he would secretly instruct his village *amfoome*, during their weekly meeting, to send *ŋkiy si* (spies) into enemy country to study the lie of the land and the location of settlements, and to draw up campaign strategies with his *anyaaŋ*. Each village, depending on its population, might produce ten or more renowned warriors for a particular expedition.[12] Certain special warriors were believed to be *aŋgaasəm*, i.e., possessing magical powers, who could make themselves invisible and escape from burning houses, or turn into birds or dogs and penetrate enemy territory and subsequently lead the forces into battle; such people could live on their own for weeks or months without needing a sexual relationship with a woman. Each village was believed to possess a few such people, and it was at their doors that messengers knocked at night to invite them to war.

Divination, in the form of a sacrifice, was usually carried out in the Palace to determine the outcome of the war before fighting began. Each village *manjoŋ* had its own diviners. The diviner placed the war spears on the ground, the blades facing the sunrise and touching a heap of stones. A cock or a goat was slaughtered and the flow of its blood read as a good or bad omen. If in the context of an offensive war the omen was bad, it was called off until such a time as a good omen was obtained. In the context of a defensive war, if the omen was bad then women and children were evacuated to friendly territory or hidden in the forests and only able-bodied men remained to fight. The omen for the Nso'-German war of 1906 was bad, but it was decided that it was better to stay and fight than allow themselves to be captured without a struggle.

The Nso' fighting force never moved in daytime. The combatants assembled around midnight at a spot near the border with the group to be attacked. They were divided into columns, each led by a *nyaaŋ* to whom orders were given to direct the attack. A sacrifice to assure victory was then made over the weaponry and each warrior took an oath on *ŋgem li'* to fight until victory was gained. At daybreak *Mfoome* and his assistants would lead the fighting men into enemy territory carrying the *ciciwar* (white flag) and a *soŋ rər* (war trumpet of elephant tusk), and striking *ŋgem li'*. The signal to attack was *Mfoome* firing his gun; in earlier times, before guns were available, it was the sounding of the war trumpet. When fighting began the white flag was pinned to the ground in a conspicuous place and the sounding of the war trumpet maintained; while the flag stood all must go on fighting.

Taken unawares by the war trumpet and early-morning gunshots, the people rushing out of their houses were rounded up and taken captive; any men who were already armed to fight were over-powered or killed in single combat, and their heads cut off and taken away for victory celebrations. If the enemy was discovered to be more powerful, casualties on the Nso' forces heavy and defeat imminent, *Mfoome* would remove the flag and all the Nso' would flee.[13]

Nso' warriors fought for Fon and country; and also to bring honour and prestige to their village. Although all offensive expe-ditions were supposed to be declared or sanctioned by the Fon, this was not always the case. Stories are rife that occasionally, especially in the wars of expansion in Noni territory, a group of renowned fighters in a village wanting to impress the Fon with a surprise victory would secretly organise an expedition to subdue a small group or chiefdom for the Fon. If they succeeded, the domain of the Fon of Nso' was extended and the village *manjoŋ* and its fighters accorded royal decorations. If defeated, however, shame fell on Fon and country. The story is told of a son of Fon Tamanjo, known as Taraŋge' and resident in the village of Meluv, who took about eighty fighters on a secret expedition to attack Nchanti in Lower Noni. His entire contingent was killed and only he escaped. When he reported his defeat to the Fon and asked for an official expeditionary force, the perplexed Fon refused.[14]

The two most renowned wars in which the entire *manjoŋ* Nso' was engaged were the Nso'-Bamum war of 1886 and the Nso'-German war of 1906.[15] Both were fought on Nso' soil. During the 1886 encounter the Bamum were heavily defeated, their ruler Nsa'ŋgu slain and his head cut off and taken away. The Ba' contingent attacked first from the Dzəkwa' (Ŋkar) side and Gham, coming via Mba', attacked from the rear. The two contin-gents soon encircled the Bamum warriors, inflicted very heavy casualties, and the war was over in a few days. In the 1906 encounter, which lasted over two months, the Ba' contingent under *Mfoome* Njola' again attacked first from the Ŋkar side and Vekovi, and Gham's contingent, under *Mfoome* Bamgha, attacked from Ndzən in the rear. The Germans and their Bamum allies were very powerful and steadily pushed the Nso' contin-gents into the capital, Kimbo', after inflicting heavy losses. It soon became an all-out war in which the Germans chased the Nso' warriors from village to village looting, destroying and killing men, women and children. The work of *Mfoome* Ba' and *Mfoome* Gham became that of assembling the remnants of their forces and organising them to assist villages which were under attack from open combat or from ambush. After two months the Germans completely overpowered the Nso' forces and the Fon surrendered and agreed to pay tribute.[16]

Smith has observed that in West African warfare, the ruler himself seems only exceptionally to have led his nation in battle, and that most of them delegated their authority to their field generals (1976: 74). This is true of Nso'. The Fon and the great lords of the kingdom, along with smiths, smelters, diviners and the *ataanto'* (hereditary court officials), never participated in combat and were always advised to stay far away, although they might watch the war from a safe and distant place. We note the contrast between Bamum and Nso' in around 1886, when Nsa'ŋgu fought and was killed in a war which Səmbum II watched from a distance. At the beginning of the Nso'-German encounter of 1906, the Fon watched the early battles from a hill-top near Yer from where he could view the whole of Ŋkar. By contrast, Njoya personally accompanied his Bamum troops into the battlefield on the side of the Germans.

The size of the Nso' contingent in any war depended on the type of war being fought. The military force was smaller in raids and skirmishes and larger in major expeditions and general wars. Except, perhaps, in the German war of 1906, the Nso' contingent was never fully deployed in any war. If both sectors were involved, there were still the tributary chiefdoms and the fraternal fondoms of Mbiame and Oku whose forces were ready to lend support when necessary.

One very important aspect of Nso' military organisation and warfare concerned logistics. This, as Smith rightly remarks, was always a limiting factor in West African wars. The problem of provisions, he adds, 'was greatly simplified by the general requirement that troops should provide and carry with them their own food' (1976: 85). Nso' warriors, like the Zande of northern Zaire, brought an initial supply of food with them, and those who were not far from their homes went back for more when they needed it (Mair 1977: 67). *Wonle ŋgwa'* (adolescent boys) carried additional provisions, mostly boiled maize, cocoyams, yams and drinking water. Each boy carried 'one or two bags of meal' and all of them stayed together 'well to the rear' of the military force.

Moreover, women of the villages nearer the war front were also
organised to supply food to the troops when it became necessary.
Food might also be sent from the Palace if the contingent was
large and the war long. Warriors might also live on wild fruits and
roots when further provisions were not available, and each warrior had to forage for himself, as was likely the case during the
Nso'-German war.[17] The supply of provisions was never really a
problem because, except for 'wars of capture', e.g., by Bamum in
imitation of the Ba'ni and Fulbe, wars did not last more than a few
days.

Weaponry included clubs, stones, catapults or slings and long
wooden shafts with sharpened edges; and also spears, cutlasses or
swords and iron-tipped arrows. There were shields of woven reed
to protect the body. All these weapons were manufactured locally. With the increasing specialisation of Babungo in the smelting
and smithing of high-quality iron goods for export (Warnier and
Fowler 1979; Fowler 1990) and the development of the Oku slag-
recycling industry (Fowler 1995) Nso' had easy access to supplies
of spears and cutlasses close at hand. Shuufaay Lun in Kimbo'
operated a palace smithy, *kilam ke fon*, which was principally for
making spears and cutlasses, especially in times of war.[18] The
standard weaponry, therefore:

> consisted of a handful of throwing spears, a shield and a cutlass carried to the
> side in a sheath. ... The primary use of the cutlass ... was to sever the head
> of a dead enemy and bring it back for display and to win the rewards
> bestowed on a good fighter. (Warnier 1980: 88)

Any adult Nso' man travelling out of his neighbourhood was thus
always armed with weapons that were as much for war as symbols of manhood and honour. Any man travelling without these
weapons was said to be travelling naked, like a woman.

The most costly weapon, and the only firearm, the musket or
flintlock, began to be available in very limited quantities shortly
after the Kimbo' settlement, from the time of Fon Tamanjo. Guns
had reached Bornu, Hausaland and elsewhere in the Sudan by the
end of the seventeenth century (Smith 1976:106–118), and we
cannot exclude the possibility that they had reached Nso' from the
north before the end of the eighteenth or the beginning of the
nineteenth century. They could also have reached Nso', then or
earlier, from Calabar in the south, where guns began to be imported shortly after 1713 and became a standard article of trade by
1763, and from where most Grassfields guns seem to have been

obtained. However, it was not until the 1870s, when Belgian gun-makers 'turned out thousands of very low quality muskets for the Calabar trade', (Warnier 1980: 84–6) that guns began to be plentiful. It appears that, until the late nineteenth century, the importation and distribution of guns to heads of lineages and renowned fighters was a royal monopoly. They were acquired via neighbouring states, principally Babungo, by bartering ivory or war captives, or by direct purchase using cowries. A family that had received a share of captives after an expedition might prefer to surrender them to the Fon in exchange for a gun or two for warfare, power and prestige. When it became possible for ordinary individuals to buy and own guns, they 'manufactured household and farm equipment, reared small livestock, kept bees, grew tobacco, or acted as middlemen in the kola trade' in order to acquire them (Chilver and Kaberry 1960: 86).

Whatever the case, guns do not appear to have been greatly used and may not have had a very significant impact on Nso' warfare in the nineteenth and early twentieth centuries. The strong possibility of a gun misfiring or exploding made it an unreliable and risky weapon, although 'it was the only effective means to keep spearmen at bay'. Thus, few warriors using the gun took aim: 'it was far too dangerous as the gunman could receive the burning on his right forearm or in his eyes' (Warnier 1980: 88). Once they began to be used in Nso', guns remained most popular for use in displays at death celebrations and festivals. In other words, no matter how easily available the gun became, the spear in its various forms was still the major weapon: 'it served to engage an enemy at arm's length by thrusting or at a much greater distance when thrown' (Smith 1976: 94).

Casualty rates in Nso' wars depended on the type of campaign waged. Casualties in raids upon neighbouring territories to capture slaves or women to be kept as concubines were exceptionally low. However, it should be noted that 'wars of capture' were few, usually retaliatory and, more often than not, private enterprises. Wars of territorial expansion were also not very costly in lives, unless the group being subdued proved powerful and resisted for long. On the other hand, casualties in punitive expeditions and general wars (e.g., wars with the Nsungli, the Bamum and the Germans) were heavy. Specialists in treating serious wounds always accompanied the warriors to the field to handle serious cases. The bodies of those fallen in battle were buried there and not brought back. Special marks were cut on the door-posts of the houses of those who had fallen in battle as a signal to their relatives that they had been killed. Officials were sent to do this at night, before the troops returned. A day of remembrance was always chosen to mourn their deaths (Mzeka 1980: 69).

When the war was over and victory achieved, the troops returned triumphantly to the capital with their captives and the heads of enemies killed for celebrations and decorations on *Kaavi*, the market day in Kimbo'. They would sing *manjoŋ* songs and dance *nsii*, the victory dance,[19] on the Palace dance field; some would show off with their spears and cutlasses and shields, or with their guns, demonstrating how the war was fought; others, holding heads of slain enemies or carrying *kighaa* (jawbone calabashes) on their left shoulders and holding cutlasses in their right hands, would run to the marketplace where the Nso' public would admire them. At the end of the day the Fon would decorate the heroes with *fə nsii* (a red feather in the cap) for a captive or slain enemy and *kighaa* for a man slain in face-to-face combat; and feast the entire *manjoŋ* with food and palm-wine. More decorations for bravery were continued in the two headquarters' *manjoŋ* lodges: there the state Mfoome tied *koonte* (creeper *Passiflora sp.*) on the right arm of each warrior who killed or captured an enemy. Celebrations continued in the different villages when the heroes returned with enemy heads. There the party moved from the compound of one lineage head to another singing and dancing *nsii* songs, rolling the enemy heads on the ground and jumping over them, drinking and eating heavily. It was considered that women, children and the aged should not be killed in wars, for their heads could never be used as trophies or for victory celebrations. Interestingly, Nso' warriors avoided killing people of equal rank or status to their Fon, preferring to take them captive. The only skulls that might be given ritual treatment, preserved with care and treated with reverence, were those of a slain Fon or *Mfoome*.

Conclusion

The reorganisation of the Nso' military system in the nineteenth century put it on a firmer foundation. From the level of the state through that of the sector to village level, *manjoŋ* was well organised and well led. While the Fon remained the supreme commander, the organisation and conduct of wars was left entirely in the hands of his officers, *Mfoome* Gham and *Mfoome* Ba', and their senior assistants in the centre and in the villages. These war leaders met periodically during the dry season to discuss matters of security on the Nso' borders. During such meetings, care was always taken to know the military prepared-ness of each border village, especially those in the direction of neighbouring groups with which relationships were strained. When campaigns were organised, adequate arrangements were always made for the supply of provisions. Above all, when victory was achieved in any encounter, the bravery of the fight-ing men was bolstered through elaborate celebrations and decorations both at the centre and in the villages.

Notes

1. See: DKB, 15 Xof 1906 and V.G. Fanso and E.M. Chilver, forthcoming.

2. *Deutsche Kolonialzeitung* 15, 1908, p. 271.

3. DKB, 16.

4. See Fanso and Chilver, forthcoming. Another version of this anecdote states that it was the Fon of Babungo who used the millet to demonstrate the large population and consequent power of Nso'.

5. According to the late Fon, Səm III (1947–72), on 27 May 1960, there was no *Mfoome* in earlier times, only a *taamanjoŋ*; but, according to the late Mfoome Ba', John Ŋgo (d.1987), on 31 August 1958, there was only one *Mfoome* at Kovvifəm who organised war and hunting together with *taa manjoŋ*. See: Nso' Working Notes (henceforth NWN), IX and XV, Epitomes of and extracts from P.M. Kaberry's fieldnotes and taped records (1945, 1946, 1958, 1960 and 1963), deposited at the London School of Economics, transcribed and sent to V.G. Fanso, Department of History, University of Yaoundé, by E.M. Chilver.

6. The assumption that they were the Fulbe of Adamawa is not supported by any evidence. In reality, the Fulbe were nowhere near until much later. The iden-tity of the culprits is uncertain, but the regional evidence taken as a whole points to precursors of Gawdbe's Ba'ni and their allies (variously called Mudi, Mute, Peere, Pyere, Peli, Potopo and Montə).

7. Animals caught anywhere and destined for the Palace were first presented to the state *Mfoome* of the sector before being taken to the Palace. See: Benedict Tata, 18 March 1946, NWN, XV(1946).

8. See NWN, 27 May 1960 (1960). According to Mzeka (1980: 70), it was brought by the people of Ŋgomrin led by Faay Ŋga' Njavkoy.

9. Mzeka 1980: 68; Ba', 31 August 1958, NWN V(1958).

10. Faay Taaŋkumkuy, 9 September 1960, NWN, XIV(1960). *Maleri* became extinct in the 1930s.

11. Mfoome Ba', 17–18 September 1960, NWN, XIV, 1960.

12. Mfoome Gham, 29 March 1958, NWN, VII(1958); Chilver and Kaberry 1968: 103.

13. Mfoome Gham, 29 March 1958; Mfoome Ba', 31 August 1958 and Faay Kilam (nshiylav) 22 August 1958, NWN, V and VII (1958); also conversations between Fanso and Paa Felix Tah of Kikaykela'ki (d. 1988), Paa Paulinus Lukoŋ of Ŋkar (d. c. 1980) and Shuufaay Ŋgoorin (d. 1980s).

14. Narrator of story, Mfoome Gham, 29 March 1958, NWN, VII (1958).

15. We would like to state here that, apart from the 1906 war with the Germans, the narratives of fighting are hearsay and we have little from the other side except some confirmation of inroads into Bamum from von Wenckstern (DKB 1907); the chronology is necessarily uncertain.

16. For a fuller account of the Nso'-German war of 1906 see Fanso and Chilver, 'Nso' and the Germans.' Information about the Nso'-Bamum and the Nso'-German wars was compiled from NWN and conversations Fanso had with many informants.

17. Faay Kilam, 22 July 1958 and Mfoome Gham, 29 March 1958, NWN, V and VII (1958); conversations Fanso had with several other informants.

18. Shuufaay Lun, 1960, NWN, XIa (1960).

19. *Nsii* is a ritual and ceremony for men who had demonstrated their bravery in war or hunting by bringing home the head of an enemy killed in battle, or a leopard or buffalo killed in whatever manner. Its members who received decorations for bravery belong to the cult of heroes, *kidzə'*. *Nsii* songs are generally war songs and songs of victory.

CHAPTER SIX

Rebellion, Defection and the Position of Male Cadets:
a Neglected Category

Jean-Pierre Warnier

In 1973 I was making enquiries in the small chiefdom of Songwa, where I was talking with a notable. An old woman was following the conversation. She stood up, grasped her ancient pull-over with both hands and pulled it up to reveal her stomach. I saw a deep scar, that of a serious wound to judge from the length and jagged depression it had left on her lower body. The woman explained that towards the end of the German occupation a small band of 'Kamenda' armed with breechloaders had fallen upon them, taking off women and cattle at Mauser-point, and that she had been wounded in the scuffle.

I recall the uncomfortable feeling I had at the time. The episode was not unconnected with the appropriation of women and the prestations of game, camwood and other resources embedded in the very regional hierarchy that I was discussing with the Songwa notable. Moreover, the woman recognised this. However, at that time, the scar and the scrimmage did not fit into any of my ethnographic frameworks. It could not be fitted into any analysis of pre-colonial political systems. Rather, for me, the scar bore witness to a painful event which belonged to the colonial past. It gave rise only to embarrassment and a sense of guilt on my part. Neither the incident nor the feelings it aroused were recorded in my notes. These were ethnographic notes in the strict sense of the term.

Now, twenty years later, that scar has become domesticated. It has lost its disturbing and opaque character as the evidence for an exceptional drama. It has undergone the fate of the countless events the social sciences feed on. It has become an ethnographic fact which can be included in an overview of ancient political systems. It bore witness to the disorderly rebellion of the young unmarried men (cadets) at the start of colonisation and, in consequence, to their enforced subordination in the Grassfields chiefdoms in still earlier periods. It threw light on these systems with the help of new approaches that were not available to me when I began my work in 1971. In the interval I had, among other things, read and thought about Sally Chilver's paper (1967) on the relationships between Bali-Nyonga and the representatives of German colonial power.

In its essentials, Grassfields ethnography has been constructed from the point of view of the hierarchy of chiefs and notables. Women, since the classic work of Phyllis Kaberry (1952), have been the subject of some detailed studies. In contrast, the mass of young bachelors have never, unless I am mistaken, been the subject of special studies, despite the crucial role they played in underpinning the former hierarchies, as labour during the colonial period, as recruits to the Christian missions and, from the inception of the colonial period onwards, as rebels. This lacuna is the result of four combined effects. First, an effect of social structure: speech is monopolised by the hierarchy. The cadets constituted a category of persons reduced to silence (a muted group), as were women. The ethnologist does not hear them. Secondly, a double effect of a theoretical approach; anthropology, since 1940, in pursuing its interest in political systems paid more attention to the hierarchy than to the *vulgum pecus*, with the exception of slaves. Thirdly, the Marxist anthropology of the years 1960–70 was more concerned to single out the relationships of production than to give voice to a dominated group. Finally, the effect of a disciplinary bias: as N. Thomas has shown (1989), Radcliffe-Brown in basing anthropology on the monopoly of the professional ethnographer over the collection of facts discarded the testimony of the missionary, the trader, the colonial officer, the schoolmaster, the convert and, by so doing, dispensed with history.

In casting a historian's eye over Grassfields society, Elizabeth Chilver helped to neutralise this quadruple effect. One example is the history of the Bali 'irregulars' and the 'Tapenta' who made their appearance along with the German penetration of the high plateau. The episode of the scar belongs here. From 1891 onwards notables and cadets, nominally attached to the chiefdom of Bali-Nyonga, began to hold the region to ransom on their own account. This phenomenon became more widespread after the punitive expedition of the *Schutztruppe* Commander Lt. Col. von Pavel against Mankon and Bafut in December 1901. Armed brigandage was taken up by cadets who had broken away from authority and who were known in Pidgin as 'Kamenda', 'Tapenta'[1] or 'Free Boys'. Here is a description given by Fr. Spellenberg of the Evangelical Mission, who was in charge at Bandjoun in 1914 (cited by van Slageren 1972: 84):

> [The] appearance [of the Tapenta] bodes no good. The youths in particular, who form the tail of the troop, are the bane of the country. Corrupted by the magic of the Whites, they attack men, women and children like wild beasts. They steal anything that isn't nailed down – fowls, goats and foodstuffs. Their organisation has ramifications everywhere. When they are checked they cry: 'Lef mi, mi big boy, mi bi Tapenta boy.' (In Pidgin: Leave me alone, I'm important, I'm a Tapenta).

At this period, the phenomenon is attested from Bafut to Bandjoun. Its epicentre was the chiefdom of Bali-Nyonga. However, it is likely that its equivalent was to be found throughout the so-called Bamileke chiefdoms, with a resurgence during the Independence period from 1956 to 1970.

At the heart of the phenomenon lies the dissemination in the Grassfields of breechloaders taken from the Germans. Elizabeth Chilver (1967) has restored some of the history of this in the course of her analysis of Bali-German relationships. We start with the attack on Mankon mounted by Zintgraff on 31 January 1891. The forces assembled by the explorer consisted essentially of Bali warriors accompanied by Zintgraff and his five German companions, their Vai bearers from Liberia, and warriors from some small chiefdoms more or less closely allied to Bali. The attack proved disastrous for the Germans, four of whom lost their lives. The Vai carriers, beating a hasty retreat, abandoned their arms and provisions.

There is little doubt that the booty found its way to the Mankon and Bafut palaces, nor that the guns were redistributed to those henchmen of fons and notables known by the Bali term of *Bigwe* (pl.), masters of the arts of brainwashing and deception.

Subsequently, the dispersal of German arms increased. Following his defeat, Zintgraff called for reinforcements. These arrived in August but their bearers mutinied at the approaches to the Grassfields and made off with their arms, pillaging the villages in their path. Zintgraff's Bali allies managed to recover a good part of the material. The explorer distributed one hundred Mausers and ammunition to the Bali warriors. Meanwhile, however, the stores of the staging post of Barombi, on the Mungo, had been pillaged by bearers, who exchanged several hundred looted Mausers and carbines for women. One can see why Zintgraff said little about this reverse, more resonant of future trouble than any military defeat. There is little information about the fate of these guns. Chilver (1967: 491) records that oral traditions collected in the 1920s by British colonial officers suggest that a large number were retained by the Bali and used until the ammunition ran out.

In 1910 the German Station Commander Menzel estimated that the number of breechloaders dispensed by Zintgraff in the Grassfields amounted to between 2,000 and 2,500. Both the Fons and the administration were worried and attempted to repossess them; but in 1910 the Station had only succeeded in recovering three hundred. One should distinguish between two cases. First, that of the *Basoge* or Bali irregulars who came under the authority of the Fon of Bali-Nyonga. Zintgraff, followed later by the colonial administration, had made a treaty of protection under which the Fon of Bali-Nyonga became a colonial agent. As such, he was expected to perform two essential but contradictory tasks: the maintenance of order and the recruitment of labour. Second is the case of the Tapenta who acted quite independently, accompanied by bands of young folk. In practice it is likely that the boundary between these groups was hazy. Grassfields customs consider it perfectly proper for an executive to take a percentage of every transaction. The notables controlled the networks of matrimonial exchanges, successions and marriages. They were less careful managers in other matters and could readily close their eyes to other affairs provided they got their due share. The same collusiveness was evident in the case of the traffic in children and adults.

In the course of time the notables began to realise that the Tapenta movement formed part of a larger phenomenon: the cadets, doubtless for the first time in Grassfields history, were escaping from their control. They took note of the favour which the missionaries enjoyed among young people; of the unbelievable fact that the white man baptised converts – literally initiated them – without paying any regard to their social rank; and they remarked that the cadets fled to the coast to avoid the constraints to which they had to submit in the chiefdoms. The notables were aware of this in 1911. Chilver (1967: 505) records the anxiety of the Bali who, in 1912, complained to the Governor at Buea that 'many people are leaving. Nine out of ten, when they go the coast don't come back and don't send money to Bali'. The missions, who on the whole welcomed young people, were not troubled by the fons and notables. The disquiet of the latter with the missions was constrained by their fear of the administration, and also by the active friendship between the Basel Missionary Ernst and the Fon of Bali. However, in 1916 the internment of all the German missionaries by the allied forces gave the notables a chance to carry out what they had been contemplating for some fifteen years: to destroy the chapels, books, Christian emblems and schools, to disperse Christian meetings and to take the young men in hand again. The Christians were accused by the notables of being rebels. Out of spite, but not without deeper reasons, they were identified with the Tapenta. In the event, the Grassfields hierarchy had not misidentified their real adversaries: these were indeed the cadets.

Readers of Hirschman (1970) will have recognised two of the four options available to individuals in declining organisations – rebellion (that of the Tapenta) and defection (into the Christian churches or the market economy and its most important space: 'the coast'). The scar displayed by the old woman, the Mausers, the red berets and the confused indiscipline of the cadets who exacted redress from the notables by appropriating women, cattle and anything else they could lay their hands on, indicates a rift which divided Grassfields societies on the eve of colonisation. It might be objected that this crisis was caused by colonisation and did not precede it. In my view, this objection does not withstand a close examination of the multiple and convergent events which accompanied the colonial episode. Certainly, by escaping to the coast the cadets were fleeing forced labour and the death which was all too often its sole remuneration. Even so, taken all together, the instances of defection and rebellion[2] and the suddenness of that phenomenon, as well as the determined resumption of authority by the fons and notables from 1916 onwards, indicate that the 'traditional' chiefdoms were already subject to serious tensions on the eve of colonisation. An effort of imagination is required to envisage the extreme demands which the fons and their notables placed, by all sorts of practical and symbolic means, upon wives and bachelor cadets. It is, of course, inappropriate to speak of a 'crisis' since, all things being equal, political organisations such as Mankon's could have gone on reproducing themselves for a good while longer.

In my view this conflict has been insufficiently brought out in Grassfields ethnography. This remark applies in particular to my 1975 thesis and my larger work published in 1985, both influenced by functionalism. To counter a description of the chiefdoms of the high plateau which emphasises the harmony of their parts, one should underline that these chiefdoms rested on the shoulders of cadets, who were subjected to obligatory celibacy and to austere and meritorious work. Rewards were only enjoyed by a minority of cadets, who were destined for a polygamous marriage, to succeed to a household or lineage headship or office, and to engage in the biological and social reproduction of the chiefdom. The reconstruction of these political systems by means of ethnographic enquiry, such as my own of the early 1970s, gives no access either to the situation or to the subjective experience of the cadets; an ethnographic inquiry of this kind does not expose lines of tension or potential cracks in the system.

On the other hand, when the coloniser arrived and, independently of the control of persons by notables, distributed Mauser rifles, sacraments and employment, the cadets immediately saw opening up to them opportunities for protest for which words were found ('Lef mi, mi big boy, mi bi Tapenta boy') and for action at the point of a Mauser. They could also now discern the pathways and opportunities for defection: the mission and the coast.

To summarise Hirschman (1970), individual members of organisations allegedly 'in decline' have not only the two alternatives of protest and defection, but four options in all: protest, defection, loyalty or apathy. The first two could only be offered after the arrival of the Europeans. Before 1891 they hardly existed, if at all. We have no evidence of a collective revolt of the cadets before colonisation. The only recorded historical event which resembles it is the revolt of the retainers of the Bamum palace under the leadership of Nguwuo, which Nsa'ngu and his supporters managed to put down.[3]

On the other hand, cases of individual rebellion and conflicts between fathers and sons are well attested. Pradelles de Latour (1991) has exposed the intensity of parental domination among the Bamileke. In that case, a son would be devoured by the narcissism and all-mightiness of his father were it not for the role of the bride-giver, 'the distant father'. It has struck me that the hostility felt towards fathers, and the deep frustration of celibate cadets excluded from reproduction, transpose themselves into rivalry between sons for access to either marriage or succession. Such rivalries between sons are so strongly felt that the notables themselves found it difficult to contain them within acceptable limits. Those rivalries also involve their mothers, the wives of polygamous notables. There is plenty of evidence that they competed against one another over the advancement of their respective sons.

Defection before the colonial period was probably less difficult than might be supposed, in that chiefdoms were relatively open, and individuals or kin groups could migrate from one to the other. However, this option was not really viable for the great majority of cadets, who were likely to retain their status wherever they went. An unsuccessful contender for an important succession could obtain the status of notable in another chiefdom only if he brought a large household or a sizeable group of lineage members with him. One could argue that such people were no longer 'cadets'.

Having reached this point in the argument, we shall advance some provisional conclusions. The revolt and defection of cadets from 1891 onwards suggests strong pre-existing tensions, and supports the hypothesis that before the colonial period the only options open to cadets were the two remaining ones described by Hirschman, loyalty and apathy. Ironically, it is the colonial situation that may supply the information required to complete the ethnography of the category of celibate cadets.

Within the limits of the present paper only a quick sketch is feasible. In the past, cadets were loyal to the hierarchy. This is seen as a praiseworthy loyalty, expressed by work, submission and attachment to the imaginary world of a notability which is conceived of and conceives itself to be a vessel brimming over with the vital substances required for social reproduction: breath, sperm, camwood, oil and so on. The cadet, on the other hand, is defined and defines himself as an empty vessel lacking the means to fill itself, which means he strives to deserve. However, in the absence of reward or personal qualities, loyalty wears itself out; and then apathy sets in. Local fictions blame the losers for their misfortune (*ndon*) or for the various depleting afflictions which they are seen to suffer (*atchul*).[4]

In the past, as in the present, one would have come upon a large number of men who were dependent on others, women in particular. Supernumerary men are to be found in all hierarchised societies, and accommodate themselves, as Ortner (1981) expresses it, by diversion or retrenchment. The conversations I have had with young unemployed men have made me realise that their situation is not novel, although the present economic situation has multiplied their number and increases their unhappiness as other options are now disappearing before their eyes. Loyalty no longer pays, the escape routes are blocked, and the experience of rebellion in the *maquis* and, more recently, in the *villes mortes* operations have shown the cadets the brutal face of power which, even before the colonial period, had identified them as dangerous categories in the population. The leader of the Social Democratic Front, John Fru Ndi, appeals to these categories. The preceding analysis explains why most of the fons and neo-notables are hostile to Ndi and maintain their alliance with the President, Paul Biya. Indeed, their hostility to the cadets predates colonisation and has merely been subsequently confirmed.

To conclude: this brief article is intended to illustrate Chilver's particular contribution to the anthropology as well as the history of the Grassfields. Her work provides a powerful antidote to the 'pure' ethnography put in hand by Radcliffe-Brown and continued in the tradition he founded. Chilver introduced systematically into our field of studies the sources disqualified by the famous founder of social anthropology. Among these were the accounts of the explorers and travellers (Flegel, Zintgraff, Hutter), colonial publications (Pavel, Conrau and the articles which appeared in *Globus, Deutsches Kolonialblatt* and *Deutsche Kolonialzeitung*) and German and British archives, among the latter the *Assessment* and *Intelligence Reports*. She placed all these in the context of the development of anthropology in the 1920s and 1930s and the courses attended by British Colonial Officers in Oxford and elsewhere, which were followed by the studies undertaken under the auspices of the Colonial Social Science Research Council (Chilver 1971). To these she added missionary archives and, finally, the biographies of prominent Grassfielders, schoolmasters, and the *literati* straddling two worlds, such as Max Gabana Fohtung (Chilver 1962 reprinted as Fohtung 1992).

Notes

1. According to E.M. Chilver, this is a pidginisation of 'interpreter' (pers. com.).

2. By religious conversion, providing service for Europeans, the market economy, the 'Kamenda' adventure, the disregard for the hierarchy, the reference to the White man rather than to the Fon.

3. The analysis of this complex incident, which took place in a kingdom which was in many ways atypical of the rest, would involve too long an excursus. An account of it is to be found in Tardits' monograph of the Bamum kingdom (1980: 170–99) and Tardits (this volume).

4. I have described these in Warnier (1993).

CHAPTER SEVEN

Catholicism & Nso' Traditional Beliefs

Joseph Lukong Banadzem

Introduction

Nso' lies in the north-east corner of the North West Province of Cameroon.[1] The 1987 national census recorded a population of 217,000 for Nso' and its neighbours, Oku and Mbiami. Nso' homogeneity has been enhanced by the adoption of its main dialect for primary instruction. Kumbo (properly Kimbo'), the capital of Nso', is a sizeable city, in which the Palace of the Fon (or king) and the lodges of the main men's secret societies are situated. It is also the seat of a Catholic bishopric and an important commercial centre for the region.

Nso' was defeated by the Germans after a three-month war in 1906, and received its first missionaries at the end of December 1912. Despite this history, Nso' people have resisted total incorporation into the world religions. In 1988 the Bishop of Kumbo stated that some fifty to sixty percent of the population of the diocese were still engaging in 'traditional religious practices'.[2] In this paper I shall reconstruct some of the principal observances that were maintained in the colonial period, before discussing the influence of foreign religions on practice and belief. Most of what follows derives from insider participant observation in the postcolonial period, and more especially from enquiries made in the field in 1987 and 1988.

Nso' Religion

As in other pre-literate societies, Nso' traditional religion lacked a formalised creed and places of worship open to all. It centred on beliefs in superior, invisible beings, and rested first and foremost upon a First Cause, *Nyuy* or 'God'. Compare two attempts to describe this concept. Following his stay in Nso' (1913–15) Fr. Emonts SJ wrote: 'My own experience fortifies my opinion that the highland peoples, though pagan through and through, did not worship idols or a plurality of gods. In their own pagan way they believe in a Supreme Being, *Nyuy*, and honour it'. As time went on it became more and more clear that this was the case in Nso'. Puzzled by the importance attached to particular natural features, he went on to ask if they were gods and received the reply: '*That is not God; God is there*' (see Chilver 1985b). Chilver states: 'I shall render this term (*Nyuy*) as Breath rather than Spirit since it was formless, impersonal, immanent and genderless ... was partible in its manifestations in all life and nature and made itself felt in unexpected events and numinous places' (1990: 230). On the other hand, as she confirms, people also believed in *anyuy*, divinities and divinised ancestors. These powers elicited two main observances,[3] *cu*, directed especially to *nyuy*, and *ntaŋri*, directed at ancestors. The principal country-wide *cu* is made at the beginning of the Nso' year, *shuu-san*, the first rains in about mid-March.

Country-wide *cu* involved journeys to a number of sacred sites, some a considerable distance from the city, by a royal sacrificial team including the Fon, his sacrificial deputy the *Taawoŋ* and his female counter-part the *Yeewoŋ*, and occasionally both the previous holders of these offices. The party also included: the officiants at royal burials (*vibay ve duy* or *ve kpu*), cadet royals supposedly descended from much earlier *ataawoŋ*, the classificatory sisters' sons of the Fon (*won jemer ve Fon*), who have duties both at royal burials and in detecting treasonable witchcraft; and the palace stewards, *ataanto'*, to whom certain ritual duties are often delegated, among them the care and carriage of objects used in the ritual. At certain points, the presence of the installer and most senior councillor, *Ndzəəndzəv*, is required. The objects carried in the procession comprise palm-wine in the 'calabash of the country' (*sho'woŋ*), camwood (*bii*) in the 'bag of the country' (*kibam ke woŋ*) and the 'double-bell of the country' (*ŋgem woŋ*). The sequence of site visits is not fixed, although those I recorded in the early rains of 1987–88 partly overlap with those noted by Kaberry in 1958. *Cu* journeys of great importance[4] finish with the sacrifice of a ram, as Kaberry also records. Nowadays the remains of the ram are divided between the installer *Ndzəəndzəv* and the *vibay ve duy* . The Fon does not partake of it. Kaberry's notes offer an interesting variant, witnessed in 1958, when the Fon and his installer had been at odds. The ram, sacrificed by the Fon himself at Kovvifəm, was slaughtered over the 'hole of the country' (*mfiŋ woŋ*) in the centre of the dynastic shrine (*lav woŋ*), the blood dripping into it and on the stones which surrounded it, then dragged by the *Taawoŋ* to the old royal graveyard (*fəm*) where it was presented to, and allowed to bleed over, each stone grave marker, and finally taken to the point called *ntamer*, which term implies a magical barrier. Here it was thrown to the assembled commoner (*mtaar*) lineage heads of the north assembled outside the precinct who received it with loyal cries of praise. They were then blessed, as described below, with camwood. Nowadays the departure from the last site visited is marked by the blessing or medication (*shiv*) by the Fon of his companions: he applies camwood from the *kibam ke woŋ* to each person's forehead while each shouts his eponym (*menkfem*), the name by which his ancestor, the first titleholder, was known to the past Fon who had elevated him, and by which he is again addressed by the Fon when he offers allegiance after his succession.

Cu is taken up in each lineage-tract by the lineage heads. The *taala'* of each compound makes a round of his ritual sites (*virə ve anyuy*). His tour is characterised by generosity, for it was habitual for him to dispense wine from his sacrificial calabash or give out kola nuts to everybody he met on his way. The belief was that he could meet a god (*Nyuy*) disguised as a human being, in particular a travelling stranger. At each sacrificial site he said prayers similar to those recited by the Fon or his deputy. Here are two such prayers:

Taawoŋ recites:

Nyuy woo Fon-Kilaa,	God of the Fon's bridge,
Ver Fon fen si fen wir adzəm.	I am here with the Fon.
Dzə san ben mo wu javnin	This is the beginning of the year
ver men fee foo lon nyaaŋ fo woŋ Nso'.	and we have come out to beg for peace in Nso' land.
Ben a melu' mo ver wiyyin ne sho,	We have brought you palm-wine

Keeri woŋ Nso'o	Take care of Nso' land. Take care of our land.
Wir a tum Buy e kinyo ke juŋ ki	If somebody crosses River Buy with good intentions
Ven men se si. Wu waa wiiy a kinyo ke biki	Welcome him. If he does so with evil intentions
Ven tsem nsay e si wo.	Blind his eyes with earth [dust].
Ben a bii wo: wan wiy, wan lumen,	Here is your camwood. Give us male and female offspring,
Koŋ a mensə mensə.	Let our spears always be wet with animal blood.
Fo kiseevi kejung ki e woŋ Nso'	Give peace and blessings to the people of Nso'.

On another occasion, the Fon recited:

Nyuy woo way taa,	God of Way [market] Taa,
Ver ben si fen wir adzəm,	We are all present here,
Bo wu mo' yo' dzə bam,	No one is left behind,
Ji sanne javvane.	That, as it is the beginning of the planting season.
Ver men wiy fo wiy suŋnen	We have then come to speak
Mo atar ver ee yii suŋnen for mbiy	Just as our fathers used to speak in the past
Ku likiwu kee sho fo lon ji sanne javanne	For our sake we implore as the planting season has come.
Ver lon vifa veyi, kfen lon ki ŋgooy.	We appeal for abundant food and offspring
Kfen lonne ji woŋe waa du fo mbiy.	We also appeal that our land should progress
Bara' wo wu wiyyin ji wun a Nso' wa lim,	The white man who has come to work with us
Ver a wune lim a shu mo'on.	Make that we work in a common accord.
Wir tum Buy wun a shiliv she juŋ shi,	If somebody crosses River Buy with a good heart
Wu wiy akijuŋ.	Let him be very welcome
Wir tum Buy wun a shiliv she bishi	But if he crosses Buy with an evil heart
ven tsem nsay e si wo.	blind his eyes with soil.
Fo wan wiiy e fo wan lumen,	Give us male and female children,

fo kong mensə mensə.	let our spears constantly be wet with blood.
Ko bii e bar woŋ Nso' sho.	Take camwood and smear Nso' land with it.
Ver men alon vifa ve juŋ vi fo ven	We are begging for good things
E foo Nso'.	To give to Nso'.

At the Kumbo site such prayers were said at several places, starting behind the Palace (*bam nto'*), and passing through sites in and outside it, including a symbolic bridge (mentioned in the first prayer above), a spot above the old market (mentioned in the second prayer above) and ending at a stream. Similarly the route to Kovvifəm was marked by several sacred sites, some by streams, another by a grove, another at an old marketplace, and ending at the royal graves.

There were other sites such as Taavisa', already mentioned, and Mba' and Mbuluv, sources of the Fon's wine. Baba', a separate chiefdom to the west of Nso', is the scene of a covenant which fixed a boundary and permanent alliance. At one such site, Wvə, it is thought that the spirit of the late Fon Sem III Mbinkar Mbinglo (1947–72) may have established himself.

The second main observance, *ntaŋri,* was directed to ancestors. Subsumed within this term are the sacrifices offered to the dead in funerary ceremonies, and the more specific intercessory sacrifices made when occasion called for it or diviners so prescribed.

For these rites palm-wine, a fowl, camwood, and palm-oil were needed. The bodies of the dead were always prepared for burial with camwood, as a symbol of communion and blessings. It was also employed at entry points to sacrifice sites, designed to honour or propitiate the dead. A mixture of oil and camwood was sprinkled on the threshold of the main lineage house (*faay-woo-ku'un-ne*) where the sacrifice took place. At Kumbo Palace the family dead are propitiated by smearing the threshold of the *nggay,* the assembly hall of the dynastic group: this is done by a *taanto'*. For dead Fons, sacrifices are performed in their grave-huts, usually by the *Taawoŋ* on the Fon's behalf.

These sacrifices involve killing a fowl, by tearing its beak apart, as invocations are uttered. Omens are read from its death-throes and the final position of the chicken; all present watch its movements closely. The ancestors or dead are supposed to have accepted the sacrifice if the beak tears easily and the dying fowl hops towards the sacrificer.

During the burial of important persons, the ancestors are invoked to bestow peace, abundant food, good health and also many children on the officiant and the lineage at large. These formulae, described as the 'three hands', are also observed in Kom and Bum, close neighbours of Nso'. The same invocation is repeated when palm-wine is poured at the door of the lineage house (*faay-woo-ku'un-ne*); this is served from a special earthenware vessel, the pot of the dead (*kiikpu*). The act of pouring the palm-wine at the door, on the floor or threshold of the lineage house symbolised softness, the approach of rains and water. The ancestor was asked to bestow blessings and 'good things' for the officiant.

Such sacrifices are often only attended by younger members of the patrilineage. These, referred to as *anyuy*, must spread the news of the *ntaŋri* among all other members of the lineage: the more widespread the news, the more successful it is held to have been. The officiant takes as his portion the neck and entrails of the fowl, considered the most prestigious parts. All other participants receive a piece, no matter how small.

Three other forms of sacrifice need to be mentioned briefly. *Saay anyuy* (lit. graves of the gods) is performed following the death of those individuals who had had 'baptismal pots', *kiing anyuy* set up in their compounds. These pots are used in the final naming of twins or other children born with special signs, and also for their medication. Such individuals[5] were offered sacrifices at a road junction leading to their compound, rather than at their graves. They were held, in their after-life, to prevent evil from entering their lineage homestead.[6]

Ntaŋri-meŋwer was a sacrifice offered to the remotest ancestor traceable, to mollify him or her when some offence or neglect was presumed, and which still needed to be resolved and forgiven.

Finally there was *sov-kidiv*, lit. 'piercing the calabash' – piercing in the metaphorical sense of discovering the truth. This ceremony was called for when a breach had existed between an ancestor and his or her descendants. The same sacrificial objects were assembled as for a normal *ntaŋri,* but in addition a small calabash was filled with palm-wine and heated to boiling point so that a straw put into it could by its movement indicate the failure or success of the ceremony. If the central vortex kept the straw upright, the sacrifice was accepted. This was a rarely performed ceremony. It should be noted that the officiant was, in most cases, not the lineage-head but a 'specialist', a *ngaa-shiv*.

Səm

I will now examine beliefs concerning the intrinsic properties of animate and inanimate objects. These rested on a theory of human nature and the directing power of words over matter. Nso' society was deeply influenced by these beliefs, and their further study is important for the elucidation of the social and political structure and world-view of the Nso'.

Foremost among these beliefs was that concerning *səm*, a psychic power possessed by some people. Chilver (1990: 235) has described it, as follows:

> This is the innate power to project a multiform co-essence in the belly which, according to most of the older informants, old men in authority, was well-intentioned; according to others it could become 'bad' under the influence of malice, greed or treasonable ambition, a reason given among others for removing adult princes from the vicinity of the palace in the past. Its more ethereal imagery [than that of *Virim*, witchcraft. JLB] is associated with high winds, travel by night under the stars ... translocation, clairvoyance, teleportation. The *Fon*, who was ... shortlisted by divination and is subsequently selected for good intentions (Emonts, 1922) is publicly credited with *səm* of the highest order, royal *səm* [*səm vifon*, JLB] which is sharply contrasted with the *səm* of human witches, *səm-arim.*

Other persons in Nso' society, besides the Fon, were seen as endowed with *səm vifon* and they, like the Fon, undertook to do good deeds as diviners and medicine-men (*aŋgaaŋgang* and *aŋgaashiv*) to counteract the misdeeds of witches whose *səm* led them to attack the community and their own kin and affines.

Səm was acquired through the uterine line, but could be modified or reinforced. The latter was the case with 'children stolen by God' (*nyuy shoŋ wan*) who disappeared from their homes and returned, after an interval, in the early morning, standing mute, close to green plants, banana stems or raffia, with clenched fists. These had, during a trance experience, reinforced their psychic powers and acquired *səm vifon* and other, mostly curative, powers. They had to be well received and properly trained if they were not to become dangerous. They became medicine-men with powers superior to those of witches, who were believed to cause famine, torrential rains, droughts, and also to transform their close kin into meat which they gnawed, resulting in the death of the victim. Those with *səm vifon* were held to overcome the *arim* in other-worldly battles.

Connected with the belief in psychic power were beliefs associated with hunting. Certain royal animals, the buffalo (*nyar*), leopard (*baa*) and especially the lion (*bvara'*, see below), were also thought to be endowed with *səm*. They were difficult to kill except by persons with *səm* and additional powers. Hunters who shot these animals obtained extra powers by acquiring a black pebble-like object which the animals ejected into the earth and buried before death. Hunters took great pains to rush in and extract this before the animal died. When acquired it could be used for many types of treatment. The bones of such royal animals also had special virtue and were used as splints to heal fractures. Hunters who killed royal animals underwent a protective rite, *kaani*. This entailed immersing and washing the hunter in a stream. Then cowries were given him by his mother's father, which he put into a white bag as he came out of the stream. A sacrificial goat was released and left to stray until it died. It was believed that if this rite was not performed the hunter would fall sick, mostly from blisters which left him spotted and looking like a leopard. Among these animals, the lion was viewed rather differently and not hunted. The same reverence was due to lions as the Fon, and they in turn behaved majestically.[7]

Shiv

We turn now to *Shiv*, 'medicine'. I shall distinguish, on one hand, between natural or man-made objects held either to be endowed with intrinsic power or to have had power introduced into them in the course of their manufacture, and, on the other, curative plants. The first category includes an enormous variety of objects which are manipulated or directed by words for beneficial or punitive purposes. Many of these objects were used defensively to protect property from thieves and were often buried in packets or snail-shells, or hung in horns or bags over doorways. They were held to intercept any malevolent person who approached or attempted to tamper with them, and even to counter-attack, inflicting illness or misfortune on the trespasser. Medicine in liquid or powdered form could also be rubbed into cuts to protect individuals from witchcraft – some believe this renders their flesh bitter to the taste of cannibal witches. Other powdered concoctions were blown off the palm of the hand, with imprecations, to be carried away by the wind and to seek out and deter approaching enemies. The preparation of such *shiv* might involve the use of either right or left hands, or stirring or grinding in a certain direction, to produce the desired effect – either to mollify or to punish. Among the best known *shiv* was the *shiv se ntamer*, barrier medicine, prepared in the Palace and distributed to house entrances and road junctions throughout the land 'to avert the overflight of hostile *səm* which caused blighted crops, barrenness and wasting diseases' (Chilver 1990: 236). The masquerade societies, their sites, paraphernalia, treated masks and musical instruments were also described as *shiv*. Each society possessed an inner core open only to initiates with *shiv*. This was believed capable of inflicting punishment on non-initiates who transgressed its rules.

The second category of local curative techniques, employing herbal remedies, massage and reduction of stress, are successfully used in many more cases than modern western biomedicine, and with more rapid relief. Practitioners deal successfully with fractures, use herbal remedies to relieve rashes, burns, asthma, haemorrhoids and other common conditions and cope better with mental disorders than hospital psychiatrists by reassuring their patients and often removing them from stressful situations to 'herbal homes'. Even though the beneficial result of herbal remedies is accepted, and is scientifically explicable, many practitioners, some of whom combined herbal practice with divination or worked with diviners, preferred to maintain a mystificatory and secretive attitude and to demand unconditional belief in their mystical powers from their patients.

Nsay

For the people of Nso' the earth (*nsay*) was endowed with extraordinary powers. Informants perceive it as both an animate and inanimate object with stronger powers than those of other animate objects. The earth is constantly referred to as the ultimate resolver of issues. Chilver epitomises the general notion of the role of the earth in these words: 'in the past, the earth was viewed, rather, as the place where the ancestors, the important dead, were and that they pervade it: they were said to "sleep" underfoot and could be awakened'. The earth rendered justice when human proceedings were deficient; likewise, it dealt severely with defaulters who had wrongfully sought its intervention or had made false appeals to it. The earth was the bestower of godly gifts. It was seen as the source of products on which human life depended. Embedded within it were the ancestors; the apotheosis of some was desired and made evident in dreams and inner voices, and they intervened both in the course of natural events and in human life.

Vifon

Kingship (*Vifon*) and its attributes were also surrounded by notions of sacredness. Neither the person of the Fon nor any of his 'things' – his stool, staff or calabash – could be touched by ordinary people. These, like the earth, possessed powers which could render judgment: oaths could be taken on them and, if false, punishment was held to follow. If people without a special mandate to handle these 'things' were obliged to do so, they first had to prostrate themselves, placing the palms of their hands on the earth which then attenuated or interrupted the powers of kingship.[8]

This summary has not touched on many aspects of Nso' traditional belief and practice which have had to be omitted in order to conserve space. It is hoped to include them in a separate study.

World Religions in Nso'

I now turn to 'foreign' religions which have been introduced to Nso'. The largest Christian denomination is the Roman Catholic Church, in which the first Nso' was ordained as priest in 1949, after some thirty-six years of Catholic presence. There are two main Protestant churches, the Presbyterian (formerly Basel Mission) Church and the Cameroon Baptist Church, both of which have considerable followings, the first long established in the north of Nso'. All three denominations have latterly been involved in the translation of the New Testament into the Lam Nso' language. Some other groups, such as Jehovah's Witnesses and the Baha'i, have a presence in Kumbo, but have made little impact upon the Nso' population.

Islam is, of course, the world religion with which Nso' has been longest in contact, by way of trade and war. The chronology of early direct trade contacts between Nso' and Hausa merchants must remain hypothetical. We know from Barth (1857) that Hausa merchants had reached 'Mbafu', the western Grassfields across the Mbam, by the 1840s, and there may well have been earlier contacts. The followers of Modibo Adama do not appear to have reached Banyo before the 1830s. However, they had been preceded by Bali-Chamba raiders (with whom they are confused in both folk memory and many early European accounts). Perhaps by the mid-nineteenth century or later, the Banyo Fulani had intervened in a civil conflict close by in Ntem, which became subject to Banyo. Ndu followed suit and was obliged to provide a base for raids: many Ndu refugees found shelter in Nso'. There is no memory of Hausa settlement in Nso' before the German occupation, after Fulani raids on Nso' had been stopped.

By the 1880s there was contact with Hausa trade in another direction, through Bum, a main kola depository, to the Takum and Benue markets. Apart from passing graziers heading for German posts, Fulani graziers only arrived in any number after the advance of the British forces in 1916, leading to farmer-grazier disputes. The Hausa had settled in the Kumbo quarter known as Gazata, and also symbiotically with Fulani at the cattle-trading and veterinary centre of Jakiri. While elsewhere intransigent, proselytising and with a low regard for unbelievers, the Moslems (all Sunni) of Nso' have been accommodating and have made quite a number of influential converts, in particular among traders. The Hausa exercise some influence through their own versions of healing medicine and protective amulets, and because of their commercial honesty and hospitality. For a time in the 1960s, following his *rapprochement* with the Bamum and the Tikar of Bankim, Fon Səm III (Mbinkar Mbiŋlo) favoured the Moslems, gave them a site near the Palace for a mosque, and adopted some of the outer forms of Islam (he died a Christian, though retaining his one hundred wives). The Fon at the time of my later fieldwork (who died in September 1993) started as a Christian but turned towards Islam, constrained perhaps by the requirement of royal polygamy and the example of other important rulers. However, there have been no mass conversions as a result.

Some surface similarities between Moslem and Nso' custom – blood sacrifice, the levirate, polygamy and some features of matrimony and inheritance, would lead one to expect its easier acceptance as a new religion. Its ideology of power, the fusion of temporal with spiritual power, is very similar, but that in itself presented problems since it could well involve a total replacement of rulers; this fate had already been opposed in the Nso' resistance to the Fulani slave-raids which the *Jihad* became. Commercial relationships involved both cooperation and rivalry, and had not the least effect on religious belief, even where contact was closer, as in Bum. In general, only those chiefdoms which were vassalised, conquered or which received a large Moslem immigrant population have adopted Islam.[9] In Nso' it soon became clear that Islam had less to offer than Christianity, which was somewhat distant from the colonial power and which was seen to offer positive improvements and attractive ethical values.

The Catholics, the last of the denominations to arrive in Cameroon, in 1890, were directed by the German Government to areas where Protestant missions were not firmly established, and were forbidden to proselytise in the Moslem north. The Basel Presbyterian Mission was already established in Bali, Fumban and Bagam, so the new Mission, from the German Province of the Sacerdotes Cordis Jesu, or Sittard Fathers, was encouraged to make for Nso', arriving in the last days of 1912, after which they acquired some land at Shisong. Their promise of a school was agreeable to the Fon, Ŋga Bi'fon I (1910–47), who sent young royals and retainers to be educated at Shisong. The Sittard Fathers accomplished much in their brief stay – a boys' school, teaching of handicrafts and building, and, briefly joined by religious sisters, a girls' domestic science class: their larger economic plans were cut short by the First World War. After a gap of nearly three years, broken by one visit by a priest from Nigeria, the Christian remnant, held together by two catechists, was first intermittently and then regularly visited by the so-called 'French Fathers' of the same order from Fumban. At the same time, in 1919, former soldiers and carriers were repatriated from internment in Fernando Po where they had been indoctrinated by military Chaplains and Spanish Capuchins. These were zealots, intolerant of 'pagan practices'.

Violence broke out between the traditionalists, looking to the British, and the new Christians, looking to the French Fathers to intervene. This led to a visit by the Resident, with soldiers, to restore order, reopen the Church and pacify both parties. In 1923, after the British Mandate had been agreed, the French Fathers were withdrawn by the Vatican which replaced them with 'Mill Hill Fathers'. If open conflict was avoided in Nso', underlying tensions remained, particularly concerning the flight of wives and wards to the Mission. To learn 'doctrine' was one thing, but flight to a Christian partner was another, for the Fathers did not recognise at that time that 'pagan' marriage had any sacramental character. Such flights to safe territory, as Kaberry's unpublished material suggests, had been quite frequent in the past; nevertheless the Mission was now blamed.

Both chiefs and missionaries tried to circumvent the influence of the British officers. The British response was to forbid direct exchange marriage, to encourage bridewealth marriage (to little avail in Nso'), to reduce the powers of chiefs to exact excessive punishments, to refuse to accept witchcraft as an offence except in terms of harassment or a public-order misdemeanour and to persuade the mission that runaway royal wives should leave the chiefdom. They licensed herbalists, and if they paid some attention to beliefs in their reports, they were inclined to leave them alone unless they offended their conception of morality, as in the case of poison ordeals. However, with these exceptions the British system of Indirect Rule which left these regions to manage their own affairs served to conserve local practices.

However, to regard the establishment of Roman Catholicism in Nso' in terms only of the play of foreign authorities on an inert mass is to mistake the situation. How and why Nso' people were attracted to the new religion, their motives, and the ways in which they resolved conflicts between 'doctrine' and customary obligations have seldom been examined in historical and missiological literature; a truer picture is perhaps to be found in the novels of Kenjo Jumbam and Jedida Asheri. One factor was the affection and respect in which particular priests were held, but their flocks were not uncritical of them all. The adoption of the religion involved many different individual trajectories and experiences, but many might say that its works – in education and healing and in some fields of economic progress – were elements in conversion in a social situation which had become irreversible.

Conclusion

Christian faith is professed in a learned creed, but in daily life it is experienced in sacraments and sacramentals. Some of the Catholic sacraments have counterparts in traditional rites. Sacramentals, signs used by the Catholic Church as sources of grace, such as blessings (of persons, property and articles of devotion) and the use of holy water and incense were associated with Nso' conventions and habits. Also, local ways of showing reverence or expressing joy or sorrow were incorporated into the liturgy, and this helped to popularise the Christian message. However, the critical factor in the introduction of Christianity was that it occurred after Nso' was conquered by the Germans in 1906 and was thereafter increasingly and forcibly 'opened up', both in practical terms and in terms of access to alternative kinds of knowledge. Individuals were confronted with new experiences and a larger world, after which they were presented with a means of independently accommodating themselves to it and finding some security in it. Greater familiarity, after the Second World War, allowed the Catholic Church to become increasingly indigenised both in style and personnel.

The 'old religion', as described above, was associated with local sacred spots[10] both at the level of the fondom and at that of the lineage. They were served by a very limited group of officiants and surrounded by mystery; most people did not take part.

Its officiants, the Fon and *ataala'*, were the intermediaries with divinity and prayed for good health, good food and many children. Their roles are now marginalised by the effects of biomedicine, of new, better-bearing crops and labour-saving equipment, and the large increase in population which these factors caused. Now the Fon retains his importance as a focus of ethnic identity and for more secular activities, rather than as the country's highest religious authority.

If the notions of *səm* and *shiv* are still entertained, often with expanded modern imagery, and remain active, they have lost much of their force and their social attachments and have tended to degenerate. Particular rituals, such as those associated with twins and special children, have been fading away and the names associated with them have been replaced with names compatible with Christian connotations such as *Kinyuy*, *Berinyuy*, *Suinyuy*. These began to be used some two decades after the introduction of Christianity.

The most easily detectable reciprocal influences are in the domain of language and symbolism. Accommodation and then 'inculturation' have been encouraged by the Church itself in liturgical matters and in sacramentals. Lam Nso' is used in church services, and its religious vocabulary has been borrowed in order to transmit Christian concepts; for example, the church building is spoken of as *ŋgay*, the chalice as *sho'*, the Mass itself as *cu* and the priest is described as *ŋgaa-cu*.

The corn or boundary plant *kikeŋ* (*Dracaena deisteliana*), a widespread symbol of peace and inviolability, has been adopted wholesale by Christians. Altar cloths, chasubles and other Mass vestments are decorated with this symbol. It is carried in church processions and during the reading of the Gospel when the reader is flanked by two people carrying it. The white bag, emblematic of pure-heartedness in Nso' society, ennobled with cowry shell decorations, has been incorporated in Christian religious practice. Moreover, some Christian practices are seen to have their counterparts in Nso' custom: Chrism oils and the Sacrament of extreme unction is likened to the use of camwood and oil in rituals of blessing and incorporation, for example. At the beginning of the planting season the priests of both religions bless the seed to be sown. The sacramental blessing with holy water has its counterpart in Nso' custom. It would not be fanciful to compare the church bells with the *ŋgemwoŋ*: indeed the analogy was spotted long ago by one of Fr. Emont's informants. The concepts of sin and penance are found in both religions. The list could be lengthened, but I have mentioned some of the factors that help explain why many Nso' could enthusiastically embrace a foreign religion. Yet despite strong external influences, traditional practices continue side-by-side with Western and Christian practices.

Notes

1. Further background information about Nso' may be found in Emonts (1922); Kaberry (1952, 1959); Chilver & Kaberry (1960, 1968); Mzeka (1980); Aletum & Fisiy (1989); Goheen (1988).

2. Esua, F.C. (Bishop). Closing speech of the first Synod of Kumbo Diocese, 31 August to 4 September 1988. Kumbo Diocese comprises parishes in the fondom of Nso', the related fraternal chiefdoms of Oku, Mbiame and Noni and the parishes of Nkambe, Ako, Tabenken and Sabongari in the Donga Mantung Division. The Bishop's estimate of fifty to sixty percent needs careful analysis. We can only take it as indicative, and acknowledge the presence of a large unchristened population in the Diocese. However, readers should note that, on the whole, Nso' has become more christianised than Wimbum, Mbembe, Yamba and other areas to its north and north-east.

3. It should also be noted that another ritual (*Jaŋ saar* lit. 'calling the finger millet') has completely disappeared. The presence of maize and other of grains with higher yields has eclipsed the *jaŋ saar* rite. Also worthy of note is the fact that two other ritual sites (Nzennso' and Mbonso') have not been visited for a long time. In 1983 there were preparations for the boundary rituals at Mbonso' but this did not and still (1994) has not taken place.

4. For example, those ending at the old Palace site at Kovvifəm, and the present Palace and its surrounding area in Kumbo, as well as those ending at 'the house of the country and royal graveyard at Kovvifəm, at the refuge site of Taavisa' where there is a royal grave, and at the Palace in Kumbo.

5. They may be recognised by their twin-parent names such as Tanle (father of twins), Yenle (mother of twins) and Tabiy (m), Yeebiy (f), Takoŋ and Yeekoŋ for single children.

6. Fr. Emonts says that this road-junction sacrifice will mislead a ghost (*Kimaleŋ*) who wishes to do harm, while a well intentioned one will find the way (1922: 166).

7. The hunter was automatically given the highly coveted rank of *tavnjoŋ* (dignitary of the men's war club, the *manjoŋ*). Note the similarity of the rite of *kaani* to the *nyuy shong wan* rite already described. They share the same symbol of purity – the white bag – and the replacement of the royal animal with the straying goat.

8. Note that the earth is seen as being the stronger power.

9. The Bamum are a notable exception to this generalisation.

10. For example, by waterfalls, river pools, ravines, clumps of forest and bush.

CHAPTER EIGHT

Pursue to Attain:
a Royal Religion

Claude Tardits

In December 1915 the British army reached Fumban, the capital of the Bamum Kingdom in Cameroon. The Christian missionaries, mostly German, had to leave the country. The sovereign, King Njoya, was faced with an unforeseen situation, as he had first introduced and familiarised himself with the practices of Islam in 1906 before accepting the settlement nearby of members of the Basel Protestant Mission. He had then distanced himself from Islam and followed the Protestant mission's teachings; he had biblical texts translated into the Bamum language.

The religious situation in the kingdom at the beginning of the twentieth century was complex. The King's entourage – the counsellors of the kingdom, the great officers of the Palace and many servants – followed Njoya in his practice of the prayers and fasts of Islam; when the King decided to listen to the Christian preaching, some parents, including the King himself, sent their children to the Mission school, without necessarily abandoning the practice of Islam. Nevertheless, whatever its involvement with the religions of salvation introduced into the country, the population never ceased to observe its own religious traditions. These were never condemned by the King.

The missionaries' departure, which followed the German retreat, no doubt led the King to ponder which course to follow. The British advised him to return to Islam, which he seems to have done for a few months (Njiassé-Njoya 1981: 171). That return was brief, and in 1916 Njoya elaborated a religious doctrine of salvation, the inspiration for which came from what he knew of Islam but which, in his view, would be better adapted to the way of life of his people.

The title of the text, composed in the latest form of the writing created at the end of the nineteenth century by the King and his entourage – the *a ka u ku mfe mfe* alphabet – is *Pursue to Attain – nuǝt ŋkuǝtǝ*. The title indicates that, by a prolonged effort, the people would accept the religious foundations of the religions of salvation, Christianity and Islam, whose similarities Njoya had been struck by, and would respect the practices which the King had borrowed from the Mâlikite rite.

Njiassé-Njoya carefully compares the King's text with Islamic orthodoxy in his thesis: 'Naissance et évolution de l'islam en pays bamoun'. In this he concentrates on the borrowings from Islam, shows which were Njoya's innovations in relation to Moslem orthodoxy and traditional practices, and underlines the heretical element in the King's approach.

Here I shall consider those Bamum traditions which were retained by the King in his text and attempt to grasp the difficulties he obviously faced as an African king invested with a traditional religious role. One of the interests in *Pursue to Attain* is that its writer had intimate experience of the beliefs of his people and was familiar with ritual practices and their ideological implications, which were liable to influence his selection. This situation differs from those in which salvation religions were imposed from the outside. This objective will involve recalling traditional ritual practices and the beliefs which accompany them.

The royal initiative can only be understood in the context of the history of the kingdom in the nineteenth century and of the situation which confronted the monarch at the time of writing.

The Tragic Decades of the Nineteenth Century

The Bamum kingdom was probably founded at the end of the sixteenth or the beginning of the seventeenth century by migrants said to have come from the Tikar area, to the east of the Mbam River. During the first two hundred years, the Kingdom only covered an area of some four hundred square kilometres around its capital, Fumban. Its territory was occupied by a few small political units which had submitted to the Bamum kings, and by the members of the patrilineages founded, in each reign, by the sons and servitors of the King and who received an endowment of land and women from him. In the 1960s, a list of two hundred and thirty lineages could be recovered which dated back to this early period.

At the beginning of the nineteenth century, King Mbombwo, the eleventh sovereign, conquered the area between the Mbam, Mapé and Nun Rivers. He thus enlarged the size of the Kingdom almost twentyfold, subjugated more than sixty groups and dispersed those who had not managed to flee the conquered lands. These lands were divided into hundreds of domains cultivated by the war captives, now reduced to serfdom, for the benefit of the land-holding heads of lineages and of the King. The royal court assumed an unprecedented importance: the King was served by numerous captives and supporters whose loyalty he tried to ensure by the same means. The traditions reported in the manuscript by Njoya which deals with the history of the country clearly states that it was Mbombwo who made the Bamum rich (Njoya 1952: 26).

A series of tragedies were to start with the end of his reign. The sons of the ailing King, divided over the forthcoming succession, started to kill each other. The servitors of the Palace, whose great numbers gave them power, also killed many of the sons and, as a reward, appropriated some of the wives of the dying King.

One of the few sons of Mbombwo to escape the massacre succeeded to the throne, but the Palace servitors, fearing his retaliation, killed him. A young son of the dead King succeeded briefly to the throne before being murdered by the Palace servitors. The chief of the King's guards, formerly a war captive, seized power. This slave reigned for several years before being eliminated by the son of a daughter of King Mbombwo. There were no more male descendants and therefore, in accordance with custom, it was Nsa'ngu, the son of a princess, who reigned. In the eyes of the Bamum, the elimination of the male lines issuing from Mbombwo was due to the initial violation of custom when the sons of the King had killed each other. Therefore, to bring the country back to order, Nsa'ngu set about executing all those who had taken part in various violations of Bamum laws. A still more tragic episode took place at the end of the reign of the very man who had recently restored the dynasty. Certain brothers of the King had manifested an ambition to succeed him, even though the law restricted the sovereignty to a son or a son of a daughter of the reigning King. Nsa'ngu then started a war against his neighbours, the Nso', thinking that his ambitious brothers would be killed in it, which is in fact what happened. However, he was himself decapitated and his head taken by a Nso' in enemy country. Hundreds of Bamum died during this confrontation. Nsa'ngu and his brothers were dead and one of his sons succeeded him. The Bamum succession law had been saved and Njoya acceded to the throne (Tardits 1980: 168–99).

The Reign of Great Initiatives

Njoya, who was to become the most famous Bamum King, was too young to govern when he succeeded his father in 1885 or soon after. The reign started with a few years of regency, until the young sovereign became the true master of the country, some time between 1892 and 1896. Having heard many tales of the history of the nineteenth century, Njoya was aware of the fragility of political power.

The first great officer of the Palace, the *Titamfon* Gbetnkom Ndombuo, had safeguarded the regency, along with the young King's mother, and ought then to have retired to the country, as was the custom. Njoya had barely taken on the government of the country when the *Titamfon*, intending to replace the young King by one of his brothers, plotted a revolt. The troubles continued unabated and the country fell into civil war. Fumban, where the King had stayed isolated, was threatened by famine. Njoya decided to call on the Moslem Fulbe for help. The Fulbe had come from Nigeria in the nineteenth century and occupied the Adamawa Plateau. Some had settled a few hundred kilometres to the north of the Bamum. The Fulbe Lamido of Banyo agreed to intervene on behalf of the Bamum King. There were probably several reasons for this decision: the Fulbe were attracted by a country which produced kola nuts, and their chief probably preferred to help another king rather than the rebellious royal servant who had also solicited his help. Moreover, the Emir of Yola, his suzerain, is said to have dreamt that a white mosque would one day be erected in Fumban.

The Fulbe intervention took place some time between 1895 and 1897. The military action was brief: in accordance with

Islamic tradition, the Fulbe invoked God and then charged on the enemy. The enemy were immediately defeated, the former *Titamfon* captured and burned alive in the capital. This brief battle, which the Bamum call the 'victory of the horse', had important consequences. The Bamum, who were proud of their own fighting abilities, had been impressed by the Fulbe's show of strength. When asked about the reasons for their power, the Fulbe had answered that it came from the prayer to God, the *dùâ'*.

The young Njoya decided to acquire what, in his eyes, gave the Fulbe their strength: horses, writing and knowledge of the rites that they had mentioned. His plan was quickly realised. He organised a cavalry force. With the help of his entourage he devised, before the end of the century, a writing system which he wished to distinguish from the Arabic used by the Hausa and Fulbe *marabout*; he then had the Lamido of Banyo send him a few *marabouts* to instruct him in the practices of Islam. For Njoya these three elements all served the same purpose: procuring a power comparable to that of the Fulbe who then dominated the Adamawa Plateau.

We have at our disposal a text which reports the statements of witnesses of the period as to the reasons for adopting the Moslem rites:

> Njoya decided to take some war medicine from the Fulbe so as to increase the Bamum territory like his predecessor King Mbombwo had done. This was reported to the Sultan of Banyo who sent to the sultan Njoya a large white gandoura, a long turban, a pair of baggy trousers and prayer beads and then told him to pray to God, as it was out of this prayer that the war medicine would come. From then on Njoya started the practice of Moslem prayers, not in the name of God but as a war medicine (extract from the manuscript Mouclùlì 1956).

In order better to understand the significance of this text we need to recall that, before going to war, the Bamum always ingested a substance, the 'war medicine', which was supposed to protect them and stimulate their fighting spirit. As the Fulbe had told the Bamum that their prayers were the reason for their victory, the latter understood that this rite was the equivalent of their medicine but even more potent.

The King and his entourage learned to pray and familiarised themselves with Islam, taught them by Hausa *marabouts* who practised the Mâlikite rite. Njoya erected a mosque in front of the Palace, and the first fast of Ramadan took place before the end of the nineteenth century.

These new practices remained largely the concern of the royal court. The King, faithful to his vision of Islam, did not wish his new instruments of power to become known to persons other than himself and those close to him. In any event, the lineage heads did not show much enthusiasm for these new practices which seemed to them very restricting, especially the fasting they enjoined. Throughout this period the Bamum never abandoned their own religious practices.

The arrival of the Germans in 1902 put an end to Njoya's first encounter with Islam. Protestant missionaries of the Basel Mission had settled in the nearby kingdom of Bali-Nyonga, where the German colonisers had installed their first military post in the Grassfields (see O'Neil, this volume). Some of them visited Njoya with the aim of spreading their activity to Fumban. The King agreed that a Protestant mission might settle in his capital. His wish was to see the opening of a school similar to that which had been established by the missionaries in Bali-Nyonga. Moreover, the strength of the German Christians was impressive.

In 1906 the Protestants settled in Fumban and, in accordance with Njoya's wishes, built a school. The mosque was replaced by a church. An excellent relationship was forged between the missionaries and the Bamum king, who took an interest in the progress of the pupils, attended classes, followed the preaching of the Pastor at Sunday services, and even listened to a few catechism classes. Meanwhile, his entourage had considerably polished up the Palace script and this enabled them to translate extracts from the Bible, a catechical text and some hymns.

Knowledge of Christianity remained, for the King, a purely intellectual pursuit; this new religion of salvation involved him less than Islam. The missionaries, wishing to effect a 'conversion from the top', initially hoped to baptise[1] the King. There remained only one obstacle: the king had several hundred wives. Custom did not allow him to part with them and the counsellors of the kingdom opposed his baptism. The King himself did not allow his daughters, whom he had sent to the Mission school, to marry Christians: princesses' marriages had political implications. The missionaries, it seems, realised the limits of their influence around 1910. Nevertheless, Njoya continued, during the last years of their presence, to attend their sermons and to take an interest in Christianity.

A year after the First World War broke out the German forces came under pressure from the British troops moving in from Nigeria, and had to leave Bamum country. The missionaries were taken prisoner and deported.

The Bamum were surprised to see Indians of the Moslem faith in the British Army, and the British officers even encouraged Njoya to return to Islam. It is possible that the victorious strength of the newcomers provoked in Njoya the same reactions that he had experienced during the Fulbe intervention. According to the testimonies recorded by Njiassé-Njoya, the King returned to Islam for a while (1981: 171). That return was short-lived because, as early as 1916, the King decided to compile a work of religious doctrine largely inspired by Islam but adapted to Bamum society.

Traditional Practices and Beliefs

Bamum society was heavily marked by hierarchy and stratification. It may be represented as a social pyramid at the summit of which was the King and his entourage; next, we find more than five hundred patrilineages, descended from the princes and Palace servitors of successive reigns, which constituted what, given the origin of their founders, can be called a princely and a palatine nobility. Rights to political incumbencies and to lineage land and domains were inherited within the patrilineages. Finally, at the base of the pyramid was the large population of male and female captives reduced to servitude, who were used to work the land.

The King distributed male and female captives, seized during war expeditions in which he participated, to princes and Palace servitors. He meted out justice and he was the priest of the cult dedicated to the royal ancestors who had transmitted their power to him at his enthronement. The King governed with the assistance of the counsellors of the kingdom. These were the peers of the King and the guardians of tradition but could decide, together with the King, to alter the customs of the country. The Bamum Kings told them in confidence the name of the son they had chosen as their successor. Six great Palace officials were constantly with the King, three of princely and three of palatine origin.

These, for reasons that will become clear, had particular cultic roles.

The Palace housed several hundred wives and their children, with as many servitors; many secret societies, open either to the princes or to the Palace servants, as well as a society concerned with justice and discussion of policy, the *mutngu*, were to be found there.

At the rear of the royal residence, which was reserved to the King, were many houses containing shrines assigned to particular cults: the house called *ruop*, where the King met his wives in the evening, the house of the *küšuop* where protective objects and powders were prepared and kept, finally the royal graveyard where the Bamum sovereigns were interred and the 'house of the country' where their skulls were kept. The front part of the Palace was largely occupied by the quarters of the secret societies in the courtyards of which were set up the stones at which libations and sacrifices were made.

Some hundreds of patrilineages occupied the centre of the kingdom. Each had a head, called *nži*, who allocated plots of lineage land to their agnates and led members of the kin group to war. The *nži* had authority over all the agnatic branches descended from lineage heads. They tried to settle those disputes within this group which family heads had not managed to resolve. They punished violations of custom, unless they were a matter for the King, and were responsible for the cult of their ancestors, thereby protecting their lineage and ensuring its prosperity. The residences of family heads included an altar and all the lineages had a graveyard reserved to the *nži* dead.

The Bamum population depended essentially on agriculture, and agricultural activities were necessarily determined by the rhythm of the seasons. Regular ritual performances followed the same pattern: at the end of July the first harvest, a part of which was taken to the Palace as insurance against possible future shortages, was the occasion for a ceremony intended to end all the ills which might afflict the population and of rites of thanksgiving and propitiation at the grave sites. Another festival, marked by important displays of maskers, followed the second harvest in October and was another occasion for sacrifices at the grave sites. Some time later came the ritual preparations which preceded the annual hunts and raiding expeditions.

To whom, and against what, were these rituals addressed in Bamum society? It must be remembered that in the 1960s, when I undertook my research, the population had long been influenced by Islam and Christianity. The information comes from fragmentary mentions in works written under Njoya's direction, some European writings of the early 1900s, whose authors had but a limited access to the domain of beliefs, and from recent Bamum works not unaffected by decades of Islamisation or Christianisation. We were able to collect a few accounts from individuals brought up at the beginning of this century and, moreover, we noted that many Bamum remained discreetly attached to their traditional practices and would occasionally speak about them. We should again stress, however, that the information we received mostly concerned ritual practices and apotropaic objects and materials; the foundations of these beliefs emerged largely from the comments provoked by our questions.

Ritual acts, sacrifices, libations and prayers were addressed to the ancestors and to divinities called *penyinyi*. The population believed in an after-life. When the King went to the royal cemetery, he visited his fathers. The dead could communicate with the living through premonitory dreams. The ancestors punished, with various ills, any transgression of the customs prescribed to regulate the social order which they themselves had helped to establish.

The *penyinyi* were little gods of unknown origin who lived in nature. They could be beneficial, but they too punished those who transgressed the laws. Belief in the *penyinyi* raises a question which is of interest to the parallels we are about to draw. The word *penyinyi* is composed of the plural affix *pe* and of the substantive form *nyi* which, in the singular, designates a single divinity. This form was therefore kept to refer to the creator god of Christianity and Islam. Some authors have been led to propose that, if the population believed in the *penyinyi* before the advent of Islam and Christianity, the singular form may have been reserved as a designation for a superior god (Njiassé-Njoya 1981: 176). The impact of the religions of salvation raises difficulties for the reconstruction in detail of the beliefs of the nineteenth century. We can only say that we have not personally found any tradition which specifically refers to this *nyi* nor to attributes peculiar to it.

The population also believed in the existence of evil elements, the *pagüm* (sing. *nzum*). They too lived in nature, but could also enter and fasten themselves within the belly of a person. It is important to note that women, but not men, who became host to a *nzum* transmitted it to their male and female descendants.

The *pagüm* caused nothing but harm: sterility in women, illness and death. The *nzum* inhabiting the body of a human being could act without the latter's knowledge in order to satisfy any grudge he might have had. There is a saying in Bamum which shows that the reason for these grudges could be very slight: 'the reason for *nzum* is the broken calabash'. It is not surprising that in a society as differentiated as that just described, fear of the *pagüm* has been ever-present, and a preoccupation with how to neutralise them.

We now come to the domain of remedies, sacrifices, libations, prayers and material means employed to fight these evil elements.

Sacrifice was a solemn religious act, its performance regulated by custom and ordered according to the social hierarchy. At the Palace the King made sacrifices on the graves of his predecessors in the royal cemetery, and on the skull of his father in the 'house of the country' during the feast which marked the end of the harvest. He also made sacrifices at the entrance of the Palace on the completion of its repair. Before hunts and wars, sacrifices took place on the weapons to be used. Sacrifices also took place at the grave sites during the 'thundering rains', thought to be beneficent because the *penyinyi* fell with them. Finally, recourse was had to divination at times of calamity in order to determine the appropriate rite to perform.

At lineage level the *nži* made sacrifices, following the same calendar, at the graves of their ancestors and at the hearths of their houses. Blood sacrifices were also made at the thresholds of their dwellings and at crossroads to bar the way to maleficent forces.

Sacrificial victims included dogs, poultry and goats and, in the Palace only, rams and cattle. Blood was a powerful vehicle that nourished the beneficiaries of the sacrifice. The rite was accompanied by libations and prayers. The liquids used, palm-wine, sorghum or millet beers, had properties similar to that of blood. The significance of prayers is developed below.

Next we examine the regulation of access to the Palace graveyard and the burial sites of the lineages, as well as to certain other sacred sites such as the 'house of the country'. Only the King, the counsellors of the kingdom, the great officers of the Palace who were of palatine origin and those twins who were responsible for guarding the site had access to the Palace graveyard. Access was strictly forbidden to the King's brothers, whatever titles they held, and to his sons. The same prohibition applied to agnates of the *nži* at lineage level. Breaches of this rule were punished by reduction to servitude.

The fear was that the kinsmen of the King, and lineage heads likewise, would take their place at sacrifice and appropriate their benefits. This concern implies that sacrifice was seen as a compelling act and that the notion of *do ut des* underlay beliefs. The religious situation which unfolded after the Christianisation and Islamisation of the country becomes understandable by reference to this notion, as we shall see later.

Libations were not only poured when sacrifices took place. The great officers of the Palace offered them in the house of *ruop* and in the 'house of the country' on a set day of the Bamum week. The heads of the secret societies did likewise at the altars under their authority. At the lineage level libations were poured at the thresholds of houses and crossroads. Maize porridge was left about for the *penyinyi* to feed on.

Next let us look at prayer. The term *nžuom* covers both prayer and oath. It is applied to the formulae of imprecation and conjuration, whereby punishment is brought down on the heads of oath-breakers and transgressors of the laws of the country. Some examples will illustrate the structure of these statements and the contexts in which they were employed. Most of my examples were collected among lineages.

Let us start with a *nžuom* pronounced by a Counsellor of the Kingdom at the death of another counsellor, when the latter's principal servitor has revealed the name of the heir the dead man has chosen:

> This heir you have presented, if he is truly the son the *nži* chose to succeed him, may you be safe and sound; but if he is not the son chosen by the *nži* and you have taken the one you like, may your belly burst when the *nži*'s belly bursts in the grave.

Let us turn now to the *nžuom* pronounced at the investiture of the heir chosen by a newly dead *nži*. All the members approach their new lineage head one by one, drink what is referred to as the 'wine of submission' and take an oath in the following terms:

If I hear things secretly spoken in a house against the *nži*, if someone pronounces his name without my telling the *nži* of it, let my belly swell and let me die. If I am going to slander him, denounce him to the king, lie so that they kill him, let me die. If I tell the truth to the *nži* let me be safe and sound.

Identical ceremonies took place at the installation of the new King. The counsellors of the kingdom and the great officers of the Palace then pledged themselves to the monarch while touching the rod of the country which he held in his hand.

The close servitors of the King were similarly enjoined never to mention the King's confidences to their family, and to report to the King all that they heard said of him. After which they pledged themselves with a *nžuom*.

New judges embarking on an important office of authority at the King's side pronounced the formula:

I am appointed *ngapasa* [judge] by the King: if I corrupt justice by giving judgment in favour of a complainant who is in the wrong so as to become rich, let the law fall on my head. If I give true judgments in the King's name, let me stay safe and sound.

Princes and servitors joining a secret society likewise pledged never to betray its secrets in a self-imprecation made before the society's altar.

In relationships between men and women there were many occasions when individuals had recourse to *nžuom*. A man anxious to resist his sexual inclinations might utter the following prayer: 'If I see the privy parts of a married woman, may misfortune fall on me'. A wife accused of adultery, before being sent to the Palace, where she ran the risk of being put to death, might say: 'If I have seen the nakedness of a man other than my husband, let me suffer'.

Theft and crimes were punishable by death, but the accused persons could affirm their innocence by pronouncing a *nžuom*. Such prayers, which invoked the punishment of the ancestors and the *penyinyi*, were never uttered by men or women who knew themselves to be guilty of their alleged crime. Warriors, in different circumstances, pronounced the following *nžuom* at the ceremony which preceded military expeditions: 'If I cause a man to be killed, may misfortune meet me; if I kill in the course of war, I am innocent'. Finally, one should note that the usual prayer which follows a dream of ill omen, is made in this form, to ward off future misfortune.

The grammatical construction of *nžuom* is always the same. The person who utters it first imagines that they have done something forbidden by the oath they have sworn or by the law of the land: disloyalty, treason, violation of secrecy, adultery, theft, murder. Then he invites an imprecisely worded punishment for the transgression, committed or envisaged. Informants agree that the sanctions refer to common afflictions – sterility, wounds, sickness, death. The *nžuom* are addressed to the ancestors and to the *penyinyi*, who were believed to have the power to punish breaches of covenants and customs.

If one considers the contexts in which these prayers are uttered, one can see that they perform two different functions, associated with their expressed form. If the *nžuom* refers to an imagined future, it serves to protect the social order, for example, so as to allow the proper functioning of a legitimately constituted hierarchy, or to guarantee good relationships between men and women. If the *nžuom* refers to a transgression for which the speaker is supposedly responsible it was a means of disculpation and was held to be a form of proof. Opinions were positive on this matter: nobody would bring misfortune on themselves by pronouncing a *nžuom* unless they believed themselves innocent. This remark leads us to an examination of the other sources of misfortune, the *pagüm*.

The people themselves had appropriate defences against these fearsome maleficent elements. If these defences were unavailing against affliction, the lineage heads and the King were obliged to examine the causes of the lesser or greater evils which beset the country.

Wooden carvings of animal and human figures were made and stored at the Palace. These statuettes, ranging in size from tens of centimetres to a metre, were coated with various substances such as clay, camwood powder (*Pterocarpus soyanxii*) or ashes, and covered with leaves or bird-feathers. They were termed *kusuop* (Tardits 1980: 675–6) which translates as 'forces which prohibit'; this succinctly describes their use. The *kusuop*, kept inside houses or placed out on the farms, were held to bar entry to *pagüm*. Powders were also made of various vegetable ingredients: these are called *fu*, generally translated as 'medicine'. Such mixtures could be rubbed on the face and body, put on the threshold of a house where a death had taken place or placed at a crossroads. *Fu* medicines were also used by individuals in what a westerner might call 'risk situations' – wives and husbands used them when the wife was pregnant, and men took them before engaging in war or hunting.

Fu pit, the 'medicine of war', was usually made up of ground leaves, salt and oil but also of the flesh of a species of weaver-bird (*Textor cuculatus*) because it was a dawn songster, and of the heart of a buffalo and sometimes that of a leopard. There is clearly some relationship between the ingredients used and the effects attributed to them.

The Palace had such great need of protection that *kusuop* and *fu* were made there and kept in the most secret lodges of the royal residence – 'the house of *kusuop*' and the 'house of the country'. A royal privilege was involved, since lineage heads were forbidden to keep a storehouse of statuettes and protective medicines.

The *nžuom*, as a mode of proof, was connected with the apotropaic measures employed against the *pagüm*. Men and women could be the unconscious carriers of a *nzum*. In a lineage, whenever goods were destroyed or stolen or when people fell ill, the lineage head was obliged to seek out the cause. It sometimes happened within the family that one of its members would admit to being the cause of the trouble. It would be enough, for example, if a person invited to do so refused to pronounce a *nžuom*, thus accepting his guilt. The *nži* then had to require the individual to repair the damage done, so that a reconciliation could be arrived at. On the other hand, if every person required to pronounce a *nžuom* did so and thus all had proclaimed their innocence, the lineage head consulted a diviner, following which he publicly announced the revelations of the earth-spider, the creature of divination. This made it possible to detect the presence of a *nzum* carrier who, ignorant of his or her condition, had earlier pronounced a *nžuom* in good faith.

As we saw, the *nzum* was activated when in daily life its host felt slighted or abused. This explains why it was the wives of agnatic members of the lineage, as well as their servants, who were so often accused after spider divination. A society in which large-scale polygyny was practised – lineage heads had an average of eight wives at the start of the century and the more important might have fifty or so – and which was to a large extent composed of former captives taken in war and their descendants, amounting to two-thirds of the population – offered particularly fertile ground for abuse and frustration.

If the accused person accepted the outcome of the spider divination, he or she was usually sold outside the lineage. If they rejected it, they were led to the Palace to take the 'proof drink' at the secret society of *mütngu*. A member of this authority pronounced a *nžuom*, as follows, just before the poison ordeal: 'You have told the truth you are safe and sound; you have lied, then you fall'. Vomiting the liquid was proof of innocence, falling down after drinking it was proof of guilt which called for judgment and sentence. If the carriers of *nzum* were held to have caused illness or death, they were executed (Tardits 1980: 824). If the drinking ordeal had established that the accusation was groundless, divination was repeated and the process of enquiry was continued.

We shall conclude this brief account of the methods and practices used by the Bamum to protect themselves and to ensure respect for their customs with a short description of the great festival which followed the first harvest.

This festival was called *nguon*, a term which refers to the friction drum given by kings to lineage heads as a mark of royal confidence; there were ninety of them in Njoya's reign. The lineage heads placed the drum in the keeping of one of their relatives or servants. It was accompanied by a bag of *fu* made from ground roots and barks, resin and shining specks[2] which were believed to have fallen from the moon. This powder stimulated the germination of plants, helped the sick to recover and protected people against the *pagüm*. At the market women bought it to mix it with their seeds, while the *nguon* holders blew it in various directions to bar maleficent elements.

The drummers arrived at the Palace by night, and, next day they assembled in the 'courtyard of war' where the King, the counsellors of the kingdom, and all the lineage heads of the kingdom were present. Next, three men introduced themselves to this assembly. These were persons appointed for life by drum-owning lineage heads; it was said of them that they had 'four ears and four eyes'. They had, in the preceding months, travelled about in the 'core of the country', that is to say the territory conquered when the kingdom was founded where all lineage heads were established on their estates. They had collected all the complaints voiced by the population and had informed themselves about the malfeasance complained of. Each of them gave the assembly a full account of the complaints they had collected, enumerated the abuses often committed in the King's name, and finally predicted the misfortunes which might follow, with suggestions about the amending measures which needed to be taken to deflect them. The King was obliged to listen without any overt reaction. The King then took up the 'rod of the country' and the Counsellors renewed their pledge of fidelity to him with a *nžuom*.

A little later, the drum-owning lineage heads formed two opposite lines in the courtyard fronting the Palace. The Counsellors of the Kingdom advanced between the two serried ranks and, having made a round of the market, one of them announced the measures decided upon to end the misdemeanours which had caused the evils complained of.

A huge banquet was then offered to all present in the courtyard of the royal residence. The day after this great communal feast, the King and lineage heads repaired to their respective family graveyards to offer sacrifices and libations to the dead. Animals were also slaughtered at all the sacred sites. This great ritual of blood-sacrifice marked the end of the unifying Bamum celebration.

This great public festival thus linked together the protective acts and means of defence against the *pagüm* and the appeasement of and thanksgiving to ancestors and divinities: it involved the use of *fu*, the denunciation of abuses, the reparation of wrongs and reconciliation, the renewal of allegiance to the King, and finally prayers, libations and sacrifices.

To sum up, let us try to identify the general themes of those practices in which religion and magic co-exist (although this distinction is not made by the Bamum themselves).

The prevention or elimination of misfortune are the purposes, always stated by the people, in their explanation of the uses of *kusuop* and *fu* and recourse to *nžuom*. Many evils afflict the people: scarcity and even famine, the destruction and theft of property, adultery, sterility, wounds, sickness, death, disloyalty, treason, violence and murder. They affect the family, the lineage, the Palace; indeed, the whole community.

These evils are inflicted by *pagüm* who are dispersed throughout nature, or who are attached to individuals and then activated by the anger of the latter when they feel offended or wronged. Misfortunes are also sent by the ancestors and the *penyinyi* when these are neglected, or when the laws of the country are transgressed or promises are betrayed.

The aims of the interlinked procedures are clear. The first measures are taken, either at family or lineage level to reconcile their members, or country-wide, when the political hierarchy makes decisions to deal with the complaints of the people, which could be openly voiced every year at the *nguon* festival.[3] When reconciliation or reparation was impossible or insufficient, there followed the procedures intended to identify persons guilty of the neglect and transgressions punished by the ancestors and *penyinyi*. They range from *nžuom*, available to everybody, to the 'proof-drink'. The guilty are eliminated, usually killed. Finally, libations and sacrifices are sometimes made to placate the ancestors and *penyinyi*. In every case the sources of misfortune are then held to have dried up.

The great sacrificial rituals conducted on two annual occasions, characterised by various festivities, communal meals and dances, express the thanksgiving of the people, who take part in them to ensure continuing prosperity.

An initial observation is called for: apotropaic measures and ritual activities aim to guarantee health, prosperity and the maintenance of social order. There is no existence to take into consideration or protect other than that of the living. A second observation can be inferred from the description we have given: the use of protective materials and recourse to ritual acts seem to complement each other, to anticipate, and put an end to, any situation likely to threaten the well-being of the population. The procedures can be lengthy and there is no limit to them: the carriers of *nzum* and those responsible for transgressions are eventually identified, sent away or eliminated. Did not King Nsa'ngu put an end to dozens of years of violence arising from the misdeeds of the reign of Mbombwo?

So the beliefs of the Bamum leave no room for what we call uncertainty; neither do they attribute to the ancestors and to the *penyinyi* any powers of an absolute character which could oppose human interventions.

Pursue to Attain

In the light of the preceding summary of Bamum history and religion, we now consider the religion that Njoya created early in this century. Our main evidence is the text he wrote. This text consists of thirty chapters; some, including the early ones, are restricted to an exposé of the doctrinal foundation of the cult, others to the enumeration of the laws of God, the things that he condemns and those he loves, and the consequences of human conduct. The influence of Mâlikite dogma, as presented in the *Risâla* and diffused by Hausa *marabouts*, is clearly evident. We shall respect the sequence of the text, but regroup statements referring to the same topic.

The first chapter establishes the reality of God's existence: 'He has neither father, mother nor children. Nobody knows where he lives. It is he who created mankind' (ch.1). After the text announces the creation of the world by an unengendered god, it goes on to describe its violent end:

> God will destroy all this world... only God knows how he will set about it. There will be many murders and wars. Wild beasts will kill each other and go from village to village killing many people...(ch. 2).

Then come the resurrection and last judgement:

> After that God will bring back to life all men and animals. ... And then God will weigh the acts of men: those who have done more good than evil he will despatch to Ajana and those who have done more evil than good he will send to the fire where they will be burned in reality. (ch. 4).

Some remarks scattered throughout the work develop aspects of creation: 'All the great things men fear were created by God' (ch. 19). Then comes a list of them: a mountain 'from which a terrible fire suddenly springs', earthquakes, epidemics, floods, meteors, fiery rains. God also created the *pagüm*: 'The *pagüm* really exist. God created them. The *pagüm* who kill people to eat them are wicked' (ch. 18). Finally, God created Chedani: 'Chedani [Satan] really exists. It is he who incites men to commit all sorts of sins' (ch. 9). Ajana is more precisely described than the fire:

> A good man who, after death, goes to Ajana is put in a very fine place; exempt from death, he is showered by God with all the good things he wants: finery, beautiful women... he gets all these things as free gifts. In Ajana there is no misfortune, weariness or sickness... (ch. 5).

These brief extracts show that of several basic themes of the religion of salvation co-exist with the affirmation that the *pagüm*, maleficent beings, had real existence: belief in a creator god, an end of the world and a post-mortem existence in which mankind will be divided, some enjoying a permanent well-being, the rest eternal torment after God has judged them. However, one must not forget that several thousand Bamum, at the time when Njoya was compiling his text, were already familiar with Moslem and Christian teachings. On the other hand, could the King ignore the deeply rooted belief in the *pagüm* and their importance in accounting for the events which confronted mankind? The ancestors, whether in Ajana or the fire, did not cease to exist, and the King had predicted that one could continue to communicate with them through dreams. If the *penyinyi* are no longer present, a *nyinyi* is now before us.

The difference between the human condition on earth and that after death, where either eternal bliss or torment awaited them, was the most innovative part of the royal doctrine for the greater part of the population.

Let us next examine the rules of conduct laid down by God for men who, whether they obeyed them or not, determined their destinies. There are, on one hand, a set of prohibitions, and on the other the actions beloved of God.

Chapter six enumerates the sins which prevent men from entering the Kingdom of God: to desert one's wife in order to take another man's wife, to go to live with a prostitute or servant, murder, lying, jealousy, theft, lack of respect for the name of God, failure to practice the Moslem prayers regularly, belief in the efficacity of the *kusuop*, disobedience towards father, mother and the King. These sins correspond largely to acts already prohibited by Bamum tradition. Their sexual morality was less strict, however, and relationships with a 'free woman' or female servant were not condemned (Njiassé-Njoya 1981: 188–9). The break with the past was marked by the interdiction on the use of the *kusuop* and the obligation to repeat the Moslem prayer and respect the one God.

We next briefly rehearse the rites which had to be undergone to enter Islam and show obedience to the Will of God. Whoever accepted the royal doctrine had first to undergo a rite of purification. He had to wash his genitals, saying he was washing away slavery, then scrub his head and neck several times. After that he pronounced the *chahada* and proceeded to wash his shoulders and forearms. However, before turning to the list of obligations which an adherent of the royal religion had to undertake, it should be recalled that Njoya had a mosque near the Palace rebuilt and had set aside a space for prayer outside the city walls.

The royal text calls for five prayers a day; that of the middle of the day on Fridays was to be said at the mosque. Ablutions were necessary before prayer and their form followed that of the *takbîr* (chs. 22, 23, 24).

Fasting was to be practised in three circumstances determined by the Moslem ritual calender: one must fast on the ninth day of the first month, in the month of Ramadan, and on the second, sixth and ninth days of the last month of the year.

A sheep must be sacrificed at a date corresponding to *Aïd al Kebir* and one must practise alms, the *zakat*.

All these obligations are set out in chapter 11 of the work. The directions are brief and insufficient in comparison with Islamic texts. For example, Njoya says nothing about the conditions surrounding fasts, while in Moslem tradition these are dealt with in regulations which take account of, among other things, the situation of travellers, the exhausted and the sick, and which lay down exemptions, compensations and expiations.

In Njoya's text the sacrifice is one of the obligations, whereas that of the *Aïd al Kebir* is of a traditional rather than divine order. The *Risâla* is very clear on this point (Al-Qayrawani 1914: ch. 19). On the other hand, the *zakat* is described very precisely. Njoya repeats the text of the *Risâla* almost word for word (ch. 29; Al-Qayrawani 1914: 127–41). Njoya's work is certainly brief, with many gaps. Its author sometimes distances himself from Islam: he ignores the pilgrimage to Mecca and makes Bamum the language of the cult. He justifies his decision with vigour:

> Those who opine that God cannot hear those who pray in their national language because it is not that of the ancients [i.e., classical Arabic] which is the language of free men, such are liars (ch. 14).

Njiassé-Njoya does not hesitate to speak of this as a major blasphemy (Njiassé-Njoya 1981: 201–2). Could it have been otherwise, though, in an enterprise aimed at converting a population to beliefs and practices adapted to its mode of life?

The doctrinal basis of *Pursue to Attain,* and the important part played by ritual borrowings from the Mâlikite rite, are such that several writers have spoken of a 'Bamum Islam' to refer to a short-lived religious policy – one which, perhaps, eased the reception of Islam by the people of Bamum.

Several chapters of the work deal with men's conduct in the light of divine commandments. The King does not hesitate to write: 'That which men most love at the bottom of their hearts is that what God does not love. What they do not love at the bottom of their hearts, that God loves' (ch. 10). Moreover, Chedani intervenes:

> It is he who incites men to commit all sorts of sins. Chedani will flee from you if, when he approaches you, he hears the name of God invoked. Chedani tempts a man seven times a day and seven times by night. (ch. 9).

How then will humans fare, torn between their desires, satanic solicitations and the hope of eternal blessedness? Njoya is clear:

> A man who lives on earth committing sins is accursed: he suffers misfortunes in his lifetime (ch. 7). Such a man sows discord, he loses his wealth, his wives will leave him.

However sins can be forgiven:

> If a man takes another man's wife and later renounces his action because he has realised it is a sin and asks God to forgive his sin, God will pardon him.
> If he has killed a man and then repents of the murder because he has realised it is a sin and asks for God's pardon for it, God will forgive him.
> If a thief gives up stealing because he has realised it is a sin and asks pardon from God wholly truthfully, God will forgive him (ch. 8).

Prayers invoking God are set out; they concern the speaker, his family and close kin:

> O my God, I know that you want all humankind to come closer to you. That is why you sent your prophet Mahamadu to teach Islam to men. I have broken one of your commandments. Sometimes my body transgresses your law. O my God, let your holiness come to my brow today; let my heart be filled with your breath today so that from now till my death all mankind will see your glory and holiness shine in me and be astonished. O my God make this sin depart which invades me like a wind (ch. 20).
> … May God remove all your sicknesses and grant you good health. May my God spare you from discord and fill your spirit with goodwill. May God take from you the spirit of hatred so that you remain at peace. May my God give you the will to love your children as you love yourself, to love your wives as you love yourself, to love your brothers and sisters as you love yourself (ch. 21).

However, God does not always forgive, as Njoya makes clear:

> He who prays every day, without letting a moment slip, gives alms every year, never prays with dirt on his body, offers much adoration to God, takes no forbidden food, helps the poor, the sick and the unfortunate and yet does not observe God's laws prays in vain. When he prays the wind carries away and scatters his words before they reach God. In truth he will not enter God's Kingdom (ch. 12).
> A man who, when in a happy situation, commits sins without thinking of praying to God for forgiveness but who, when he falls sick and feels death approaching starts to pray that he be saved, God cannot save him (ch. 8).
> Hypocrisy and duplicity are not pardonable.

These are, to some extent, the different imaginary cases which the King offers in the chapters we have drawn from. What is remarkable is the freedom left to men to choose their path. The notion of destiny makes no appearance whatsoever.

Finally, we shall summarise some aspects of Njoya's doctrine so as to relate them to some final observations on traditional beliefs and practices. One fundamental feature must be emphasised from the start, for it determines human behaviour: eternity is promised to humans, and their fate after the Last Judgment depends on their conduct. The blessings and pleasures of Ajana awaiting good men are recalled. Bamum tradition on the other hand, only mentioned the misfortunes which such men had to guard against.

Misfortunes come to punish sins and ritual neglect. The existence of *pagüm* is recognised but nothing is said about their interventions. A good life and eternal beatitude rewards those who have observed God's laws. Even if justice is God's affair, man, who is aware of his duties, must be judged on his conduct, and punished or rewarded accordingly.

Finally, man, who is inclined to evil, may sin but can repent of his sins and omissions. Except in the case of hypocrisy, repentance will elicit God's clemency. Njoya writes more than once: 'he will be pardoned'.

The creator God is never presented as the holder of absolute power. His clemency depends on human behaviour. Does this divine dependence echo that of the ancestors propitiated by sacrifices? Is the will of men, in both cases, the key to their destiny? Or is God too great?

The royal doctrine was apparently disseminated during some of 1916 and 1917. The King at this time displayed some hostility towards Christianity. The royal schools in which the Bamum script and the history of the country were taught replaced the Christian establishments, and some of their pupil teachers were obliged to go into royal service. There were even some violent incidents (Tardits 1980: 240). There was a similar struggle between the monarch and the Moslems. For example, Njoya forbade his sons to attend the Koranic school (Njiassé-Njoya 1981: 174).

The King gave up his project in the course of 1917: in 1918 he returned to Islamic orthodoxy. The opposition of his own family and the remonstrances of the Hausa *marabouts* must have carried weight. No doubt the King realised that his knowledge of Islam was limited and that the criticisms of the representatives of orthodoxy were well founded. The short-lived aspect of the royal enterprise matters little.

What strikes us is of a different order: the convergence between some features of Bamum tradition and certain passages of *Pursue to Attain*. The limited character of the ancestors' powers, constrained by sacrificial practices, corresponds to that of a creator God likewise constrained by the fact that it is men who decide their own fates by their conduct; moreover his clemency operates in a frame of reference in which men have knowledge of how to obtain it.

A short extract from the *Risâla* demonstrates the distance between orthodoxy and the royal text:

> It is necessary to believe in the predestination (*al qadar*) of bad as well as good, of what is sweetness as well as what is bitterness. All result from a decree of Allah, our Lord. It is he who is sovereign and disposes of all things and they happen only as he has decided. He has knowledge of all things before they exist and they only exist to the extent that he has conceived them (Al-Qayrawani: 21).

A question needs to be formulated: can the representation of one God, merciful but all-powerful, be accepted and make its way against traditions in which people are offered means (e.g., things or actions) by which they hope to maintain good health and the proper functioning of their society?

Njoya, writing at the beginning of this century, did not explicitly engage himself in this direction. Fifty years later, in the 1960s, there were many persons in his country who were wary of *pagüm* and still had recourse to *nžuom*. A lineage head living not far from Fumban, for example, confided to me that he had visited his ancestors' graves in the traditional graveyard when his prayers in the Moslem mode had gone unanswered.

The co-existence of recourse to traditional African practices and those allowed for in the missionary religions of salvation (Islam or Christianity) is commonplace. Perhaps the special interest of the Bamum case is that, thanks to Njoya's text, we can identify the points at which the articulations between them are difficult to make.

Notes

1. They had chosen Solomon as his Christian name.

2. Editors' note: This may refer to feldspar, a crystalline silicate of alumina, found abundantly in local igneous rocks.

3. At this festival the senior lineages repeated their oaths of loyalty to the King, and the country was 'closed' to witches.

CHAPTER NINE

Political Dress:
German-Style Military Attire and Colonial Politics in Bamum

Christraud M. Geary

In 1967 Elizabeth Chilver analysed the changing relationship of Bali-Nyonga and the Germans between 1889 and 1913 in one of her most important essays about German colonial rule in the Cameroon Grassfields. She traced the shifts in German policy and, by extension, changes in German perceptions of the Bali-Nyonga kingdom. Initially the Germans considered Bali-Nyonga under Galega I (ruled c. 1858–1902) and his successor Fonyonga II (ruled 1902–40) a staunch ally. This favourite status allowed Fonyonga II steadily to increase his realm of influence (Chilver 1967: 498–9).[*]

However, by 1908 the Germans had begun to question Bali's growing sub-imperialism. The ruler of Bali-Nyonga appeared to abuse his privileges, and it became obvious to the Germans that he was following his own agenda. Ultimately, the German administration adjusted its policies to these newly perceived 'realities,' and began to curtail Fonyonga II's power.

This policy shift was in part provoked by the observation that Fonyonga II and several other rulers in the region, among them the rulers of Bamum, Bangangte and Ngambe, had established bodyguards or troops armed with breechloaders (Chilver 1967: 498; Menzel, 5 September 1908). The possession of guns by Grassfields rulers deeply worried the small German contingent at the military station in Bamenda and the German administration in Buea, especially when they encountered such weapons during their campaigns against Babadju and the kingdom of Kom in 1904 (Glauning, 29 March 1905). The origins of some of the guns could be traced to the expedition of Eugen Zintgraff who had reached Bali-Nyonga in 1889 and stayed there until 1892 (Chilver 1966; Menzel, 4 August 1910). In addition, the German administration had occasionally issued guns as well as ammunition to loyal rulers in recognition of their services.[1] Action needed to be taken to remove these weapons, a process which lasted well into 1910.

Some indigenous troops were not only armed with guns, they were also clad in locally created, German-style military attire. Thus, German documents also contain references to German-style military dress in Bali and other kingdoms. Its existence is *visually* documented in historical photographs which show Fonyonga II's and other kings' troops in uniforms resembling those of the German *Schutztruppe* (Fig. 1). Why did the rulers introduce these German-style uniforms for their troops? What was their meaning?

Figure 1: *Fonyonge's Soldiers, Bali.* Bali-Nyonga, Cameroon. Photograph by Bernhard Ankermann, 1908. No. VIII A 5325. Courtesy Museum für Völkerkunde, Berlin, Germany.

It should be noted that, although German efforts were primarily directed towards the removal of the guns, the Germans also considered the prohibition of German-style military dress among their African subjects. While the German concern with arms in the hands of the local population is understandable, the question arises of why the Germans were concerned with the Africans' use and display of German-style military attire.

Unfortunately, the documentation of German-style military dress in Bali-Nyonga is scant. Therefore, this paper will suggest some answers to the above questions by tracing the process of adoption, modification and ultimately rejection of German-style military attire by the King and elite of another Grassfields kingdom which the Germans counted among its allies: the Bamum kingdom of King Njoya (ruled c. 1886–1933). This encounter with the colonials at the beginning of this century teaches much about meaning and transformations of dress and its political implications. The paper will also reveal that the political meaning and symbolism of this style of attire was not lost on some German observers. Finally, it will address the German colonialists' notions of the appropriate dress for their African subjects.

The multiple meanings of dress have been acknowledged in writings on the subject. Most authors share a common interest in dress and adornment as 'a communicative symbol that serves crucial functions within human lives' (Roach and Eicher 1979: 20). Among the functions considered are dress indicating social roles, establishing social worth, symbolising economic status, and serving as an emblem for political power. Dress, the cultural arte-fact, is a system whose symbolism provides cueing for the wear-er and observers alike (Smith and Eicher 1982: 28). In order to unravel and understand this system, dress needs to be set into the wider cultural matrix, and its symbolic associations and intricate meanings need to be explored (Biebuyck 1982). The focus on the construction of identity, a recent theme in anthropological enquiry, adds another dimension to the exploration of dress and adornment. In situations of rapid political, religious and econom-ic change, choices of dress may represent meaningful statements about identity. Such considerations form the basis for studies of *political* dress.

An examination of the introduction, transformation and ulti-mate rejection of German-style military dress and regalia as a result of the colonial experience in Bamum needs to explore first the role of dress and adornment in general. It requires an understanding of earlier forms of dress and adornment and their meaning. Therefore, this chapter begins with the principles underlying dress, and by extension military dress, in Bamum.

Students of dress and adornment in Bamum may draw on multiple sources, which permit a detailed analysis covering transformations in dress and adornment from the middle of the nineteenth century to the present. The Palace Museum at the Bamum court in Fumban and many German museums contain items of nineteenth-century Bamum dress and adornment, in particular head-dresses, ceremonial garments, and accoutrements of Kings and Queen Mothers (Geary 1983a).[2] Another excellent source on nineteenth-century dress are the china ink, pencil and crayon drawings created by Bamum artists after 1920 (Savary 1977, 1979). These drawings consist of king-lists and genre scenes, and present a reified Bamum dynastic history. The king-lists depict the nineteenth-century kings in their royal attire. However, nineteenth-century royal and elite dress changed dramatically in the 1897 when King Njoya and the court converted to Islam and adopted Hausa-style clothing (see below). When the Germans reached Bamum in 1902, they encountered the King, his courtiers, and most of the royal wives in Hausa-style attire. For the early twentieth century, abundant written and photographic German records serve as good sources for the discussion of elite dress in Bamum.

From these sources, one gets a good sense of dress and adornment for Bamum elite men and for the King in the second half of the nineteenth century. It should be noted that only about one-third of the Bamum belonged to the elite, constituted by the royal lineage, the Palace nobility and their descendants. The basic attire for the male elite consisted of a loincloth held by a string or belt. Elite men wore head-dresses at all times. Leather or wooden sandals protected their feet during long journeys (Rein-Wuhrmann 1925: 38). Bracelets, anklets and necklaces adorned the wearer. Elite women wore narrow belts around their hips, and occasionally small cloths covering the pubic area. They too displayed necklaces and bracelets. Both male and female slaves went bareheaded and wore, if anything, small cloths held by fibre strings (Rein-Wuhrmann 1925: 40).

The materials used in the production of dress and adornment reflected a person's rank in Bamum society. A measure which set one wearer apart from another was rarity and value of the materials. To give one example: towards the end of the nineteenth century loincloths could be made from locally produced bark cloth, cotton cloth imported from the north or highly valued imported cloth from textile mills in Europe. Loincloths could be plain or patterned in the complicated technique of indigo resist-dyeing. Adornments such as bracelets were produced from fibre, beads or brass. Head-dresses could be fibre, cotton or leather and could be embellished with cowries, beads or feathers. The King held the monopoly over all precious and imported goods, and he alone granted the elite the right to use and display brass or bead adornments. In fact, the King mandated which type of attire and adornment the royals and the elite at the court should wear. Dress and adornment (or the lack thereof) were thus indicative of a person's rank and closeness to the King in the hierarchically organised Bamum society.

In the second half of the nineteenth century, warriors would don splendid feather head-dresses, and wear elegant and valuable accoutrements, such as beaded bracelets, anklets and necklaces, during warfare. Splendidly decorated weapons (cutlasses, spears, shields, and knives, and flintlock guns after c. 1860) were taken to battle. Some fine examples of such weaponry are now in the Palace Museum in Fumban (Geary 1983a: 175–85). Displaying flamboyant dress and exquisite weapons was part of a deliberate strategy. The Bamum army wanted to impress opponents with their wealth, and might thus intimidate them psychologically.[3] In addition, any warfare was accompanied by numerous rituals, which assured the positive outcome of a military campaign. Indeed, parallels might be drawn between nineteenth-century military dress and the exalted nature of some types of ritual/ceremonial attire. When a war was successfully concluded, victory celebrations took place in the dancing field in front of the Royal Palace at Fumban. Warriors performed dances in similar outfits, echoing the notion of 'uniform'.

Other structural and aesthetic principles underlying nineteenth- and early twentieth-century male dress (and thus military dress) became more obvious when King Njoya and the royal court converted to Islam in 1897. This conversion brought about a dramatic change in dress and adornment of the Bamum elite. It occurred as a result of an alliance with Lamido Umaru, the Islamic ruler of the Fulbe kingdom of Banyo to the north of Fumban. Umaru's troops had been called by King Njoya, when he faced unrest and the threat of a usurper in his kingdom, and needed to suppress the opposition. The Islamic foreigners fought side by side with troops loyal to Njoya and ended the revolt. In exchange for Umaru's support, King Njoya and his courtiers showered him with presents and converted to Islam (see Tardits, this volume; Njoya 1952: 39). According to accounts gathered by Njiassé-Njoya in Fumban, the admiration for Banyo military efficacy and the desire to be equally strong was the major reason for the King and the court's conversion to Islam. Elite Bamum began to wear Islamic (Hausa-style) attire, initially imported by Hausa traders from the north. Some fifteen years later, Islamic dress had been widely, if sometimes unwillingly,[4] adopted by the Bamum elite men and women.

When fighting together with soldiers from Banyo, the Bamum observed how the Moslems prayed before battle, how they were dressed in splendid cavalry outfits and war smocks covered with protective amulets. These ritual gestures, the attire, and the proud demeanour of the new allies deeply impressed the Bamum (Njiassé-Njoya 1981: 58). King Njoya subsequently introduced new Islamic-style military garments, and began to import horses to create a cavalry. While Bamum military tactics remained the same, the novel military dress for the royal army visually represented the new alliance, and the sharing of the symbolic power contained in this type of dress.

As with earlier dress and adornment for the elite, the hierarchy of materials and the restricted access to them (through the King) remained one of the fundamental principles, even after Islamic dress had been adopted. Fabric types, imported by Hausa traders from the north, increased in number, as did the embellishment of these fabrics through dyeing and Hausa-style embroidery. In a report about a visit to Fumban in December 1905/January 1906, the Basel missionary Stolz described a market with Hausa traders:

> When we entered Bamum, it was just market [day]. We saw well above two hundred people. The soul of these markets are of course the Hausa. One can simply buy everything in this market, cloth, Hausa garments, shoes, leather, then all kinds of foods, also fresh beef, rancid butter, firewood, and shells which take the place of money, and much more. (Stolz 22 January 1906)[5]

After the turn of this century, European cloth also reached Fumban.

Besides the use of distinguishing types of materials, another characteristic of both elite and military dress was the great variation within its particular elements. The variants and patterns of nineteenth- and early twentieth-century elite and royal head-dresses, for example, provide a good case in point (Geary 1983a: 160–5). These ranged from caps to the extravagant *mpelet*-style royal head attire.[6] Cotton, both white and indigo-dyed, beads, cowries, leather, feathers and brass ornaments, such as hat-pins, constituted the most common materials. Some head-dresses also displayed zoomorphic icons in their design, such as frog/toad, spider, buffalo, snake, lizard or leopard motifs. Within the Bamum world-view, all these animals had certain characteristics paralleling and alluding to human qualities and society (Geary 1992: 229–31). Even after the introduction of Islamic clothing, the importance of the head-dress remained. In fact, as can be seen from numerous photographs of the King and the Bamum elite taken in the first two decades of this century by European photographers, new models were added to the already astonishingly wide repertoire, among them turbans.

Accumulation of elements of dress and adornment were used visually to make statements about the wealth and access to power of the wearer. While many early photographs clearly demonstrate this tendency towards accumulation, the (literal) depth of this phenomenon can perhaps best be gauged from one of Anna Rein-Wuhrmann's observations, made while a Basel Mission teacher in Bamum from 1911 to 1915:

> Rich gentlemen indulge in extreme luxury and wear several expensive garments on top of each other, for example during festivities and particularly during horseback parades. I once asked the uncle of the king to count for me all of his [garments]. He wore six of them and certainly was not freezing, but said in all seriousness that it was appropriate for horseback riding to wear many garments, because the horses would be unpredictable and would like to throw the rider, so the fall would be softened a little bit by clothes with folds. (1925: 38–9)

The King's 'uncle', most likely *nži*[7] Monkuob, who was friendly with Rein-Wuhrmann, gave a practical explanation. However, this phenomenon may well relate to the consistent pattern of accumulating elements of dress and adornment; that is, the higher ranking the person, the greater the accumulation of garments and of single items such as bracelets and necklaces, and the more ostentatious the display. Besides, accumulation was an aesthetic strategy.

In Bamum, the visual language of dress placed an individual into a certain relationship with the King who bestowed the privilege to wear these forms of dress and adornment. It reflected and constituted a person, a person's achievement, and a person's standing within the strict hierarchy of Bamum society. Wearing special types of dress and adornment were constructive and reflective of a person's identity. Any Bamum observer of these elite dress ensembles could 'read' all the elements. The King was well aware of this power of dress and adornment and closely controlled access to and distribution of certain types. German-style military dress, as bestowed by the King on his loyal soldiers, was among those types, and needs to be examined from this perspective.

Why did King Njoya adopt German-style uniforms for himself and his guards? The relationship between the Germans and King Njoya was similar to their relationship with the Fon of Bali-Nyonga. The few Germans stationed in the Cameroon Grassfields had to rely on the support of allied chiefs. Ever since its 'discovery' in 1902, the Germans thought of the Bamum kingdom as a future key economic centre in the colony. While Bali-Nyonga's fortunes declined, the Germans increasingly relied on Njoya's cooperation in supplying labour for the coastal plantations and porters for the frequent transports of rubber and other products to the coast. Many German policy decisions depended on individuals such as Captain Hans Glauning, who was impressed with King Njoya's loyalty and creativity and was one of his most ardent supporters among the Germans (Geary 1994).

The Bamum King in turn, much like Fonyonga II, seized the opportunity to secure Bamum's leadership in the region, to follow his own strategies and even to wage his 'own' wars with the approval of these new allies. In 1906 Njoya supplied auxiliary troops for a German military campaign, which served both his own and the Germans' expansionist strategies. The Bamum troops supported Captain Glauning in a punitive expedition which defeated the neighbouring kingdom of Nso' (Glauning, 25 June 1906). This proved to Njoya the military prowess of the German allies, who, like the troops from Banyo in 1897, helped him to achieve a strongly desired victory.

From the Bamum perspective, the alliance with the Germans was confirmed through an intense gift exchange. The Germans gave portraits of the *Kaiser*, flags, firearms, music boxes and mugs, while the King reciprocated with ivory and art works.[8] A document dated 8 February 1904, less than two years after the Germans arrived in Fumban, throws light onto the continuous exchange:

For the third time in six months, on the twenty fourth of October last year [1903], appeared here a fair-sized delegation from the paramount chief (Sultan) Joia of Bamum. This time, it brought two medium-size elephant tusks and a smaller tusk, sent by the mother of the Sultan, and several other small things for the Governor, begging him to come to Bamum himself; in addition two very large and magnificent elephant tusks and a rather original-ly carved small table embroidered with [cowry] shells and beads as present for his Majesty, the *Kaiser*. [...] On the fifteenth of this month [February 1904], chief justice Ebermaier will travel to Bamum on my orders, to render a return visit to the Sultan and to bestow praise on him for his proven loyal-ty and reliability towards the government. Mr. Ebermaier will take the Sultan some things he especially requested, thus for example, a used tent with tables and chairs, and flags, a uniform hat, embroidered epaulets, etc. [...] He also wishes in particular champagne [*Sekt*] with glasses in order to host his European guests, an especially beautiful flag, a decorated sabre, etc. (von Puttkamer, 8 February 1904)

According to indigenous diplomacy between neighbouring chiefs, valuable and often exotic presents were an established part of gift exchange, and symbolised in tangible form political alliances between equals, in this case the Kaiser and the Bamum King. Both German and Bamum expectations of appropriate gifts were perfectly met by these items. Again, there are clear parallels with Njoya's earlier relationship with the Lamido of Banyo.

As the previous quotation shows, military regalia were among the German presents. In the eyes of the Germans, these were well suited as tokens of alliance for Grassfields chiefs. The chiefs themselves often used them to their advantage in the local com-petition for power, because they were able to intimidate their rivals by visual allusion to their mighty allies (Busch 1988). Njoya was 'rewarded' with several shipments of uniform parts, such as helmets and breast-plates for his soldiers.[9]

King Njoya, albeit himself in Islamic dress, posed with his courtiers in these authentic military regalia in front of the tent he had requested, upon receiving an official portrait of the Emperor in 1906 in recognition of services provided during the Nso' campaign (Fig. 2). In the composition of the soldiers' uniforms, the original German items, such as the helmets, breastplates and broadswords, were combined with indige-nously made ones – in this case the trousers. It is noticeable that the guards do not wear any shoes, a common element in most other pictures of German-style military regalia as used in Bamum. German-made shoes were an indicator of status and wealth and a highly desirable commodity. The helmets with the eagle finial and the breastplates of the Bamum soldiers were

Figure 2: *King Njoya Receiving an Oil Print of Kaiser Wilhelm II for his Support of the German Military Campaign Against the Nso'*. Bamum, Cameroon. Photograph by Martin Göhring or Lieutenant Edler von der Putlitz, 1906. No. Kam 201. Courtesy Linden-Museum Stuttgart, Germany.

those of the *garde du corps* under the command of *Kaiser* Wilhelm II, an elite regiment, admitting only noblemen as officers.[10] Seven pairs of these (now rather dilapidated) German helmets and breastplates are still part of the Bamum Palace Museum collection (Geary 1983a: 205, Figs. 147, 148).

The combination of German-made and locally produced uniform parts is depicted in several other images. In late 1905 or early 1906, Inspector Friedrich Lutz, in the same travelling party as missionary Stolz (see above), arrived in Fumban (Lutz, May 1906). He included several photographs with his report, one showing King Njoya with the throne of his father, King Nsangu (Fig. 3). Njoya sports what looks like an elegant officer's uniform, complete with proper pith helmet, leather boots and German

Figure 3: *King Njoya and his Father's Throne in Front of the Old Palace at Fumban*. Bamum, Cameroon. Photograph delivered by Friedrich Lutz, May 1906. No. K 782. Courtesy Basel Mission Archive, Basel, Switzerland.

parade broadsword. Upon closer examination, the uniform jacket and possibly the trousers appear to have been produced by Bamum tailors, as well as the bead-embroidered epaulets. Besides the uniform-style ensembles, combining authentic and indigenous elements, King Njoya and his soldiers wore German-style uniforms, produced almost entirely by his tailors, embroiderers and bead artists.

Who produced these stunning garments? As mentioned above, Hausa traders brought clothing from the northern areas of what are now Cameroon and Nigeria to the Bamum kingdom when the King and the court adopted Islamic clothing. Hausa were prominent in Fumban, where they had settled and gained recognition as tailors, embroiderers, leather workers and even weavers, as photographs of the Hausa settlement demonstrate.[11] As far as the Palace was concerned, the King controlled access and distribution of this new style of dress and adornment to the court elite – princes and high ranking retainers. Soon, however, he established weaving and tailoring workshops at the Palace, gaining independence from the Hausa traders and tailors and allowing him to create his own style of clothing. Initially, Hausa tailors were the teachers; their students were princes, other royals and high-ranking retainers. After the Basel missionaries arrived in Fumban in 1906, the missionary wives also taught spinning and sewing to the princesses and royal wives (M. Göhring, 18 July 1906).

There are some contemporary descriptions of the royal weaving and tailoring workshop at the Palace, termed the *nda shüe*, the house of clothing. Under King Njoya's predecessors this area of the Palace was concerned with the production of bark cloth (Tardits 1980: 677). Women and princesses spun the cotton, men wove, sewed and embroidered (Rein-Wuhrmann 1925: 150–1). Missionary Eugen Schwarz, who arrived in Fumban in May 1908, described the tailoring workshop:[12]

> Another craft is tailoring. In this, too, the Bamum accomplish great things. Previously the King and his people purchased their garments entirely from the Hausa at great expense. Again and again Njoya was advised to have his own people do the tailoring since they understood it as well as the Hausa, but to no avail. Recently, however, a superior agency has been urging the king to invent his own outfit and he has now invented it and had it made in his own tailor workshops, which should inconvenience the Hausa. A consequence was that the king ordered 3,000 Marks worth of cloth from our store in Victoria for his newly active tailor workshop; the cash that used to end up in Hausa pockets may be going to Europeans more and more. The latest Bamum clothing is much more beautifully made than that they used to get

from the Hausa, particularly the embroidery, which is not only beautifully but punctually executed. When you consider that, in earlier times, the Bamum dressed in bark cloth, you cannot help calling attention to this progress. The inside of such a Bamum tailor workshop, but primarily a royal one, looks wholly European. Here there are one, two, or three sewing machines; there a cutting table; and somewhere else again people squat doing hand embroidery, of course without an embroidery frame. It instinctively makes a person feel at home when one sees the needles flying through the air and a needle deftly threaded. Or when the king himself stands in the workshop having something measured on him or trying something on, one sees how the people have to work wholly in accordance with the king's taste. (Schwarz, 25 June 1910)

In these workshops Bamum tailors produced the German-style military uniforms. The beginning of the *indigenous* creation of entire German-style uniforms can be dated to 1904 or 1905. When missionary Ferdinand Ernst described his reception in Fumban by the King in December 1903, he reported that the King, his cavalry and soldiers wore Hausa-style clothing (Ernst, 14 December 1903). In other words, in December 1903 German-style military garments did not come to attention of the missionary, indicating that their introduction very probably post-dated his visit.

A first indication of the existence of indigenously produced German military-style uniforms are two photographs in the archives of the Hamburgisches Museum für Völkerkunde, which were donated to the museum by a Fraülein Schultz in 1904/5.[13] One of these photographs, probably taken in late 1904, shows Njoya surrounded by guards in what the caption of the photograph describes as a 'daily garment' (Fig. 4). Njoya wears a hybrid outfit, consisting of a knee-long embroidered gown, what look like white, uniform-style trousers, German leather boots and a white round hat, decorated with a v-shaped dark ribbon.[14] His soldiers wore jackets, made from dark or white fabric, and dark long trousers (except for one soldier). Some of them now wear German-made shoes, while others are still barefoot. They all sport head-dresses identical to Njoya's own. Beaded emblems, resembling both Islamic amulets and German medals, decorate their uniforms, and may indicate rank within the guard. Compared to the patterns of later uniforms these outfits are rather plain, which may explain their designation 'daily garment' in the original photograph caption on the filing card. The second 1905 photograph in Hamburg depicts King Njoya and a retainer. Over white trousers of German manufacture, Njoya wears a striped jacket, with beaded epaulets. A German-style officer's hat, a leather belt

Figure 4: *The Lamido of Bamum Surrounded by his Loyal Followers (Daily Attire)*. Bamum, Cameroon. Photograph Donated by Frl. Schultz, 1905. No. 6, Box 67. Courtesy Hamburgisches Museum für Völkerkunde, Germany.

Figure 5: *Lamido Njoya with his Personal Guard*. Bamum, Cameroon. Photograph by Adolf Diehl, 1906/1907. No. Kam 74. Courtesy Linden-Museum Stuttgart, Germany.

with a buckle and shiny German leather boots complete the ensemble. The King holds a German broadsword, which also appears in later photographs (see Geary 1988: 50).

An undated photograph, also donated by Schultz, depicts eleven Bamum soldiers standing to attention in uniforms which have drawn inspiration from both Islamic and German models.[15] The same uniforms and hats appear in a photograph taken by Adolf Diehl, a colonial agent for the Gesellschaft Nordwest-Kamerun, who came to Bamum as early as 1903 or 1904. Four soldiers wear identical white buttoned gowns over dark long-sleeved shirts, the fronts of which are finely embroidered in a Hausa-inspired pattern which is the trademark of Bamum artisans (Fig. 5). Handsome dark trousers, leather belts, puttees, laced shoes and beaded epaulets complete the outfits. A fifth guard is dressed entirely in white, with a long gown covering his white shirt and straight white trousers. Although not clearly visible in the photograph, there are indications that his outfit was also richly embroidered. Finally his white round hat and a beaded v-shaped emblem on the left sleeve of his shirt seem to set him apart from the others, suggesting high rank in the Bamum military hierarchy.

Amidst his soldiers, King Njoya stands at ease, leaning slightly on his fine broadsword.[16] His uniform consists of a jacket patterned after the German style. Buttoned-down shoulder pads hold in place several embroidered (sword-) belts which are attached to an equally elaborate belt. It seems as if cotton strips made on narrow Hausa looms were used for creating these multiple belts. Intricately embroidered patterns decorate the strips. The most elaborate one has leopard claws, held in place by bead ornaments, attached to it. Since the King alone had access to leopard pelts, teeth and claws, this element of the royal uniform is a fitting, although traditional, royal emblem. A rectangular beaded 'medal' can be seen on the right of the King's chest. His cap, with a shield, is modelled after European prototypes, yet the white feather bush on top recalls both German and Bamum tufts of feathers attached to helmets and head-dresses.

The first *written* reference to German-style military uniforms occurs in missionary Martin Göhring's report on his arrival in Bamum on 11 April 1906. King Njoya met the missionary party on horseback, clad in white, richly embroidered Hausa garments, while a group of his guards wore red velvet uniforms, also embellished with embroidery (Göhring, 13 May 1906). Were these uniforms made from the velvet received as a gift from the Germans? In the same document, but in a different context, Göhring indicates that the size of King Njoya's bodyguard was about one hundred strong (Fig. 6).[17] From then on, the missionaries mentioned Njoya's soldiers only occasionally. A group of twenty or thirty uniformed and armed guards seems to have accompanied King Njoya on his excursions, including those to the mission station and religious assemblies (Göhring, 18 July 1906; Hohner, 30 August 1907). He also used them to supervise the building of roads, rest-houses for the Germans, and to guard his livestock farms.

The most famous Bamum uniforms, reminiscent of those of the Black Hussars (Fig. 7), were designed by King Njoya himself after photographs he had seen in the German magazine *Die Woche* (Wenckstern 1906: 191). In fact, besides the uniforms of the *Schutztruppe*, photographs and official imagery served as sources of information for the King and inspired these new dress forms. The Hussar-style uniforms were certainly among the most complex and most astonishing creations of the Bamum tailors and embroiderers. Rudolf Oldenburg, the representative of the Deutsche Kamerungesellschaft, who arrived in Bamum in 1907, took three interesting photographs of these uniforms depicting Njoya and five of his men in the large dancing field in front of the Palace. In the first image, the guards stand in formation in front of Njoya, their commander (Geary 1988: 58). In the second, more playful, depiction, all of them including King Njoya stand at ease in a row, right hands on their hips (Fig. 7). This photograph, according to its archival caption, was arranged to resemble the pose assumed by the German Crown Prince with his comrades in another photograph. The third image in this series, a portrait of King Njoya, belongs to the large number of royal portraits taken by European photographers before the First World War.[18]

As in the other instances, the Hussar uniforms are translations of an idealised 'German uniform' into an indigenous idiom, rather than exact copies. Yet the tailors strived for close resemblance, most noticeably in the cut and fabric, and in the rather exaggerated loops which close the jackets. Yet there is also intricate Bamum-style embroidery on the sleeves and, as can be seen in one image (Geary 1988: 58), on the back of King Njoya's jacket. Very probably, the backs of the uniforms were not visible in the picture Njoya saw – which left the elaboration open to the imagination of the King and his tailors. The hats also depart from the

Figure 6: *Military of the Chief.* Bamum, Cameroon. Photograph by Martin Göhring, ca. 1907. No. K 1934. Courtesy Basel Mission Archive, Basel, Switzerland.

Figure 7: *Jodja with his Loyal Followers Posed Accurately according to a Picture of the German Crown Prince Surrounded by His Comrades.* Bamum, Cameroon. Photograph donated by Frl. Schultz, no date. Photograph by Rudolf Oldenburg, ca. 1906. No. 64, Box 67. Courtesy Hamburgisches Museum für Völkerkunde, Germany.

Figure 8: *The Bamum King with Two of his Notables.* Bamum, Cameroon. Photograph by Martin Göhring, ca. 1907. No. E-30.29.4,4. Courtesy Basel Mission Archive, Basel, Switzerland.

Figure 9: *King Njoya in Dress Uniform*. Bamum, Cameroon. Photographer Unknown, ca. 1907. Copy of an Enlargement in the Bamum Palace Museum at Fumban, Cameroon.

German model. The cut of the busby may have been difficult to understand from the photograph. Instead, the tailors created a type of round hat, this time with beautifully interlaced embroidery, topped by a white tuft of feathers. Upon careful examination it becomes evident that only the King has proper boots, while his retainers wear the laced shoes, depicted in other images, with leather leggings, creating the effect of boots. Finally, it should be noted that two of the guards display German swords, while the King holds a Fulbe-style sword.

There seems to have been no end to variation in the uniforms, especially those worn by King Njoya himself. In a photograph taken by missionary Martin Göhring, we encounter the King in yet another outfit: the uniform-style jacket already seen in Fig. 5 and an embroidered cape with heavy, beaded epaulets (Fig. 8). A sword-belt and two rectangular amulets decorate the jacket. Njoya's most stunning outfit resembled the parade uniform which the *Kaiser* wore in the official portrait given to loyal chiefs (Fig. 2). In this photograph (Fig. 9), an enlargement of which is now in the Palace Museum at Fumban, the Bamum King assumes an authoritative pose. As in *Kaiser* Wilhelm's portrait, Njoya's hands rest on the sword and he looks serenely into the distance. Several belts, the same ones as depicted in Figure 5, and the sash with the leopard's claws embellish his white uniform jacket with broad cuffs. He wears German-made epaulets and an extravagant wisassler helmet crowned with an eagle finial, both imported in 1905: the same type of *garde du corps* helmet displayed by the *Kaiser* in his official portrait. This dress uniform, the ultimate expression of Njoya's sentiment towards the *Kaiser*, indicated King Njoya's self-perception. He clearly perceived himself as an equal of the ruler of the distant land whose retainers and soldiers had reached the Grassfields.

In January 1908, King Njoya and thirty of his soldiers, clad in their German-style uniforms, travelled to the coast to pay homage to the German Governor Theodor Seitz and to deliver a present for the German Emperor on his birthday: the fabulous, beaded two-figure throne of his father, King Nsa'ngu, which is now in the Museum für Völkerkunde in Berlin (Geary 1983b). Several photographs were taken during this visit by government photographers and by members of the Basel Mission (Fig. 10). They show King Njoya in different German-style uniforms, but never in Islamic clothing.[19] King Njoya and his soldiers participated in the Emperor's birthday celebrations, which consisted of

Figure 10: *King Njoya with his Own Soldiers in Duala*. Photographer Unknown, January 1908. No. Ph MAF 71. Courtesy Museum für Völkerkunde Leipzig, Germany.

parades and other official displays. Needless to say, the Germans considered the Bamum 'costumes' highly amusing, if not inappropriate according to their notions of how the residents of this exotic kingdom were supposed to be dressed. Nevertheless, they admired the military discipline of the Bamum soldiers who paraded in front of the Governor during the celebration. In the words of Governor Seitz:

> Yoya and his soldiers attended the religious service and the subsequent parade of the *Schutztruppe*, the 30 soldiers of Njoya, who were armed with flintlock guns, tried to march by, which did not turn out badly at all (Seitz 1908a, 10).

It is obvious from this observation that, besides wearing uniforms, the Bamum guards must also have practised drills resembling those of the German troops.

In Bamum, recollections of the performance of the troops in Buea are more vivid. In 1977, many of the oldest princes in Fumban still remembered the lively accounts of those who had accompanied Njoya to the coast. In the years of telling the story, the feats of the Bamum had become legendary. Not only had they paraded in the most accurate fashion, they also outdid the soldiers of the *Schutztruppe* in sharp-shooting, tug-of-war and wrestling matches. This caused the Germans to be so jealous that from then on they refused to provide the Bamum with guns (Geary 1983a: 66–7).

In his novel *Njoya, reformateur du royaume bamoun,* the poet and writer Adamou Ndam Njoya gives an account of the splendid and impressive Bamum displays and refers to the German spectators' divided sentiments. On one hand, he suggests, they admired the Bamum. On the other hand, they felt uneasy about blacks achieving such accomplishments (Njoya 1978, unpaginated). Both texts thus offer indigenous explanations for the shift in German attitudes towards the military aspirations of their African allies in the Grassfields.

Early German efforts to remove guns and uniforms date back to 1905. German criticism of uniformed troops of chiefs is foreshadowed in an event noted by von Wenckstern in his 1906 report on the military campaign against the Nso'. A German merchant in Fumban threatened King Njoya that Lieutenant von Wenckstern would not tolerate his new Hussar-style uniforms and would take them away (von Wenckstern, 1 September 1906). Von Wenckstern's assessment, that these Hussar uniforms did not at all resemble the uniforms of the *Schutztruppe* (as for example the Bali uniforms in Figure 1, or the so-called 'daily' uniforms in Figure 4) points to concern on the part of the Germans. They feared that uniformed Africans would try to intimidate and blackmail the local population which was not able to distinguish official from locally made uniforms.

Captain Glauning had dealt with the issue in a *laissez-faire* manner. When he died in March 1908, his successor First Lieutenant Menzel took a different stance. King Njoya felt threatened by Menzel's effort to prohibit guns and the use of armed guards in Bamum. In the autumn of 1908, a few months after Njoya and his soldiers had returned from the coast where Governor Seitz and other colonials had lavished praise[20] on the enlightened ruler from the interior, Menzel made his move to settle the gun issue. According to the biennial report for 1 April to 30 September 1908, Menzel was now convinced that his predecessor Glauning had frivolously permitted King Njoya to have an armed guard (Menzel, 26 September 1908).

In August 1908 Menzel had been in Fumban, and had ordered Njoya to abolish the uniformed guards. According to a report by missionary Göhring:

> Njoya got rid of his soldiers, bought nothing but Hausa garments, and put away anything European. We feared for our entire work here, since, in addition, our female pupils declared that they no longer wanted to learn how to sew. We therefore wrote a petition to the Governor to rescind First Lieutenant Menzel's order, because its consequences would threaten our entire work and open the door for the intrusion of Islam. We sent this letter through Bamenda Station. First Lieutenant Menzel immediately came here in person. He denied having forbidden Njoya to have soldiers. [...] He said, that as far as he was concerned, Njoya could keep as many soldiers as he pleased. [...] First Lieutenant Menzel said that everything should be laid to rest. If I had anything at all, a concern, etc., I should confide in him. Thus, the matter is finished (Göhring, 2 October 1908).

As a result of the missionary's intervention, Menzel rescinded his order and permitted the King continued use of his guards. He allowed Njoya to maintain his soldiers on condition that they did not engage in military drills, imitate military honours or carry arms. The soldiers were supposed to be messengers for the chief and could not be employed outside the kingdom (Menzel, 5 September 1908). With these restrictions, the *raison d'être* for the guards had, from the Bamum point of view, been abolished.

In addition, the First Lieutenant suggested that the guns should be confiscated and the Bamum guards be equipped with staffs (Menzel, 26 September 1908). Another report to Governor Seitz in January 1909 pertains to an enquiry by Lieutenant Edler von der Planitz about guns in Bamum. Njoya admitted to having thirty-six breechloaders, although he insisted that the late Captain Glauning had known about the weapons. The Germans subsequently confiscated these guns. In the second part of this report, concerned with the chiefs of Bamum and Bali 'playing at soldiers', Menzel described his actions. He tried to convince Njoya that his guards should no longer be armed with guns, but that spears, bows and arrows were the appropriate equipment for the Bamum warrior. He also deplored the fact that the missionaries in Bamum had meddled with administrative affairs, and that he had therefore to travel to Bamum again. He now requested that the Governor should authorise him to outlaw firearms in Bamum entirely, because, among other reasons, favouring King Njoya over Fonyonga would increase the rivalry between Bali and Bamum. Furthermore, the reversal of his earlier order as a result of the intervention of the missionaries would make it appear as if the missionaries were superior to the Military Station (Menzel, 13 January 1909). Although the original documents seem to have been lost, this change of policy towards Bamum was implemented.

The effect of the final prohibition of firearms was immediately obvious. When Governor Seitz rendered a return visit to Bamum and arrived in Fumban, Njoya received him in grand style:

> On the 26th of November [1909], I arrived in Fumban, the Bamum capital, and was greeted by the paramount chief Yoya and his entourage in the first valley behind the city walls. Yoya who has exchanged his tasteless European fantasy uniform for Fullah dress and disbanded his troops who had worn European-style uniforms, was accompanied by one hundred mounted men and perhaps a thousand foot soldiers, all in Hausa gowns and armed with spears. Only few carried bush guns which they fired now and then during my entry, however with weak charges, a sign that in Bamum, too, powder has become rare and is used sparingly (Seitz, 21 December 1909).

In Seitz' *official* memoir, there are no further references to the German-style uniforms in Bamum. Here, the reception in Fumban becomes an exotic highlight of Seitz' trip, for 'Joja and his horsemen in their Hausa attire presented a fantastic picture' (Seitz 1929b, 85). Literally overnight, King Njoya had eschewed German-style uniforms for himself and his guards.

From the German point of view, this action concluded a rather peculiar episode. The German reactions to the adoption of 'fantasy' uniforms by the Bamum King and his guards ranged widely. In fact, as noted above, the German administration had given military regalia to loyal chiefs and thus facilitated the introduction of military attire. Certain observers considered the indigenously made uniforms as playful, naive aberrations of their loyal African subjects. Others, among them the missionaries who lived in Fumban, seem to have tolerated German-style military attire because it looked proper and orderly, and because they admired Njoya's inventiveness and creativity (Göhring, 13 May 1906). Some observers, among them Station Commander Menzel, perceived these developments as threats to German rule, particularly when seen in conjunction with indigenous efforts to arm these guards with guns.

Finally, many Germans must have perceived any mimicry of European dress and adornment as inappropriate, preferring, as did Governor Seitz, exotic, lavish Hausa attire to hybrid dress forms. Anna Rein-Wuhrmann summarised this sentiment in 1925:

One would wish all natives of the hinterland a keen eye for the beauty of the practical attire of their homeland, and would like to keep from them all European doodads and tinsel. Since this is impossible, one can only cultivate their love in and pride of their homeland. Both also consist in a person's loyalty to the patrimony of his forefathers (1925: 45).

Only one German observer, missionary Göhring, seems to have had a better understanding of the indigenous meaning of the guards in German-style military dress; he asked the Station Commander to tolerate Njoya's troops in order not to jeopardise the Mission's proselytising (Göhring, 2 October 908).

From the Bamum point of view, German-style uniforms were a perfect innovation. As in the case of the Hausa-style attire worn by the Fulbe of Banyo, which the Bamum court had adopted in 1897, this type of dress was associated with the power and military prowess of a new player in the Cameroon Grassfields. It was exotic in nature: different in pattern from earlier dress forms, and made from precious materials. It was prestigious in the eyes of Bamum's neighbours, for it demonstrated the gift exchange with the Germans and thus the type of relationship maintained with the new power in the region. The cost of procuring the fabrics and accoutrements such as shoes was exorbitant. Only a wealthy ruler could afford it and only an influential king could allow his subjects to wear such powerful and beautiful attire. Creative adaptations, such as beaded epaulets and belts, heralded the inventiveness of the Bamum tailors and embroiderers whom King Njoya had brought together at his Palace.

Within the range of uniform-style attire, general principles distinguishing elite dress from other dress could be perfectly accommodated. An abundance of variation in cuts, materials and rich embroidery echoes the principle of proliferation of forms within one type of garment. Hats, which perhaps constitute the best example, ranged from authentic German hats and helmets to creatively embellished 'Hussar' and other types of head-dresses, and added to the repertoire of flamboyant Bamum elite headgear. Uniform jackets, especially the ones sported by Njoya, also showed a range of patterns and cuts. Finally, one of the elements of elite dress was accumulation, as mentioned above. Indeed, medals, belts and rich embroidery recall this characteristic of elite dress. While modelled on a foreign prototype, the Bamum-made uniforms were endowed with meaning according to indigenous categories.

Perhaps the most intriguing aspect of the adoption of German-style uniforms was their political dimension, for they alluded visually both to the alliance with the Germans and to King Njoya's ability to manipulate this alliance in internal and external affairs. Internally, the King had absolute control over the production and distribution of this style of dress. In fact, he also carefully controlled and monitored the relationship of the Bamum with the Germans. Externally, the use of the uniforms expressed his closeness to the colonial power, as well as the riches of the Bamum court. The sudden disappearance of the German-style uniforms is the clearest indication that the Bamum King and his loyal retainers perceived the attire as political dress.

While the colonialists interpreted the end of this episode as King Njoya having come to his senses, his deliberate strategy foreshadowed an increasing rift with the colonial administration, which was latent during the later part of German colonial domination and fully manifested itself under French rule. Immediately after Njoya and his court abandoned German-style uniform regalia, he turned to the Fulbe, the old/new allies, and he and the elite wore exclusively Hausa-style dress and adornment. In the first years of colonial domination, King Njoya and his courtiers had carefully constructed their identity in the German colony through dress, and had made many deliberate choices and statements. In dress, Bamum actors found one channel of expressing their agenda. In the final analysis, this examination of Bamum German-style uniforms may therefore facilitate a better understanding of African experience and actions during the German colonial period.

Notes

* This chapter is based on an earlier working paper, entitled 'Patterns From Without, Meaning from Within: European-Style Military Dress and German Colonial Politics in the Bamum Kingdom (Cameroon),' circulated by the African Studies Center of Boston University (1989).

1. In two documents, dated 25 February and 31 March 1908, a Captain Gebauer confirmed the execution of an ordinance by Governor Seitz, to issue 100 cartridges to King Njoya of Bamum, to be used with his carbine M-88, which had been accorded to him earlier by the German administration (Gebauer, 25 February 1908; Seitz, 31 March 1908).

2. During fieldwork in Bamum in 1977, I discussed media, use, function and symbolism of these garments and other accoutrements in great detail with members of the Palace elite. This research, a cultural aid project, was sponsored by the German Foreign Ministry.

3. See Tardits, this volume.

4. Tardits collected testimony among older Bamum that noblemen would only put on the new type of dress before they reached the capital of Fumban and entered the Palace. Apparently, many traditionalists preferred the earlier forms of dress (Tardits 1980: 214, 339).

5. All translations from the German are by the author.

6. *Mpelet* is a high hat, which consists of two flat leaves, held by a lateral frame. Reserved for the King and high-ranking retainers, it was embellished with beads, et cetera.

7. *Nži* is a title indicating nobility.

8. King Njoya received a revolver as early as 1902 (Sandrock 1902), and further firearms at later points in time. Considering the German effort to keep such weapons out of the hands of Africans, these gifts were an unusual departure.

9. An invoice by the company Tippelskirch & Co., that shipped 'equipment of all kinds' to overseas territories, confirms the arrival of such goods. Among the items sent on the steamer *Eleonore Woermann* on 10 February 1905, were two pieces (63.4 metres) of golden brocade, 60.5 metres of light green silk, 60.2 metres of dark green silk, 43 metres of red velvet, 2 German flags with the inscriptions 'Joia-Bamum' and 'Fonjonge-Bali' and two large oil paintings depicting the *Kaiser*. On a second steamer, the *Lucie Woermann*, Tippelskirch sent twelve cuirassier helmets with eagle and finial, twelve complete broadswords and twelve cuirasses to Cameroon, no doubt destined for Bamum (11 March 1905).

10. I thank Matthias Busch for this personal communication.

11. See for example the 1912 photograph no. 19343 by Marie-Pauline in the archives of the Rautenstrauch-Joest Museum, Cologne, Germany.

12. According to the local expression, this contained 'ninety sewing needles' (Tardits 1980: 356).

13. While the identity of the photographer is unknown, she may have been a relative of a merchant of the same name, who ran the factory of the Gesellschaft Nordwest-Kamerun in Fumban and was expelled from Bamenda District by the German administration in 1906 for offences committed in Fumban against royal women (Prange 1907).

14. This v-shape is not clearly visible in this image, but can be seen in other pictures (see Fig. 5).

15. Archives of the Hamburgischen Museum für Völkerkunde, no. 65, box K 67.

16. A second image by Diehl, taken during the same occasion, is a close-up of Njoya (Archives of the Linden-Museum Stuttgart, no. Kam 71; folder WA II). This close-up permits a better analysis of the King's dress.

17. There are few pictures showing the large number of uniformed soldiers. Rudolf Oldenburg took one such image in c. 1907 (see Geary and Njoya 1985: 193).

18. This photograph was published with an article by Hans Ramsay, one of the members of the first German party to reach Bamum in 1902 (Ramsay 1925: 293). See also Geary 1988: 59.

19. For examples see the photographs taken during Njoya's stay, published in Geary and Njoya 1985: 189–91.

20. In his 1929 memoir, Seitz described Njoya's visit to the coast in the following words 'On the Emperor's birthday 1908, the paramount chief of Bamum, Joja, had appeared in Buea. The man and his attendants made a very good impression, so that I immediately promised a return-visit' (Seitz 1929: 82).

NOTES ON CONTRIBUTORS

Shirley Ardener
Founding Director of the Centre for the Cross-Cultural Study of Women, Queen Elizabeth House, Oxford. Among her publications are *Eye-Witnesses to the Annexation of Cameroon, 1883–1887, Kingdom on Mount Cameroon* by Edwin Ardener, of which she is the editor, in this series.

Ralph A. Austen
Professor of History at University of Chicago. He has published extensively on African economic and social history based on research in Tanzania and Cameroon. In 1996 he will publish *The Elusive Epic: the Narrative of Jeki la Njambe in the Historical Culture of the Cameroon Coast.*

Philip Burnham
Lecturer in Social Anthropology at University College, London. His published work on Gbaya includes *Opportunity and Constraint in a Savanna Society. The Gbaya of Meiganga, Cameroun* (1980).

B.Chem-Langhêê
Currently 'Maitre de Conference' at the University of Yaoundé. He first undertook a B.Ed. at the University of British Colombia and then a Masters degree at Carleton University. He returned to the University of British Columbia with a university scholarship to complete his Ph.D. At that point his interests were in International Relations but he has recently developed an interest in both local political history and the problems presented by study of oral history.

Verkijika G. Fanso
Associate Professor of History at the University of Yaoundé and Sub-Dean of the faculty of Arts. He took his first degree at the University of British Colombia and a Masters at the University of Yaoundé examined issues involving the Cameroon-Nigeria boundary. His research and many publications have focused on the pre-colonial, colonial, and post-colonial history of Africa and also the history of blacks in the American Civil War.

Richard Fardon
Lecturer in Social Anthropology at the School of Oriental and African Studies, University of London, and director of the African Studies Centre. Works on Chamba include *Between God, the Dead and the Wild.*

Chamba Interpretations of Ritual and Religion (1991) and *Raiders and Refugees. Trends in Chamba Political Development 1750–1950* (1988).

Ian Fowler
Lecturer in Social Anthropology at the Oxford Brookes University. A close colleague and friend of Sally Chilver, and a former student of Phyllis Kaberry, he first undertook fieldwork in the Cameroon Grassfields in the 1970s. He is an editor of the *Bulletin of Francophone Africa*.

Christraud M. Geary
Curator of the Eliot Elisofon Photographic Archive, National Museum of African Arts, Smithsonian Institution, Washington DC. Works on Cameroon include *We – die Genese eines Hauptlingtums im Grasland von Kamerun* (1975), *Things of the Palace* (1983) and *Mandou Yenou: Photographies du Pays Bamoun, Royaume Ouest Africaine 1902–1915* (1985).

Joseph Lukong Banadzem
After obtaining a doctorate at Paris 1 University (Sorbonne Panthéon) he now teaches history at the École Normale Supérieure Annex at Bambili in the centre of the Cameroon Grassfields.

Robert O'Neil
Worked in the N.W. Province of Cameroon for fifteen years as a Catholic Priest. A member of St Joseph Missionary Society of Mill Hill (MHM), he acquired a Ph.D. at Columbia University in 1987. His publications include *Mission to the British Cameroons* (1992) and a biography of Cardinal Herbert Vaughan (1995). He is currently working on a history of the Mill Hill Missions in Uganda.

Claude Tardits
Honorary President of École Pratique des Hautes Études, Vème Section, Paris. Works on Bamoum include *Le Royaume Bamoun* (1980) and he edited *Contribution de la recherche ethnologique à l'histoire des civilisations du cameroun* (1981).

Jean-Pierre Warnier
Professor of Social Anthropology at Université René Descartes, Paris. Works on Cameroon include *Échanges, développement et hiérarchies dans le Bamenda pré-colonial (Cameroun)* (1985), et *L'ésprit d'entreprise au Cameroun* (1993).

David Zeitlyn
Formerly Junior Research Fellow then British Academy Research Fellow at Wolfson College, Oxford. Now a lecturer in Social Anthropology at University of Kent, Canterbury. Works on Mambila include *Sua in Somié. Mambila Traditional Religion* (1994). Honorary Editor of the Anthropological Index.

BIBLIOGRAPHY

a) Non-archival references

Adda, K.M. 1975. 'The Formation of the Mambilla c.1800–1926'. Department of History Research Essay: Amadu Bello University.

Afigbo, A.E. 1972. *The Warrant Chiefs* (Ibadan History Series). London: Longmans.

Aletum Tabuwe, M. & C.F. Fisiy. 1989. *Socio-Political Integration and the Nso' Institutions*. Yaoundé: SOPECAM.

al-Qayrawani, I.A.Z. 1914 (1952). *La Risala: ou, Epiître sur les éléments du dogme et de la loi de l'Islam selon le rite malikite*. Alger: Jules Carbonel.

Amadiume, I. 1987a. *Afrikan Matriarchal Foundations: The Igbo Case*. London: Karnak.

Amadiume, I. 1987b. *Male Daughters, Female Husbands: Gender and Sex in an African Society*. London: Zed.

Ankermann, B. 1910. 'Bericht über eine ethnographische Forschungsreise ins Grasland von Kamerun'. *Zeitschrift für Ethnologie* 42, 288–310.

Ardener, E.W., S.G. Ardener, & W. A. Warmington, 1960. *Plantation and Village in the Cameroons: some economic and social studies*. London: Oxford University Press for the Nigerian Institute of Social and Economic Research.

Ardener, E.W. 1965. *Historical Notes on the Scheduled Monuments of West Cameroon*. Buea: Government Printer.

Ardener, E.W. 1967. 'The Nature of Reunification in Cameroon'. In *African Integration and Disintegration: Case Studies in Economic and Political Union* (ed.) A. Hazelwood. Oxford: Oxford University Press.

Ardener, S.G. (ed.) 1992. *Persons and Powers of Women in Diverse Cultures*. Oxford: Berg.

Ardener, S.G. 1968. *Eye-Witnesses to the Annexation of Cameroon, 1883–1887*. Buea: The Government Printer.

Austen, R.A. 1977. 'Duala vs. Germans in Cameroon: Economic Dimensions of a Political Conflict'. *Revue française d'histoire d'Outre-Mer* LXIV(4), 477–97.

Austen, R.A. 1986. 'Cameroon and Cameroonians in Wilhelmian Innenpolitik: Grande Histoire and Petite Histoire'. In *L'Afrique et l'Allemagne* (ed.) K. Ndumbe, III. Yaoundé: Éditions Africavenir.

Banadzem, J. (forthcoming). 'Death, Afterlife and Funerary Rituals in Nso': Practice and Belief in a Changing Society'. In *Nso' and its Neighbours: Readings in Social History* (eds) B. Chem-Langhèè, V.G. Fanso, M. Goheen & E.M. Chilver. Yaoundé: and Amherst: Amherst College.

Barth, H. (1857) 1965. *Travels & Discoveries in North & Central Africa.* London: Cass & Co.

Baumann, H. & L. Vajda. 1959. 'Bernhard Ankermann's völkerkundliche Aufzeichnungen im Grasland von Kamerun 1907–9' (including letter from Adolf Vielhauer to Ankermann of 22 November 1910 pp. 271–76). *Baessler Archiv* (NF) 7(2), 217–317.

Berndt, C. & E.M. Chilver. 1992. 'Phyllis Kaberry (1910–1977): Fieldworker Among Friends'. In *Persons and Powers of Women in Diverse Cultures* (ed.) S. Ardener. Oxford: Berg.

Biebuyck, D.P. 1982. 'Lega Dress as Cultural Artifact'. *African Arts* 15(3), 59–65.

Bloch, M. 1990. 'What Goes Without Saying: the Conceptualization of Zafimaniry Society'. In *Conceptualizing Society* (ed.) A. Kuper. European Association of Social Anthropologists. London: Routledge.

Blu, K.I. 1980. *The Lumbee Problem* (Cambridge Studies in Cultural Systems). Cambridge: Cambridge University Press.

Böckner, G. 1893. 'Streifzüge in Kamerun II'. *Deutsche Kolonialzeitung* 6(1), 7–9.

Bohannan, P. & L. Bohannan. 1953. *The Tiv of Central Nigeria. (Ethnographic Survey of Africa: Western Africa, Part VIII).* London: International African Institute.

Broc, N., & Siary, G. 1988. *Dictionnaire illustré des explorateurs et grands voyageurs français du XIXe siècle.* Paris: Editions du C.T.H.S.

Burnham, P. 1980a. *Opportunity and Constraint in a Savanna Society (The Gbaya of Meiganga, Cameroun).* London: Academic Press.

Burnham, P. 1980b. 'Raiders and Traders in Adamawa'. In *Asian & African Systems of Slavery* (ed.) J.L. Watson. Oxford: Basil Blackwell.

Burnham, P. & T. Christensen. 1983. 'Karnu Message and the War of the Hoe Handle – Interpreting a Central African Resistance Movement'. *Africa* 53(4), 3–22.

Burnham, P., E. Copet-Rougier & P. Noss. 1986. 'Gbaya et Mkako: contribution ethno-linguistique à l'histoire de l'Est-Cameroun'. *Paideuma* 32, 87–128.

Busch, M. 1988. 'Deutsche Uniformgeschenke an Stammeskönige im ehemaligen Schutzgebiet Kamerun'. *Der Bote aus dem wehrgeschichtlichen Museum* 12(23), 38–43.

Chilver, E.M. 1951. 'The Institutes of Social and Economic Research in the African Colonies'. *Journal of African Administration* 3(4), 178–186.

Chilver, E.M. 1957. 'A New View of Africa. Lord Hailey's Second Survey'. *The Round Table. A Quarterly Review of British Commonwealth Affairs* XLVIII (189 December), 120–129.

Chilver, E.M. 1958. 'Commonwealth Studies in British Universities. 1. – Social Sciences'. *Universities Quarterly* 12(4), 407–413.

Chilver, E.M. (ed.) 1962. *Portrait of a Cameroonian. An Autobiography of Maxwell Gabana Fohtung.* Cyclostyled edition.

Chilver, E.M. 1963. Native Administration in the West Central Cameroons 1902–1954. In *Essays in Imperial Government. Presented to Margery Perham* (eds) K. Robinson & F. Madden. Oxford: Basil Blackwell.

Chilver, E.M. 1964 (revised 1970). *Historical Notes on the Bali Chiefdoms of the Cameroons Grassfields.* (Two Reports to the Bali Historical Society, Report 1 Origins, Migration and Composition. Report 2 The Bali-Chamba of Bamenda: Settlement and Composition). Cyclostyle: privately circulated.

Chilver, E.M. 1966. *Zintgraff's Explorations in Bamenda, Adamawa and the Benue Lands 1889–1892.* Buea, Cameroon: Government Printer. (Previously circulated privately in 1961).

Chilver, E.M. 1967. 'Paramountcy and Protection in the Cameroons: the Bali and the Germans, 1889–1913'. In *Britain and Germany in Africa: Imperial Rivalry and Colonial Rule* (eds) P. Gifford & W.R. Louis. New Haven: Yale University Press.

Chilver, E.M. 1971. 'The Secretaryship of the Colonial Social Science Research Council: a Reminiscence'. *Anthropological Forum* 4(2), 103–12.

Chilver, E.M. (ed.) 1985a. 'Grassfields Chiefly Palaces and Royal Households'. *Paideuma* 31.

Chilver, E.M. 1985b. 'Nso' Working Notes: Father Emonts on traditional religious concepts: death and conversion in Kitiwum (Dec. 1912 – Nov. 1915.)'. (Cyclostyle: privately circulated).

Chilver, E.M. 1989. 'Women Cultivators, Cows and Cash-Crops: Phyllis Kaberry's Women of the Grassfields Revisited'. In *Proceedings/Contributions, Conference on the Political Economy of Cameroon – Historical Perspectives, June 1988 (African Studies Centre Leiden, Research Reports No. 35)* (eds) P. Geschiere & P. Konings. Leiden: African Studies Centre.

Chilver, E.M. 1990. 'Thaumaturgy in Contemporary Traditional Religion: the Case of Nso' in Mid-Century'. *Journal of Religion in Africa* 20(3), 226–47.

Chilver, E.M. 1995a. 'Grassfields Working Notes: Some Notes from Funggom, June 1947 selectively transcribed from Phyllis Kaberry's MS notebooks'. Privately circulated.

Chilver, E.M. 1995b. 'Grassfields Working Notes: Max Moisel's Visit to Bamenda, Bali-Nyonga and Babungo, 1907'. Privately circulated.

Chilver, E.M. & P.M. Kaberry. 1960. 'From Tribute to Tax in a Tikar Chiefdom'. *Africa* 30(1), 1–19.

Chilver, E.M. & P.M. Kaberry. 1965. 'Sources of the Nineteenth-Century Slave Trade: The Cameroons Highlands'. *Journal of African History* 6(1), 117–20.

Chilver, E.M. & P.M. Kaberry. 1966. 'Notes on the Precolonial History and Ethnography of the Bamenda Grassfields (Prefectures of Bamenda, Wum and Nkambe)'. Privately circulated in cyclostyled form.

Chilver, E.M. & P.M. Kaberry. 1968. *Traditional Bamenda: The Pre-colonial History and Ethnography of the Bamenda Grassfields*. Buea, Cameroon: Government Printer.

Chilver, E.M. & P.M. Kaberry. 1970. 'Chronology of the Bamenda Grassfields'. *Journal of African History* 11(2), 249–57.

Chilver, E.M. & P.M. Kaberry. 1971. 'The Tikar Problem: a Non-Problem'. *Journal of African Languages* 10(2), 13–14.

Clozel, F.-J. 1896. *Haute-Sangha – Bassin du Tchad, Les Bayas: Notes ethnographiques et linguistiques*. Paris: Joseph André.

Copet-Rougier, E. 1987. 'Du clan à la chefferie dans l'est du Cameroun'. *Africa* 57(3), 345–63.

Coquery-Vidrovitch, C. 1965. 'De Brazza à Gentil: la politique française en Haute-Sangha à la fin du XIXe siècle'. *Revue française d'histoire d'Outre-Mer* 52(186), 22–40.

Coquery-Vidrovitch, C. 1972. *Le Congo au temps des grandes compagnies Concessionnaires: 1898–1930*. Paris: Mouton.

Davidson, B. 1992. *The Black Man's Burden: Africa and the Curse of the Nation-State*. London: James Currey.

Deutsches Kolonialblatt: Unattributed reports.

1904. 'Uprising in the Cross River districts and operations of Oberst. Müller and others from 5 February to 22 August, 1904', 15, 698–702.

1905. 'Progress of pacification of the Bamenda *Bezirk*, reporting operations by Hptm. Glauning and others north and south of the station', 16, 557–8.

1906a. 'Concerning touring by Missionary Göhring and other members of the Basel mission and a brief account of its implantation at Bali and progress to the end of 1904', 17, 353–5.

1906b. 'Uprising and banditry in the Bamenda *Bezirk* in March especially south and west of Bali; mustering of forces against Bansso in april and punitive expedition', 17, 516.

Dillon, R.G. 1990. *Ranking and Resistamce. A Precolonial Cameroonian Polity in Regional Perspective*. Stanford: Stanford University Press.

Douglas, M. & D. Hull (eds) 1992. *How Classification Works: Nelson Goodman Among the Social Sciences*. Edinburgh: Edinburgh University Press.

Emonts, J. 1922. *Ins Steppen- und Bergland Innerkameruns; aus dem Leben und Wirken deutscher Afrikamissionare*. Aachen: Xaveriusverlag.

Fanso, V.G. & E.M. Chilver. (forthcoming). 'Nso' and the Germans: the First Encounters in Contemporary Documents and in Oral Tradition.' In *Nso' and its Neighbours: Readings in Social History* (eds) B. Chem-Langhèè, V.G. Fanso, M. Goheen & E.M. Chilver. Yaoundéand Amherst: Amherst College.

Fardon, R.O. 1984. 'Sisters, Wives, Wards and Daughters: a Transformational Analysis of the Political Organisation of the Tiv and their Neighbours'. *Africa* 54(4), 2–21.

Fardon, R.O. 1985. 'Sisters, Wives, Wards and Daughters: a Transformational Analysis of the Political Organisation of the Tiv and their Neighbours. Part II: The Transformations'. *Africa* 55(1), 77–91.

Fardon, R.O. 1987. 'African Ethnogenesis: Limits to the Comparability of Ethnic Phenomena'. In *Comparative Anthropology* (ed.) L. Holy. Oxford: Blackwell.

Fardon, R.O. 1988. *Raiders and Refugees. Trends in Chamba Political Development 1750–1950* (Smithsonian Series in Ethnographic Enquiry). Washington D.C.: Smithsonian Institution Press.

Fardon, R.O. & G. Furniss. 1993. 'Frontiers and Boundaries: African Languages as Political Environment'. In *African Languages, Development and the State* (eds) R. Fardon & G. Furniss. London: Routledge.

Fohtung, M.G. 1992. 'Self-portrait of a Cameroonian, Taken Down by Peter Kalle Njie and Edited by E.M. Chilver'. (Published version of *Portrait of a Cameroonian: an Autobiography of Maxwell Gabana Fohtung*, cyclostyled for private circulation 1962). *Paideuma* 38, 219–48.

Fowler, I. 1990. 'Babungo: A Study of Iron Production, Trade and Power in a Nineteenth Century Ndop Plain Chiefdom (Cameroons).' PhD: London University.

Fowler, I. 1995. 'The Oku Iron Industry in its Regional Setting: A Descriptive Account'. *Baessler-Archiv (NF)* XLIII, 89–126.

Fowler, I. (forthcoming). 'Tribal and Palatine Arts of the Cameroon Grassfields; Elements for a "Traditional" Regional Identity.' In *Art and Contested Identity* (ed.) J. MacClancy.

Fowler, I. (in prep.) 'The War of the @phones: A Dual Colonial Linguistic Legacy for Cameroon.' In *Linguistic Conflict and Identity* (eds) S. Ardener & I. Fowler.

Fowler, I., & Zeitlyn, D. (eds) 1995. *Perspectives on the State: from political history to ethnography in Cameroon. Essays for Sally Chilver. Paideuma* vol. 41. Stuttgart: Franz Steiner Verlag.

Garbosa II (Gara of Donga), M.S. 1956. *Labarun Chambawa da Al'Amurransu, Salsalar Sarakunan Donga*: Privately published.

Geary, C.M. (ed.) 1979. 'Cameroon Grassfields Studies' (*Paideuma* 25).

Geary, C.M. 1981. 'The Historical Development of the Chiefdom of We (Southern Fungom)'. In *Contribution de la Recherche Ethnologique à l'Histoire des Civilisations du Cameroun* (ed.) C. Tardits. Paris: CNRS.

Geary, C.M. 1983a. *Things of the Palace. A Catalogue of the Bamum Palace Museum in Foumban (Cameroon)* (Studien zur Kulturkunde 60). Translated by K. M. Holman. Wiesbaden: Steiner-Verlag.

Geary, C.M. 1983b. 'Bamum Two-Figure Thrones: Additional Evidence'. *African Arts* 16(4), 46–53.

Geary, C.M. 1988. *Images from Bamum. German Colonial Photography at the Court of King Njoya, Cameroon, West Africa, 1902–1915*. Washington, D.C.: National Museum of African Art.

Geary, C.M. 1992. 'Elephants, Ivory, and Chiefs: The Elephant and the Arts of the Cameroon Grassfields'. In *Elephant: the Animal and Its Ivory in African Culture* (ed.) D. Ross. Los Angeles: Fowler Museum of Cultural History, University of California, Los Angeles.

Geary, C.M. 1994. *The Voyage of King Njoya's Gift. A Beaded Sculpture from the Bamum Kingdom in the National Museum of African Art.* Washington, D.C.: National Museum of African Art.

Geary, C.M. & A.N. Njoya. 1985. *Mandu Yenu. Bilder aus Bamum, einem westafrikanischen Königreich, 1902–1915.* Munich: Trickster Verlag.

Geschiere, P. 1980. 'Child-Witches against the Authority of their Elders: Anthropology and History in the Analysis of Witchcraft Beliefs of the Maka (Southeast Cameroon)'. In *Man, Meaning and History; Essays in Honour of H.G. Schulte Noordholt* (eds) R. Schefold, J.W. Schoorl & J. Tennekes. Verhandelingen van het Koninklijk Institut voor taal-, land- en volkerkunde. The Hague: Nijhoff.

Geschiere, P. 1982. *Village Communities & the State.* London: Kegan Paul International.

Goheen, M. 1988. 'Land Accumulation and Local Control: the Negotiation of Symbols and Power in Nso', Cameroon'. In *Land and Society in Contemporary Africa* (eds) R.E. Downs & S.P. Reyna. Hanover and London: University of New Hampshire, University Press of New England.

Goheen, M., & Shanklin, E. 1996. 'Accidental Collisions: A conversation between Sally Chilver, Mitzi Goheen and Eugenia Shanklin'. *Journal of the Anthropological Society of Oxford (JASO)* .

Goody, J.R. 1971. *Technology, Tradition and the State in Africa.* London: Oxford University Press for the International African Institute.

Gründer, H. 1982. *Christliche Mission und deutscher imperialismus: eine politische Geschichte ihrer Beziehungen während die deutschen Kolonialzeit .* Paderborn: Schöningh.

Hacking, I. 1992. 'World-Making by Kind-Making: Child Abuse for Example'. In *How Classification Works: Nelson Goodman among the Social Sciences* (eds) M. Douglas & D. Hull. Edinburgh: Edinburgh University Press.

Hamman, M. 1975. 'The History of Relations between Mambila Borderland and its Eastern Neighbours to 1901.' B.A. Research essay: History Dept. Ahmadu Bello University.

Harter, P. 1986. *Arts Anciens du Cameroun (Arts d'Afrique Noire supp. T.40)).* Arnouville: Arts d'Afrique Noire.

Hausen, K. 1970. *Deutsche Kolonialherrschaft in Afrika: Wirtschaftsinterressen und Kolonialverwaltung in Kamerun vor 1914.* Zurich: Atlantis.

Héritier, F. 1977. 'L'identité Samo'. In *L'identité: séminaire dirigé par Claude Lévi-Strauss* (ed.) C. Lévi-Strauss. Paris: Grasset.

Hirschman, A. 1970. *Exit, Voice and Loyalty: Responses to Decline in Firms, Organizations and States.* Cambridge Mass.: Harvard University Press.

Hopkins, K. 1973. *An Economic History of West Africa.* London: Longman.

Horton, R. 1961. 'Destiny and the Unconscious in West Africa'. *Africa* 31, 110–6.

Horton, R. 1971. 'African Conversion'. *Africa* 41, 85–108.

Horton, R. 1983. 'Social Psychologies: African and Western.' Introduction to *Oedipus and Job in West African Religion,* Meyer Fortes. Cambridge: Cambridge University Press.

Hutter, F. 1902. *Wanderungen und Forschungen im Nord-Hinterland von Kamerun.* Braunschweig: F.Vieweg.

Jackson, M. 1989. *Paths Towards a Clearing: Radical Empiricism and Ethnographic Enquiry* (African Systems of Thought). Bloomington: Indiana University Press.

Jaeck, H.-P. 1960. 'Die deutsche Annexation'. In *Kamerun unter deutscher Kolonialherrschaft I* (ed.) H. Stoecker. E. Berlin: Rütten & Loening.

Jeffreys, M.D.W. 1962a. 'Isaac Fielding Pefok, B.E.M: a Brief Autobiography'. *The Nigerian Field* 27(2), 81–90.

Jeffreys, M.D.W. 1962b. 'Some Notes on the Customs of the Grassfields Bali of Northwestern Cameroon'. *Afrika und Übersee* 46(3), 161–8.

Jeffreys, M.D.W. 1962c. 'Traditional Sources prior to 1890 for the Grassfields Bali of Northwestern Cameroon'. *Afrika und Übersee* 46(3), 168–99; 46(4), 296–313.

Jeffreys, M.D.W. 1964. 'Who are the Tikar?' *African Studies* 23(3/4), 141–53.

Kaberry, P.M. 1952. *Women of the Grassfields.* London: HMSO.

Kaberry, P.M. 1959a. 'Nsaw Political Conceptions'. *Man* 59, 138–9.

Kaberry, P.M. 1959b. 'Traditional Politics in Nsaw'. *Africa* 24(4), 366–85.

Kaberry, P.M. & E.M. Chilver. 1961. 'An Outline of the Traditional Political System of Bali-Nyonga, Southern Cameroons'. *Africa* 31(4), 355–71.

Kaeselitz, R. 1968. 'Kolonialeroberung und Widerstandskampf in Südkamerun (1884–1907)', In *Kamerun unter deutscher Kolonialherrschaft vol. 2* (ed.) H. Stoecker. Berlin: Deutscher Verlag der Wissenschaften.

Keller, W. 1969. *The History of the Presbyterian Church in West Cameroon.* Victoria: Presbook.

Kobler, A.H. 1956. *Einst in Berlin.* Hamburg: Hoffmann u. Campe.

Kopytoff, I. 1971. 'Ancestors as Elders'. *Africa* 41, 129–42.

Kopytoff, I. 1981. 'Aghem Ethnogenesis and the Grassfields Ecumene'. In *Contribution de la recherche ethnologique à l'histoire des civilisations du Cameroun* (ed.) C. Tardits. Paris: CNRS.

Kopytoff, I. 1987. 'The Internal African Frontier: the Making of African Political Culture'. In *The African Frontier: the reproduction of traditional African societies* (ed.) I. Kopytoff. Bloomington: Indiana University Press.

Kopytoff, I. & S. Miers. 1977. 'African "Slavery" as an Institution of Marginality'. In *Slavery in Africa: Historical and Anthropological Perspectives* (eds) I. Kopytoff & S. Miers. Madison: University of Wisconsin Press.

Law, R. 1976. 'Horses, Firearms and Political Power in Pre-Colonial West Africa'. *Past and Present* 72, 112–32.

Law, R. 1978. 'Slaves, Trade and Taxes: the Material Basis of Political Power in Precolonial West Africa'. *Research in Economic Anthropology* 1, 27–52.

Mair, L.P. 1977. *African Kingdoms*. Oxford: Oxford University Press.

Maistre, C. 1933. *La Mission Congo-Niger (1892–1893))*. Paris: Société d'Éditions géographiques, maritimes et coloniales.

Mbiba, R.Y. 1991. 'Nso' and Her Neighbours: A Study in Inter-Group Relations in the Nineteenth and Twentieth Centuries.' Maîtrise: University of Yaoundé.

Mbunwe-Samba, P., P. Mzeka, M. Niba & C. Wirmum (eds) 1993. *Rites of Passage and Incorporation in the Western Grassfields of Cameroon, Vol. 1.* Bamenda, Cameroon: Kaberry Research Centre.

McCulloch, M., M. Littlewood and I. Dugast 1954. *Peoples of the Central Cameroons* (Ethnographic Survey of Africa, Western Africa Part IX). London: International African Institute.

McKnight, D. 1967. 'Extra-Descent Group Ancestor Cults in African Societies'. *Africa* 37(1), 1–21.

Meek, C.K. 1931. *Tribal Studies in Northern Nigeria Vol. 1.* London: Kegan Paul.

Meillassoux, C. 1981 (originally 1975). *Maidens, Meal and Money: Capitalism and the Domestic Community*. Cambridge: Cambridge University Press.

Mizon, L. 1895. 'Itinéraire de la source de la Benoué au confluent des rivières Kadei et Mambéré'. *Bulletin de la Société de Géographie de Paris (Series 7)* 16, 342–69.

Mohammadou, E. 1990. *Traditions historiques des peuples du Cameroun Central. Vol 1: Mbéré, Mboum, Tikar.* Tokyo: ILCAA.

Mohammadou, E. 1991. *Traditions historiques des peuples du Cameroun Central. Vol 2: Ni-zoo, Vouté et Kondja.* Tokyo: ILCAA.

Mouclùlì, I. (ed.) 1956. *Introduction à la religion musulmane dans la réligion bamoum, tradition présentée par El Hadji Abubakar nji Kuoto.*(Fumban, unpublished manuscript; fully cited in Tardits 1980, 974–8)

Mullendorf, P. 1902. 'The Development of German West Africa (Kamerun)'. *Journal of the Royal African Society* 2(5), 70–92.

Muller, J.-C. 1982. *Du bon usage, du sexe et du mariage: structures matrimoniales du haut plateau nigérien*. Paris: L'Harmattan.

Mzeka, P.N. 1980. *The Core Culture of Nso'*. Agawam, MA.: Paul Radin.

Mzeka, P.N. 1990. *Four Fons of Nso'*. Bamenda: Spider Press.

Ngwa, J.A. 1979. *A New Geography of Cameroon*. London: Longmans.

Njiassé-Njoya, A. 1981. 'Naissance et évolution de l'Islam en pays Bamum (Cameroun).' Thèse pour le doctorat du 3me cycle: Université I, Paris.

Njoya, A.N. 1978. *Njoya, réformateur du royaume bamoum*. Paris & Dakar: ABC & NEA.

Njoya, Sultan de Foumban 1952. *Histoire et coutumes des Bamum (Redigée sous la direction du Sultan Njoya. Traduction du Pasteur Henri Martin.* (Centre du Cameroun Série: Populations, no. 5). Douala: Institut Français de l'Afrique Noire.

Nkwi, P.N. & J.-P. Warnier. 1982. *Elements for a History of the Western Grassfields.* Yaoundé: Publication of the Department of Sociology, University of Yaoundé.

Northern, T. 1973. *Royal Art of Cameroon, the Art of Bamenda-Tikar.* Hanover, N.H.

Northern, T. 1984. *The Art of Cameroon.* Washington DC: Smithsonian Institute.

Nyamndi, N.B. 1988. *The Bali Chamba of Cameroon: a Political History.* Paris: Editions Cape.

O'Neil, R. 1987. 'A History of Moghamo,1865–1940: Authority and Change in a Cameroon Grassfields Culture.' Ph.D, Columbia University.

O'Neil, R. 1991. *Mission to the British Cameroons.* London: Mill Hill Mission Press.

Ortner, S.B. 1981. 'Gender and Sexuality in Hierarchical Societies: the case of Polynesia and Some Comparative Implications'. In *Sexual Meanings: The Cultural Construction of Gender and Sexuality* (eds) S.B. Ortner & H. Whitehead. New York: Cambridge University Press.

Palmié, S. (n.d.). 'African frontiers in the Americas?' typescript.

Pavel, Oberstleutnant. 1902. 'Report on the punitive expedition against the Bangwa, Bafut and Bandeng'. *Deutsches Kolonialblatt* 13, 90–2.

Pradelles de Latour, C.-H. 1991. *Ethnopsychanalyse en pays Bamiléké.* Paris: E.P.E.L.

Pradelles de Latour, C.-H. 1996. The Initiation of the *Dugi* among the Péré. *Journal of the Anthropological Society of Oxford (JASO)* .

Price, D. 1979. 'Who are the Tikar now?' *Paideuma* 25, 89–98.

Price, D. 1985. 'The Palace and its Institutions in the Chiefdom of Ngambe'. *Paideuma* 31, 85–103.

Price, D. 1987. 'Descent, Clans and Territorial Organisation in the Tikar Chiefdom of Ngambe, Cameroon'. *Zeitschrift für Ethnologie* 112(1), 85–103.

Rabut, E. 1989. *Brazza Commissaire Général: le Congo français 1886–1897.* Paris: Editions de l'École des Hautes Études en Sciences Sociales.

Ramsay, H. von. 1901. 'GNK'. *Deutsches Kolonialblatt* 12(3), 26.

Ramsay, H. von. 1925. 'Entdeckungen in Nordwest-Kamerun'. In *Das deutsche Kolonialbuch* (ed.) H. Zache. Berlin-Schmargendorf: Wilhelm Andermann Verlag.

Rein-Wuhrmann, A. 1925. *Mein Bamumvolk im Grasland von Kamerun.* Stuttgart & Basel: Evangelischer Missionsverlag & Basler Missionsbuchhandlung.

Richards, P. 1992. 'Landscapes of Dissent – Ikale and Ilaje Country 1870–1950'. In *Peoples and Empires in African History: Essays in Memory of Michael Crowder* (eds) Ade Ajayi & J.D.Y. Peel. London: Longman.

Roach, M.E. & J.B. Eicher. 1979. 'The Language of Personal Adornment'. In *The Fabrics of Culture* (eds) J.M. Cordwell & R.A. Schwarz. The Hague: Mouton.

Rudin, H.R. 1938. *The Germans in the Cameroons, 1884–1914: a Case Study in Modern Imperialism.* New Haven: Yale University Press.

Rüger, A. 1968. 'Die Duala und der Kolonialmacht, 1884–1914'. In *Kamerun unter deutscher Kolonialherrschaft vol. 2* (ed.) H. Stoecker. Berlin: Deutscher Verlag der Wissenschaften.

Ruppel, J. 1912. *Die Landesgesetzgebung, für das Schutzgebiet Kamerun.* Berlin: E.S. Mittler.

Russell, S.W., Jr. 1980. 'Aspects of Development in Rural Cameroon: Political Transition Amongst the Bali of Bamenda.' Ph.D.: University of Pennsylvania.

Savary, C. 1977. 'Situation et histoire des Bamum'. *Bulletin Annuel de la Musée d'Ethnographie, Genève* 20, 117–138.

Savary, C. 1979. 'Situation et histoire des Bamum (II)'. *Bulletin Annuel da la Musée d'Ethnographie, Geneve* 22, 21–22 and 121–161.

Seitz, T. 1929a. *Vom Aufstieg und Niederbruch deutscher Kolonialmacht,* Vol. 1. Karlsruhe: Verlag C.F. Müller.

Seitz, T. 1929b. *Vom Aufstieg und Niederbruch deutscher Kolonialmacht. Erinnerungen von Theodor Seitz, ehemals Gouverneur von Kamerun u. Südwestafrika Vol. 2: Gouverneursjahre in Kamerun.* Karlsruhe: Verlag C.F. Müller.

Skolaster, H. 1924. *Die Pallotiner in Kamerun.* Limburg Lahn: V.K.P.

Smith, F.T. & J.B. Eicher. 1982. 'The Systematic Study of African Dress and Textiles'. *African Arts* 15(3), 36–42.

Smith, R.S. 1976. *Warfare and Diplomacy in Pre-colonial West Africa.* Norwich: Methuen and Co. Ltd.

Smith, W.D. 1978. *The German Colonial Empire.* Chapel Hill: University of North Carolina.

Soh, P. 1983. 'The Political Evolution of Ngyen-Mbo'. Yaoundé: unpublished typescript.

Strathern, M. 1985. 'Kinship and Economy: Constitutive Orders of a Provisional Kind'. *American Ethnologist* 12, 191–209.

Strathern, M. 1988. *The Gender of the Gift: Problems with Women and Problems with Society in Melanesia.* Berkeley: University of California Press.

Tardits, C. 1980. *Le royaume Bamoum.* Paris: Librarie Armand Colin.

Tardits, C. (ed.) 1981. *Contribution de la recherche ethnologique à l'histoire des Civilisations du Cameroun.* Paris: CNRS.

Terray, E. 1972 (originally 1969). 'Historical Materialism and Segmentary Lineage-Based Societies'. In *Marxism and 'Primitive' Societies: Two Studies.* New York: Monthly Review Press.

Thomas, N. 1989. *Out of Time: History and Evolution in Anthropological Discourse* (Cambridge Studies in Social Anthropology 67). Cambridge: Cambridge University Press.

Thorbecke, F. 1914–24. *Im Hochland von Mittel-Kamerun (4 vols).* Hamburg: L. Freiderichsen.

Titanji, V., M. Gwanfogbe, E. Nwana, G. Ndangam & A.S. Lima (eds) 1988. *An Introduction to the Study of Bali-Nyonga (A tribute to His Royal Highness*

Galega II, Traditional Ruler of Bali-Nyonga from 1940–1985)). Yaoundé: Stardust Printers.

Van Slageren, J. 1972. *Les origines de l'Église Évangélique au Cameroun*. Yaoundé: Éditions Clé and Leiden: E.J.Brill.

Vansina, J., R. Mauny & L. Thomas. 1964. *The Historian in Tropical Africa*. London: Oxford Univ. Press for the International African Institute.

von Stetten, Rittmeister 1893. 'Das Nordliche Hinterland von Kamerun'. *Deutsches Kolonialblatt* IV(1), 33–36.

Warnier, J.-P. 1985. *Échanges, développement et hiérarchies dans le Bamenda pré-colonial (Cameroun)*. Stuttgart: Franz Steiner Verlag.

Warnier, J.-P. 1993. *L'ésprit d'entreprise au Cameroun*. Paris: Karthala.

Warnier, J.-P. 1979. 'Noun-classes, Lexical-Stocks, Multilingualism & the History of the Cameroon Grassfields'. *Language in Society* 8, 409–423.

Warnier, J.-P. 1984. 'Histoire du peuplement et genèse des paysages dans l'Ouest Camerounais'. *Journal of African History* 25(4), 395–410.

Warnier, J.-P. 1989. 'Traite sans raids au Cameroun'. *Cahiers d'Études africaines* XXIX–1(113), 5–32.

Warnier, J.-P. 1975. 'Pre-Colonial Mankon: the development of a Cameroon Chiefdom in its Regional Setting.' Ph.D.: University of Pennsylvania, Philadelphia.

Warnier, J.-P. 1980. 'Trade Guns in the Grassfields of Cameroon'. *Paideuma* 26, 79–92.

Warnier, J.-P., & Fowler, I. 1979. 'A Nineteenth Century Ruhr in Central Africa'. *Africa* 44(4), 329–351.

Warnock, M. 1987. *Memory*. London: Faber.

Wirz, A. 1973. *Vom Sklavenhandel zum Kolonialhandel: Wirtschaftsräume und Wirtschaftsformen in Kamerun vor 1914*. Zurich: Atlantis.

Wolpe, H. 1983. *Urban Politics in Nigeria: a Study of Port Harcourt*. Berkeley: University of California Press.

Zeitlyn, D. 1992. 'Un fragment de l'histoire des Mambilas: un texte du Duabang'. *Journal des Africanistes* 62(1), 135–150.

Zintgraff, E. 1895. *Nord-Kamerun*. Berlin: Paetel.

b) Archival references

Germany: Zentrales Staatsarchiv, Potsdam

Glauning, Hptm. 29 March 1905:. 'Correspondence concerning the confiscation of guns in the Bamenda area'. In *Akten betreffend: Allgemeine Angelegenheiten Kamerun vom September 1905 bis Juni 1906*. (10.01. RKA 4290).

Glauning, Hptm. 25 June 1906. 'Bericht über die Bansso-Expedition'. In *Akten betreffend: Expeditionen der Ksrl. Schutztruppe in Kamerun vom März 1905 bis Juli 1907*. (10.01. RKA 3353).

Prange, R. 1907. 'Letter of lawyer Prange to the Imperial Government re. the Expulsion of Merchant Schultz'. In *Akten betreffend: Allgemeine Angelegenheiten Kamerun vom April 1907 bis Juni 1908,* (10.01. RKA 4292).

Puttkamer, J. von. 8 February 1904. 'Gesandtschaft aus Bamum'. In *Akten betreffend Geschenke an Häuptlinge in Kamerun und in den Nachbarkolonien, sowie Gegengeschenke* (10.01. RKA 4102).

Seitz, T. 21 December 1909. 'Reise ins Bamumland'. In *Akten betreffend: Allgemeine Angelegenheiten des Schutzgebietes Kamerun vom 1. Juli 1908 bis 6. Juni 1910,* (10.01. RKA 4293).

Tippelskirch. 11 March 1905. Rechnung der Firma Tippelskirch & Co. (10.01. RKA 4102).

Wenckstern, Lt. von. 1 September 1906. 'Bericht über die Rückgabe von Nsangus Kopf'. In *Akten betreffend: Allgemeine Angelegenheiten Kamerun vom Juli 1906 bis April 1907,* (10.01. RKA 4291).

Cameroon: National Archives Yaoundé.

Gebauer, Hauptmann. 28 February 1908. 'Überweisung von Patronen'. In *Fonds Allemands* (A 1/38 p 18).

Menzel, Hptm. 8 August 1910. 'Bericht des Hauptmanns der Schutztruppe für Kamerun, Menzel, Bamenda, über das Vorhandensein von Waffen und Munition im Bali-Gebiet aus der Zeit des Dr Zintgraff sowie deren Einzug'. In *Fonds Allemands* (1/110).

Menzel, O/lt 12 April 1910. 'Über das Vorhandensein von Waffen und Munition im Bali-Gebiet'. In *Fonds Allemands* (1/110).

Menzel, O/lt 4 August 1910. 'Bericht der Oberleutnant der Schutztruppe für Kamerun Menzel, Bamenda, über das Vorhandensein von Waffen und Munition im Bali-Gebiet aus der Zeit des Dr Zintgraff sowie deren Einzug'. In *Fonds Allemands* (1/110).

Menzel, O/lt 13 January 1909. 'Bericht des Stationschefs von Bamenda, Oberleutnant der SfK Menzel, über die "Soldatenspielerei" der Haüptlinge von Bamum und Bali'. In *Fonds Allemands* (1/110).

Menzel, O/lt 5 September 1908. 'Bericht an das Kaiserliche Gouvernement über den Besitz von Gewehren durch die Häuptlinge von Bamum und Bali'. In *Fonds Allemands* (1/110).

Menzel, O/lt 26 September 1908. 'Halbjahresbericht des Oberleutnants der SfK Menzel, Bamenda'. In *Fonds Allemands* (1/110).

Sandrock, Lt. 1902. 'Bericht über den Marsch nach Bafu (Bamum)'. In *Fonds Allemands* (1/112).

Seitz, T. 7 February 1908a. 'Übergabe des Thronsessels des Häuptlings von Bamum als Geburtstagsgeschenk für den Kaiser anlässlich der Feierlichkeiten in Buea'. In *Fonds Allemands* (1/38).

Seitz, T. 21 March 1908b. 'Anweisung an die Hauptkasse'. In *Fonds Allemands* (1/38).

Cameroon: National Archives, Buea.

1929. *Quarterly Report for the Bamenda Division.*

Duncan. 29 July 1921. *Duncan, Acting Resident, to the Secretary, Southern Provinces, Lagos.* (Ab 6).

Hawkesworth, E.G. 1926. *Assessment Report on the Bafut Tribal Area of the Bamenda Division.* (Ab 3).

Hunt, W.E. 1925. *An Assessment Report on the Bali clan in the Bamenda Division of Cameroons Province.*

Podevin, G.S. 1916. *Delimination of Boundaries, November 19, 1921. Appendix:Extracts G.S. Podevin, Official Diary, January 18, 1916.* (Ab 10a).

Sharwood-Smith, B. 1924. *Assessment Report on the Menka District, Mamfe Division.* (Af 38).

Sharwood-Smith, B. 1925. *Assessment Report on the Mogamaw and Ngemba Speaking Families of the Widekum Tribe of Bamenda Division.* (Ab 20).

Switzerland: Basel Mission Archive, Basel.

Göhring, M. 13 July 1906. 'Erster Schulanfang in Bamum'. (E-2.22.280b).

Göhring, M. 18 July 1906. 'Einen Gruss aus Bamum an die Leser des Heidenfreundes'. (E-2.22.280a).

Göhring, M. 13 May 1906. 'Erste Eindrücke' (E-2.22.279).

Göhring, M. 2 October 1908. 'Quartalsbericht'. (E-2.28.64).

Hohner, M. 30 August 1906. *Erstellung eines 2. Predigtlokals.*

Lutz, F. May 1906. *Bericht über die Bali-Bamum Reise* (E-20.20.385a).

Schwarz, E. 25 June 1910. 'Ein Streifzug durch das Gewerbe von Bamum'. (E-2.32.63).

Stolz, K. 22 January 1906. 'Reise nach Bali und Bamum'. (E-2.21.386).

INDEX

Héritier, F., 20
hierarchy, 116–22, 147, 150, 169, 172
Hirschman, A., 119–21
history,
    official, 8–9
    relationship with anthropology,
        xviii–xix, xxii, 6, 12, 39–40, 45–6,
        48, 58–60, 122
homosexuality, 21
Horton, R., xxv, 20–1
Houben, Lt., 91
Hutter, H., xxiii, 87–9, 91, 97, 99

identity, xvii, xx, xxiii, xxvii, 6, 12,
    17–41, 138, 167, 190
Ifeka, C., xiii
initiation, 21

Jackson, M., 21
Jaeck, H-P., 65
Jantzen & Thormählen, 65, 74, 88
Jeffreys, M.D.W., 6, 13, 34–5, 86, 91, 94
Joss Plateau, 67
Jumbam, K., xxv, 137

Kaberry, P., x–xiii, xviii–xx, xxii, 1, 6, 8,
    15, 35, 40, 45–6, 60, 83–4, 86, 106,
    111, 116, 127
Kaberry Resource Centre, x, 41
Kaeselitz, R., 75
Kaiser Wilhelm II, 172–4, 184
Kamenda Boys' (Tapenta) revolt, xxiv,
    117–20
Kamerun, 8, 11, 33, 92–3, 96, 99
Keller, W., 95
Kimbo' (Kumbo), 102–3, 105, 108, 110,
    112, 125, 129, 134–5
kinlessness, 23
kinship, 22, 24
Knorr, Admiral, 66
Kolm, 30, 35
Kom, 102
Konntan, 83
Kopytoff, I., xviii, 20, 22–3
Kounde, 51, 57
Kovvifèm, 103, 127, 129
Kum a Mbapé, 66

labour recruitment, 81, 89–94, 97, 99, 172
Lake Chad, 48–9, 51, 55
Lamido Abbo, 49, 52
language, 6, 11
    Arabic, 51–2, 145
    Bamum, 141, 160, 162
    Bantu, 7

Chamba, 26, 31
Chamba-Leko, 2, 6, 29–31
Fula, 51
German, 95
Lam Nso', 134, 138
Mbam-Nkam, 7
Mungakka, 2, 30–1, 34, 95
Tikar, 7
Western Grassfields, 7, 102
language death, 2
Leist, K., 74
lineage, 82, 104–5, 127, 130, 143, 147–8,
    150–1, 153–6
Lumbee, 15
Lutz, F., 174

Mair, L.P., 109
Maistre, C., 52
Mambila, 12–13
Mandankwe, 11
Mankon, 87–8, 117
Manning, O., xi
marriage, 3, 10, 22, 120, 135, 137
Massiepa, 50, 55
matriliny, 3, 22–3
Mauny, R., 45
Mbiba, R.Y., 101
Mbombwo, King, 143
Mbutu, 83
McKnight, D., 21
medicine, 104, 132–3, 153–4
Meek, C.K., 34, 40
Meeton, D., 74
Melanesia, 21–2
memory, 27
men (cadets), 116–22
Mengen, 83
menopause, 21
Menzel, Lt., 186–8
mercantile capitalism, 82
merchants, 65–7, 71
Meta', 3, 89
missionaries, xxv, 66–7, 96, 118–19, 126,
    137, 147, 176, 179–80, 187–9
    see also Basel Missionary Society
Mizon, L., 50
Miers, S., 23
Mkako (Kaka), 54, 57–8
modernity, 18, 28–9, 37–9
Moisel, M., xxvii, 102
Moghamo, xxiii, 3, 81–99
    rebellions, 98–9
Mohammadou, E., 2, 6–9, 12–15
Mullendorf, P., 91–2
Müller, Colonel, 96